COMPUTERS FOR SENIORS FOR DUMMIES®

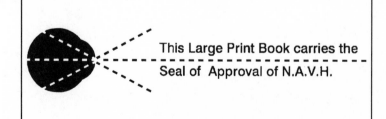

COMPUTERS FOR SENIORS FOR DUMMIES®

2nd Edition

NANCY MUIR

THORNDIKE PRESS
A part of Gale, Cengage Learning

GALE
CENGAGE Learning™

Detroit • New York • San Francisco • New Haven, Conn • Waterville, Maine • London

Thorndike Press, a part of Gale, Cengage Learning.

Thorndike Press® Large Print Health, Home & Learning.

The text of this Large Print edition is unabridged.

Other aspects of the book may vary from the original edition.

Set in 16 pt. Plantin.

LIBRARY OF CONGRESS CATALOGING-IN-PUBLICATION DATA

Muir, Nancy, 1954-
   Computers for seniors for dummies / by Nancy Muir. — Large print ed. ; 2nd ed.
   p. cm.
   ISBN-13: 978-1-4104-3408-1 (hardcover)
   ISBN-10: 1-4104-3408-7 (hardcover)
   1. Microcomputers. 2. Computers — Self-instruction. 3. Internet and older people. 4. Electronic mail systems. I. Title.
QA76.5.M766 2011
004.67'80846—dc22

2010040884

Published in 2011 in arrangement with John Wiley & Sons, Inc.

Printed in the United States of America
1 2 3 4 5 6 7 15 14 13 12 11

Dedication

To my wonderful husband, Earl, who seems to put up with all my foibles happily. Thanks, honey, for your love and support, for lots of laughter, and for letting me wander through life at your side!

Author's Acknowledgments

I was lucky enough to have Blair Pottenger, the absolute best editor in the world, assigned to lead the team on this book. Thanks, Blair, for once again making the process a pleasure. Thanks also to my friend and colleague Lisa Bucki for her always able work, in this case as technical editor. Last but not least, thanks to Katie Mohr, Acquisitions Editor, for hiring me to write the second edition of this book.

About the Author

Nancy Muir is the author of over 50 books on technology and business topics, as well as two books on Internet safety. In addition to her writing work, Nancy is the VP of Content and Curriculum for a non-profit online safety education organization called LOOK**BOTH**WAYS Foundation (ilookbothways.com). Prior to her writing career Nancy was a manager at several publishing companies, and a training manager at Symantec. Nancy lives in the Pacific Northwest where she dabbles in singing and acting in her spare time.

Publisher's Acknowledgments

We're proud of this book; please send us your comments at `http://dummies.custhelp.com`. For other comments, please contact our Customer Care Department within the U.S. at 877-762-2974, outside the U.S. at 317-572-3993, or fax 317-572-4002.

Some of the people who helped bring this book to market include the following:

Acquisitions and Editorial
Project Editor: Blair J. Pottenger
Acquisitions Editor: Katie Mohr, Tiffany Ma
Technical Editor: Lisa Bucki
Editorial Manager: Kevin Kirschner
Editorial Assistant: Amanda Graham
Sr. Editorial Assistant: Cherie Case
Cartoons: Rich Tennant (`www.the5thwave.com`)

Composition Services for Original Edition
Project Coordinator: Katie Crocker
Layout and Graphics: Ronald Terry
Proofreaders: Laura L. Bowman, Melissa Cossell, Rebecca Denoncour
Indexer: Ty Koontz

Publishing and Editorial for Technology Dummies

Richard Swadley, Vice President and Executive Group Publisher

Andy Cummings, Vice President and Publisher

Mary Bednarek, Executive Acquisitions Director

Mary C. Corder, Editorial Director

Publishing for Consumer Dummies

Diane Graves Steele, Vice President and Publisher

Composition Services for Original Edition

Debbie Stailey, Director of Composition Services

Table of Contents

17

Introduction

Conventions Used in This Book

This book uses certain conventions to help you find your way around, including:

- When you have to type something in a text box, I put it in **bold** type. Whenever I mention a Web site address, I put it in another font, `like this`. Figure references are also in bold, to help you find them.
- For menu commands, I use the ⇨ symbol to separate menu choices. For example, choose Tools⇨Internet Options. The ⇨ symbol is just my way of saying "Open the Tools menu and then click Internet Options."
- Callouts for figures draw your attention to an action you need to perform. In some cases, points of interest in a figure might be circled. The text tells you what to look for; the circle makes it easy to find.

Tip icons point out insights or helpful suggestions related to tasks in the step list.

Computers for consumers have come a long way in just 20 years or so. They're now at the heart of the way many people communicate, shop, and learn. They provide useful tools for tracking information, organizing finances, and being creative.

During the rapid growth of the personal computer, you might have been too busy to jump in and learn the ropes, but you now realize how useful and fun working with a computer can be.

This book can help you get going with computers quickly and painlessly.

About This Book

This book is specifically written for mature people like you, folks who are relatively new to using a computer and want to discover the basics of buying a computer, working with software, and getting on the Internet. In writing this book, I've tried to take into account the types of activities that might interest a 50+ year old discovering computers for the first time.

Foolish Assumptions

This book is organized by sets of tasks. These tasks start from the very beginning, assuming you know little about computers, and guide you through the most basic steps in easy-to-understand language. Because I assume you're new to computers, the book provides explanations or definitions of technical terms to help you out.

All computers are run by software called an *operating system,* such as Windows. Because Microsoft Windows–based personal computers (PCs) are the most common type, the book focuses mostly on Windows functionality.

Why You Need This Book

Working with computers can be a daunting prospect to people who are coming to them later in life. Your grandchildren may run rings around you when it comes to technology, and you might have fallen for that old adage, "You can't teach an old dog new tricks." However, with the simple step-by-step approach of this book, you can get up to speed with computers and overcome any technophobia you might have experienced.

You can work through this book from beginning to end or simply open up a chapter to solve a problem or help you learn a new skill whenever you need it. The steps in each task get you where you want to go quickly, without a lot of technical explanation. In no time, you'll start picking up the skills you need to become a confident computer user.

How This Book Is Organized

This book is conveniently divided into several handy parts to help you find what you need.

➡ **Part I: First Steps with Your Computer:** If you need to buy a computer or get started with the basics of using a computer, this part is for you. These chapters help you explore the different specifications, styles, and price ranges for computers and discover how to set up your computer out of the box, including hooking it up to a printer. These chapters provide information for exploring the Windows desktop when you first turn on your computer, customizing Windows to work the way you want it to, and getting the hang of the way Windows organizes files and folders. Finally, I provide information on using the Help system that's part of Windows.

➤ **Part II: Having Fun and Getting Things Done with Software:** Here's where you start working with that new computer. Using the popular and inexpensive Microsoft Works software, discover how to create documents in the Works Word Processor and work with numbers in the Spreadsheet. Chapters in this part also introduce you to built-in Windows applications you can use to work with digital photos, listen to music, and play games.

➤ **Part III: Exploring the Internet:** It's time to get online! The chapters in this part help you understand what the Internet is and what tools and functions it makes available to you. Find out how to explore the Internet with a Web browser; how to stay in touch with people via e-mail, instant messaging, chat, blogs; and even how to make Internet phone calls.

➤ **Part IV: Taking Care of Your Computer:** Now that you have a computer, you have certain responsibilities towards it (just like having a child or puppy!). In this case, you need to protect the data on your computer, which you can do using Windows and Internet Explorer tools. In addition, you need to perform some routine maintenance tasks to keep your hard drive uncluttered and virus free.

Get Going!

Whether you need to start from square one and buy yourself a computer or you're ready to just start enjoying the tools and toys your current computer makes available, it's time to get going, get online, and get computer savvy.

Part I

First Steps with Your Computer

The 5th Wave   By Rich Tennant

Chapter 1

Buying a Computer

If you've never owned a computer and now face purchasing one for the first time, deciding what to get can be a somewhat daunting experience. There are lots of technical terms to figure out and various pieces of *hardware* (the physical pieces of your computer such as the monitor and keyboard) and *software* (the brains of the computer that help you create documents and play games, for example) that you need to understand.

In this chapter, I introduce you to the world of activities your new computer makes available to you, and I provide the information you need to choose just the right computer for you. Remember as you read through this chapter that figuring out what you want to do with your computer is an important step in determining which computer you should buy. You have to consider how much money you want to spend, how you'll connect your computer to the Internet, and how much power and performance you'll require from your computer.

Understand All You Can Do with Computers

In just a couple of decades, computers have moved from being expensive behemoths that lived in corporate basements to being personal productivity and entertainment tools. They have empowered people to connect around the world in unprecedented ways, and they've made common tasks much easier to handle.

The following list walks you through some of the things your computer will enable you to do. Depending on what activities are important to you, you can make a more informed purchasing choice.

➡ **Keep in touch with friends and family.** The Internet has made it possible to communicate with other people via e-mail; share video images using webcams (tiny, inexpensive video cameras that capture and send your image to another computer); and make phone calls using a technology called VoIP (Voice over Internet Phone), which uses your computer and Internet connection to place calls. You can also chat with others by typing messages and sending them through your computer using a technology called instant messaging. These messages are exchanged in real time, so that you and your grandchild, for example, can see and reply to text immediately. Part III of this book explains these topics in more detail.

➤➤ **Research any topic from the comfort of your home.** Online, you can find many reputable Web sites that help you get information on anything from expert medical advice to the best travel deals. You can read news from around the corner or around the world. You can visit government Web sites to find out information about your taxes, Social Security, and more, or even go to entertainment sites to look up your local television listings.

➤➤ **Create greeting cards, letters, or home inventories.** Whether you're organizing your holiday card list or figuring out a monthly budget, computer programs can help. For example, **Figure 1-1** shows a graph that the Excel program created from data in a spreadsheet.

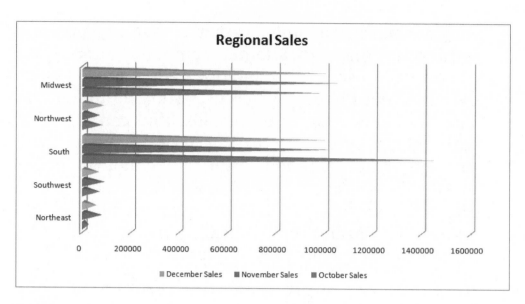

Regional Sales

■ December Sales   ■ November Sales   ■ October Sales

Figure 1-1

➤ **Pursue hobbies such as genealogy or sports.** You can research your favorite teams online (see **Figure 1-2**) or connect with people who have the same interests. The online world is full of special interest chat groups where you can discuss your interests with others.

➤ **Play interactive games with others over the Internet.** You can play everything from shuffleboard to poker or action games in virtual worlds.

➤ **Share and create photos, drawings, and videos.** If you have a digital camera, you can transfer photos to your computer (called *uploading*) or copy photos off the Internet and share them in e-mails or use them to create your own greeting cards. If you're artistically inclined, you can create digital drawings. Many popular Web sites make sharing digital movies easy, too. If you have a digital video camera and editing software, you can use editing tools to make a movie and share it with others. Steven Spielberg, look out!

➼ **Shop online and compare products easily, day or night.** You can shop for anything from a garden shed to travel deals or a new camera. Using handy online features, you can easily compare prices from several stores or read customer product reviews. Web sites such as www.nextag.com list product prices from a variety of vendors on one Web page, so you can find the best deals. Beyond the convenience, all this information can help you save money.

Figure 1-2

➼ **Handle your financial life.** You can do your banking or investing online and get up-to-the-minute data about your bank account, credit card balances, and investments.

Understand Hardware and Software

Your computing experience is made up of hardware and software. The hardware is all the tangible computer equipment, such as the keyboard and mouse, and the software is what makes the hardware work or lets you get things done, such as writing documents with Microsoft Word or playing a Solitaire game. Think of the hardware as being like your television set and the shows that you watch as being like the software.

The hardware on your computer consists of

➤ **A central processing unit (CPU),** which is the very small, very high-tech semiconductor *chip* that acts as the brains of your computer. The CPU is stored in a computer tower along with the other nuts and bolts of your computer.

➤ **A monitor,** which displays images on its screen such as the Microsoft Windows 7 desktop or a document in a software program.

➤ **A keyboard,** which is similar to a typewriter keyboard. In addition to typing words, you can use a keyboard to give the computer commands.

➤ **A mouse,** which you also use to give your computer commands, but this little device is more tactile. You move the mouse around your desk with your hand, which moves a pointer around on-screen. Using this pointer, you can click on items like buttons that cause an action, or click on the screen and drag the mouse to select text or an object to perform an action on it (such as deleting it or making the text bold).

➤ **Peripherals,** such as a printer, speakers, webcams,

and microphones. These may or may not come with your computer when you buy it, but your computer does come with slots (called *ports*) where you plug in various peripherals.

Software (also known as *programs* or *applications*) is installed on your computer hard drive, which resides in the computer casing (either in your laptop or, for a desktop computer, in the computer tower). Here are a few basics about software:

➤ **You use software to get your work done, run entertainment programs, and browse the Internet.** For example, Quicken is a financial management program you can use to balance your checkbook or keep track of your home inventory for insurance purposes.

➤ **Some programs come preinstalled on your computer; you can buy and install other programs as you need them.** For example, there is always an operating system on a computer, because it runs all the other programs. Also some programs are included with your operating system, such as Solitaire, an electronic version of the old favorite card game, which comes with Windows 7. Skype, a program that enables you to make online phone calls using your computer, is a popular program that you can find on the Internet and install on your computer yourself.

➤ **You can uninstall programs you no longer need.** Uninstalling unwanted programs helps to free up some space on your computer, which helps it perform better.

➤ **Some software programs called *utilities* exist to keep your computer in shape.** An antivirus program is an example of a utility used to spot and erase computer viruses from your system. Your *operating system* (such as Windows 7 Home Premium, which you hear more about in the task, "Choose a Version of Windows"), also includes some utilities, such as the Windows Defender program. Windows Defender protects your computer from unwanted intrusion by malicious programs called *spyware*. See Part IV for details about using utilities.

Explore Types of Computers

Just as there are many styles of shoes or mobile phones, you can find several styles of computers. Some are small and portable, some use different operating systems to make everything run, and some excel at certain functions such as working with graphics or playing games. This section explains some features you'll need to consider when choosing the type of computer you should buy.

Operating System: Windows is probably the most common computer operating system, and this book mainly focuses on its features. However, Macintosh computers from Apple are also popular. These use Apple-specific software; however, many software applications written for Windows are also available for the Macintosh, and you can also set up your Mac to run the Windows operating system, which gives you the best of both worlds. Some computers run on a freely available operating system called Linux, which has similar functionality to Windows.

Computer Design: Two types of computers you can buy are a laptop and a desktop. Here's the difference:

➤ A *laptop* is portable, weighing anywhere from two to eight pounds (the lowest weight ones are called *netbooks*). The monitor, keyboard, and mouse are built into the laptop. (Note that if the monitor is damaged, you have to pay quite a bit to have it repaired or hook it up to an external monitor.) **Figure 1-3** shows an example of a laptop, which is sometimes called a *notebook* computer. Choose a laptop if you want to use your computer mainly away from home or you have little space in your home for a larger computer.

Figure 1-3

➼ *Desktop* models typically have a large tower, such as the tower shown in **Figure 1-4**, that contains the computer's central processing unit (called a CPU). The keyboard, mouse, and monitor are separate. Desktop computers take up more space than laptops and are not portable, but they're usually less expensive.

A computer's central processing unit (CPU)

Figure 1-4

Pictures and Sound: If you work with a lot of *visual elements* (for example, photographs, home movies, or computer games), consider a computer that has a better graphics card. Games often involve sound, so a high-end sound card may also be useful. Computers with more sophisticated sound and image capabilities are often referred to as *gaming* or *multimedia* models and they typically require a larger hard disk to handle these functions. Because the capabilities of these cards change all the time, I don't give you the specifications for what's high end; instead, ask the person you're buying the computer from whether the system can handle sophisticated sound and graphics.

Choose a Version of Windows

As mentioned in the previous task, choosing your computer's *operating system* (software that runs all the programs and organizes data on your computer) will be one of your first decisions. This book focuses on computers running the current version of Windows, which is called Windows 7. Windows 7 comes in three different versions for home and business users. If you consider yourself primarily a home user, you should consider the Home Premium version of Windows 7:

➨ **Home Premium** includes entertainment tools such as Windows Media Center for playing music and movies. If you want to do more than look at photos, you'll find that this version of Windows 7 is good at working with design and image manipulation programs such as Photoshop. Also, if you choose a laptop, be aware that Home Premium includes great features for managing the battery power of your computer.

➨ **Windows 7 Professional** is great for small businesses or if you work from home. This version of Windows has ultimate security features.

➨ **Windows 7 Ultimate** provides everything that Professional provides, plus a few more bells and whistles for protecting your computer from thieves with BitLocker and handling languages other than English.

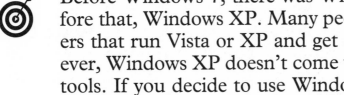 Before Windows 7, there was Windows Vista, and before that, Windows XP. Many people still use computers that run Vista or XP and get along just fine. However, Windows XP doesn't come with as many security tools. If you decide to use Windows XP, find a friend or family member who's knowledgeable about computers and can help you use XP features or other software programs that will help keep your computer secure. Note that if you're using Vista or XP, some of the steps for common tasks are different than they are if you use Windows 7; however, you can still use this book to find out about many computer basics.

Choose a Price Range

You can buy a computer for anywhere from $299 to $5,000 or more, depending on your budget and computing needs. You may start with a base model, but extras such as a larger monitor or higher-end graphics card can soon add hundreds to the base price.

You can shop in a retail store for a computer or shop online using a friend's computer (and perhaps get his or her help if you're brand new to using a computer). Consider researching different models and prices online and using that information to negotiate your purchase in the store if you prefer shopping at the mall. Be aware, however, that most retail stores have a small selection compared to all you can find online on a Web site such as Dell.com.

Buying a computer can be confusing, but here are some guidelines to help you find a computer at the price that's right for you:

➤ **Determine how often you will use your computer.** If you'll be working on it eight hours a day running a home business, you will need a better quality computer to withstand the use. If you turn on the computer once or twice a week, it doesn't have to be the priciest model in the shop.

➤ **Consider the features that you need. Do you want (or have room for) a 20-inch monitor?** Do you need the computer to run very fast and run several programs at once, or do you need to store tons of data? (Computer speed and storage are covered later in this chapter.) Understand what you need before you buy. Each feature or upgrade adds dollars to your computer's price.

➤ **Shop wisely.** If you walk from store to store or do your shopping online, you'll find that the price for the same computer model can vary by hundreds of dollars at different stores. See if your memberships in organizations such as AAA, AARP, or Costco make you eligible for better deals. Consider shipping costs if you buy online, and keep in mind that many stores charge a restocking fee if you return a computer you aren't happy with. Some stores offer only a short time period, such as 14 days, in which you can return a computer.

➤ **Buying used or refurbished is an option, though new computers have reached such a low price point that this may not save you much.** In addition, technology gets out of date so quickly, you might be disappointed buying an older model. Instead, consider going to a company that produces customized, non-name-brand computers at lower prices — perhaps even your local computer repair shop. You might be surprised at the bargains you can find (but make sure you're dealing with reputable people before buying).

➤ **Online auctions are a source of new or slightly used computers at a low price.** However, be sure you're dealing with a reputable store or person by checking reviews others have posted about them or contacting the Better Business Bureau. Be careful not to pay by check (this gives a complete stranger your bank account number); instead use the auction site's tools to have a third party handle the money until the goods are delivered in the condition promised. Check the auction site for guidance on staying safe when buying auctioned goods.

Some Web sites, such as Epinions.com, allow you to compare several models of computers side by side, and others, such as Nextag.com, allow you to compare prices on a particular model from multiple stores.

Select a Monitor

Monitors are the window to your computer's contents. If you're buying a desktop computer, it may come with a monitor that suits your purposes, or you might upgrade to a better monitor. A good monitor can make your computing time easier on your eyes. The crisper the image, the more impressive your vacation photos or that highly visual golf game will be.

Consider these factors when choosing a monitor:

➡ **Size:** Monitors for the average computer user come in all sizes, from tiny 10-inch screens on smaller laptops to 22-inch desktop models. Larger screens are typically more expensive. Although a larger monitor can take up more space side to side and top to bottom, many don't have a bigger *footprint* (that is, how much space their base takes up on your desk) than a smaller monitor.

➡ **Image quality:** The image quality can vary greatly. You will see terms such as LCD (liquid crystal display; also referred to as *flat panels*), CRT (cathode ray tube), flat screen, brightness, and resolution. Today, CRT screens, though still available, are old technology.

Look for an LCD monitor, preferably with a flat screen (see **Figure 1-5**) to ease glare.

An LCD monitor with a flat screen

Figure 1-5

➤ **Resolution:** A monitor's resolution represents the number of pixels that form the images you see on the screen. The higher the resolution, the crisper the image. You should look for a monitor that can provide at least a 1,024 x 768 pixel resolution.

➤ **Cost:** The least expensive monitor might be the one that comes with a computer package, and many of these are perfectly adequate. You can often upgrade your monitor when you buy if you customize a system from a company such as Dell or Gateway. Monitors purchased separately from a computer can range from around $100 to $3,000 or more. Check out monitors in person to really see whether their image quality and size are worth the money.

Choose an Optical Drive

You've probably used or seen a DVD used to play movies at home. Computers can also read data from or play movies or music from DVDs. Your computer is likely to come with at least one *optical drive,* which is a small drawer that pops out, allowing you to place a DVD in a tray, push the drawer back into the computer, and use the contents of the DVD. If you buy a software program, it will come on a CD or DVD, so you also need this drive to install software.

When you buy a computer, keep these things in mind about optical drives:

➨ **DVDs versus CDs:** DVDs have virtually replaced CDs as the computer storage medium of choice, but you might still find a CD floating around with music or data on it that you need to read. For that reason, you might want a DVD/CD combo drive.

➨ **DVD drives:** DVD drives are rated as Read (R) or Write (W). A readable DVD drive only allows you to look at data on it, but not save data to it. A writeable DVD drive allows you to save data (or images, or music) to it. A RW, or read-writeable, DVD drive lets you both read and write to DVDs.

➨ **DVD standards:** In the earliest days of DVDs, there were two different standards, + and –. Some drives could play DVDs formatted + but not those formatted –, for example. Today, you should look for a DVD drive that is specified as +/– so it can deal with any DVD you throw at it.

 One of the first things you should do when you buy a computer, if it doesn't come with recovery disks, is to burn recovery disks that you can use if you have to restore the computer to it's factory settings. You might need to do this, for example, if a virus corrupts your settings. Your computer should offer this as an option when you first start it, but if it doesn't, check your computer's help system or the manufacturer's Web site to find out how to burn recovery disks.

Understand Processor Speed and Memory

You computer contains a processor contained on a computer chip. The speed at which your computer runs programs or completes tasks is determined in great measure by your computer's processor speed. Processor speed is measured in *gigahertz* (GHz). The higher this measurement, the faster the processor. I won't quote the speed you should look for because these chips are constantly getting smaller and contain more and more power. However, when you shop, know that the higher numbers give the best performance and factor that into your decision depending on your needs.

In addition, computers have a certain amount of storage capacity for running programs and storing data. You'll see specifications for RAM and hard drive memory when you go computer shopping. Again, the specific numbers will change, so the guideline is to look for higher RAM numbers if you feel you need more storage capacity.

➤ **RAM is the memory needed to simply access and run programs.** RAM chips come in different types, including DRAM, SDRAM, and the latest version, DDR2. Look for a minimum of 1 gigabyte (GB) of RAM for everyday computing.

➤ **RAM chips are rated by *access speed*, which relates to how quickly a request for data from your system can be completed.** You might see RAM speed measured in megahertz (MHz). Today, 800 MHz could be considered good access speed.

➤ **Your hard drive has a certain capacity for data storage measured in gigabytes (GB).** These days you should probably look for a minimum of a 160GB hard drive, but hard drives can come with a range of huge capacities, with the largest being measured in terabytes (TB, measured in thousands of gigabytes).

➤ **Your computer will require some RAM to run the operating system.** Windows 7 requires 1GB of main memory and 16GB of hard drive space.

Determine How You'll Connect to the Internet

You have to decide how you'll connect to the Internet. You can use a dial-up connection over a standard phone line or pay a fee to get a broadband connection such as DSL. (Check with AARP to find out if they offer discounted connections in your area.) However, if you want a wireless connection that works like your cell phone to pick up a signal in certain *hotspots,* you have to be sure to buy a computer with wireless capabilities. Here's how these work:

➤ **Dial-up:** If you intend to use a dial-up connection (that is, connect over your phone line), your computer has to have a dial-up modem either built in or in an external model. Dial-up connections can be very slow, and while you're using them, you can't use your phone to make or receive calls. I'd discourage you from using dial-up unless you absolutely have to.

➡ **Wireless:** Wireless connections require that you have a computer equipped with wireless capability. You can access the Internet wirelessly when you're near a wireless *hotspot* (a place that offers wireless service), and many hotspots are appearing at public places such as hotels, airports, and restaurants. You can also subscribe to a Wireless Wide Area Network (WWAN) service from a mobile phone provider to tap into its connection. Check the computer model you want to buy to be sure it is wireless enabled. There are various techy standards for wireless such as 802.11a, b, or g. The very latest standard to look for is 802.11n, which delivers better wireless performance.

➡ **Broadband:** Broadband connections can be DSL (digital subscriber line) or cable modem. In both cases, you pay a fee to a provider, which might be your phone company or cable company. DSL works over your phone line but doesn't prohibit you from using the phone when you're online. Cable runs over your cable TV line and is a bit faster than DSL, though connections can be less dependable. Both are considered always-on connections, meaning that you don't have to wait to dial up to a phone connection or connect to a wireless network — you're always connected.

 See Chapter 16 for more about setting up your Internet connection.

Buy a Customized Computer

You can buy prepackaged computer systems online or in an electronics store. An alternative is to buy a customized computer. Companies such as Dell (see **Figure 1-6**) and Gateway offer customized computer systems. When you buy the computer, you can pick and choose various features, and the provider will build the system for you.

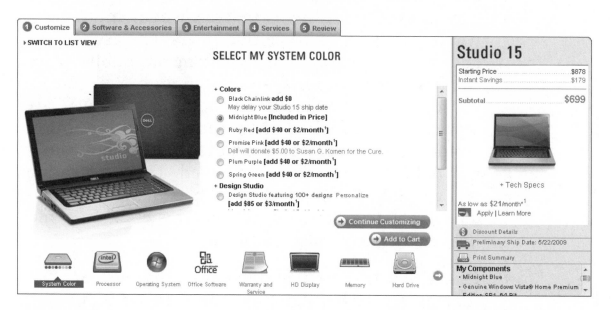

Figure 1-6

Here are some of the variables you'll be asked about when you purchase a customized system, many of which are discussed in this chapter:

➤ Type and speed of processor

➤ Amount of RAM or hard drive capacity

➤ Installed software, such as a productivity suite like Microsoft Office or Microsoft Works, or a premium version of an operating system

➤ More sophisticated graphics or sound cards

➤ Peripherals such as a printer or an upgrade to a wireless mouse or keyboard

➤ Larger or higher-end monitor

➤ Wireless capability

➤ Warranty and technical support

These all add to your final price, so be sure you need an option before you select it. Most of these companies provide explanations of each item to help you decide.

Chapter 2

Setting Up Your Computer

Once you unpack your new computer, you may need help getting it set up. Here I cover the basics: connecting your computer to a monitor, keyboard, and mouse (if you bought a laptop computer, you can skip these tasks as they're all built in!); turning the computer on and off; and mastering the basic use of your mouse.

Next you can set up the date and time in your computer's internal clock so they match your time zone, and you can apply daylight savings time settings properly. Finally you get to work with your user accounts. Windows allows you to create multiple user accounts; each account saves certain settings and allows you to control files and folders separately. When each user logs on with a particular user account, it's like accessing a unique personal computer.

Here, then, are the procedures that you can follow to get going with your computer.

Connect the Monitor, Keyboard, and Mouse

Your computer comes with a monitor, keyboard, and mouse. You should connect these before turning on the computer. Your computer will offer several types of connection ports, though USB ports are becoming the most common. Wireless keyboards and mouses use a small transmitter that you insert into a USB port, for example.

Use the following table in conjunction with **Figure 2-1** to identify device-to-PC connector ports.

Connection	Location	What It's Good For
VGA port	1	Connect your monitor.
USB port	2	Connect various USB devices, such as a digital camera.
Parallel port	3	Connect a non-USB printer.
Audio	4	Connect speakers.

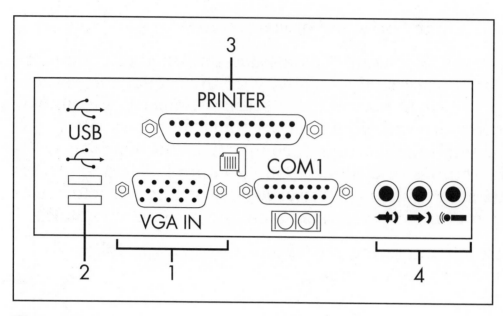

Figure 2-1

Log On and Off Windows 7

1. With your computer set up, you're ready to turn it on. Start by pressing the power button on your computer to begin the Windows 7 start-up sequence.

2. In the resulting Windows 7 Welcome screen, enter your password, if you have set one, and click the arrow button or click Switch User and choose another user to log on as. (If you need help with using the mouse to make your selection, see the next task.) Windows 7 verifies your password and displays the Windows 7 desktop, as shown in **Figure 2-2**. (**Note:** If you haven't set up the password protection feature for more than one user, you're taken directly to the Windows 7 desktop. For more on adding and changing passwords, see Chapter 21.) The icons on your desktop may vary depending on what programs your computer manufacturer may have installed.

The Windows 7 desktop

Figure 2-2

3. Once you're logged in, to change to another user account, first save any open documents, close any open applications, and then choose Start. Then click the arrow next to the button, labeled Shut Down, in the bottom-right corner of the Start menu and choose Log Off. Windows 7 logs off and displays a list of users. To log on again, click a user icon.

 To create another user, choose Start⇨Control Panel, and, under the User Accounts and Family Safety heading, click Add or Remove User Accounts. Then click Create a New Account. Follow instructions to enter a name for the account and set a password for it, if you like.

 After you set up more than one user, before you get to the password screen, you have to click the icon for the user you wish to log on as.

Use the Mouse

Unlike using a typewriter, which uses only a keyboard to enter text into documents, with a computer you use both a keyboard and a mouse to enter text and give commands to the computer. Though you might have used a keyboard of some type before, a mouse might be new to you, and frankly, it takes a little getting used to. In effect, when you move your mouse around on your desk (or in some models, roll a ball on top of the mouse), a corresponding mouse pointer moves around your computer screen. You control the actions of that pointer by using the right and left buttons on the mouse.

Here are the main functions of a mouse and how to control them:

➼ **Clicking:** When people say "click," they mean "press and release the left mouse button." Clicking has a variety of uses. You can click while in a document to move the insertion point, a little line that indicates where your next action will take place. For example, you might click in front of a word you already typed and then type another word to appear before it in a letter. Clicking is also used in various windows to select check boxes or radio buttons (also called option buttons) to turn features on or off or to select an object such as a picture or table in your document.

➥ **Right-clicking:** If you click the right mouse button, Windows displays a shortcut menu that is specific to the item you clicked. For example, if you right-click a picture, the menu that appears gives you options for working with the picture. If you right-click the Windows desktop, the menu that appears lets you choose commands that display a different view or change desktop properties.

➥ **Clicking and dragging:** To click and drag, you press and continue to hold down the left mouse button and then move (drag) the mouse to another location. For instance, you can click in a document and drag your mouse up, down, right, or left to highlight contents of your document. This highlighted text is selected, meaning that any action you perform, such as pressing the Delete key on your keyboard or clicking a button for bold formatting, is performed on the selected text.

➥ **Scrolling:** Many mouse models have a wheel in the center that you can roll up or down to scroll through a document or Web site on your screen. Just roll the wheel down to move through pages going forward, or scroll up to move backward in your document.

Set the Date and Time

1. The date and clock on your computer keep good time, but you might have to provide the correct date and time for your location. To get started, press the Windows key on your keyboard (the one with the Windows logo on it) to display the taskbar if it isn't visible.

2. Right-click the Date/Time display on the far right of the taskbar and then choose Adjust Date/Time from the shortcut menu that appears.

3. In the Date and Time dialog box that appears (see **Figure 2-3**), click the Change Date and Time button. In the Date and Time Settings dialog box that appears, enter a new time in the Time field or use the up and down arrows next to that field to change the time. If you wish, click on a new date in the calendar display. Click OK.

4. To change the time zone, click the Change Time Zone button, choose another option from the Time Zone drop-down list, and click OK.

5. Click OK to apply the new settings and close the dialog box.

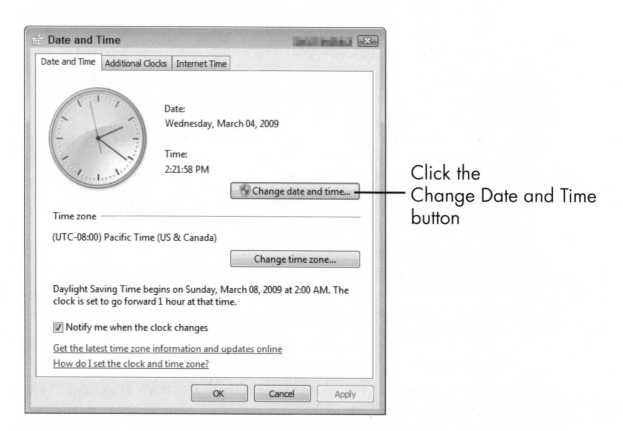

Click the
Change Date and Time
button

Figure 2-3

If you don't want your computer to adjust for Daylight Saving Time, click Change Time Zone and click the Automatically Adjust Clock for Daylight Saving Time check box to turn this feature off.

Another option for displaying the time or date is to add the Clock or Calendar gadget to the Windows desktop. See Chapter 10 for more about using gadgets.

Create a New User Account

1. Choose Start⇨Control Panel.

2. In the resulting window, click the Add or Remove User Accounts link.

3. In the resulting Manage Accounts dialog box, shown in **Figure 2-4,** click Create a New Account.

4. In the next dialog box, shown in **Figure 2-5,** enter an account name, and then select the type of account you want to create:

    • **Administrator,** who can do things like create and change accounts and install programs

    • **Standard user,** who can't do the tasks an administrator can

5. Click the Create Account button and then close the Control Panel.

    After you create an account, you can make changes to it, such as assigning a password or changing the account type, by double-clicking it in the Manage Accounts window you reached in Step 3 (in the preceding step list) and following the links listed there.

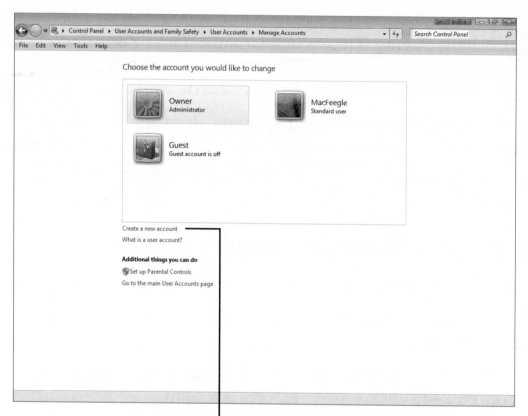

Click Create a New Account

Figure 2-4

Choose an account type

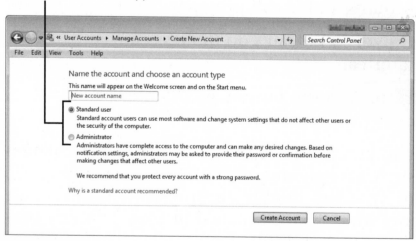

Figure 2-5

Switch User Accounts

1. Click Start and then click the arrow on the side of the Shut Down button (see **Figure 2-6**).

2. Choose Switch User. In the resulting screen, click on the user you want to log in as.

3. If the user account is password-protected, a box appears for you to enter the password. Type the password and then click the arrow button to log in.

4. Windows logs you in with the specified user's settings.

> If you forget your password and try to switch users without entering one, Windows shows your password hint, which you can create when you assign a password to help you remember it.

Click this arrow

Figure 2-6

You can set up several user accounts for your computer, which helps you save and access specific user settings and provide privacy for each user's files with passwords. To find out about setting up user accounts and changing their settings, see earlier tasks in this chapter.

Change Your User Account Picture

1. If you don't like the picture associated with your user account, you can change it. Choose Start⇨Control Panel⇨ Add or Remove User Accounts.

2. In the resulting Add or Remove User Accounts dialog box, click the account you want to change.

3. In the resulting window, click the Change Picture button and click another picture (or browse to see more picture choices) to select it (see **Figure 2-7**).

Click the Change Picture button

Figure 2-7

4. Click the Change Picture button; the dialog box closes.

5. Click the Control Panel's Close button to close it.

Shut Down Your Computer

1. To turn off your computer when you're done, you need to initiate a shut down sequence in your operating system instead of simply turning off the power. Choose Start and then click the Shut Down button.

2. If you prefer to stop your computer running but not turn the power off, click the arrow to the right of the Shut Down button and, in the resulting shortcut menu shown in **Figure 2-8,** choose Hibernate on a laptop (or simply close the lid of your laptop) to shut the computer down; if you want to *reboot* (turn off and turn back on) your computer, choose Restart.

 If you're going away for a while but don't want to have to go through the whole booting up sequence complete with Windows 7 music when you return, you don't have to turn off your computer. Just click the Sleep command instead (in Step 2) to put your computer into a kind of sleeping state where the screen goes black and the fan shuts down. When you get back, just click your mouse button or press Enter, or in some cases (especially on some laptops) press the Power button; your computer springs to life, and whatever programs and documents you had open are still open.

 If your computer freezes up for some reason, you can turn it off in a couple of ways. Press Ctrl+Alt+Delete twice in a row, or press the power button on your CPU and hold it until the computer shuts down.

Don't simply turn off your computer at the power source unless you have to because of a computer dysfunction. Windows might not start up properly the next time you turn it on if you don't follow the proper shut down procedure.

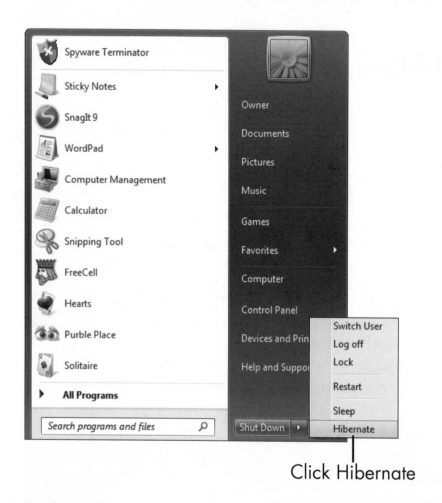

Click Hibernate

Figure 2-8

Chapter 3

Getting Around the Windows 7 Desktop

Get ready to . . .

Just as your desk is the central area from which you do all kinds of work, the Windows 7 desktop is a command center for organizing your computer work. The desktop appears when you log on to a Windows 7 computer. The Start menu is located on the desktop; you use this menu to access your computer settings, files, folders, and software. On the desktop, there is also a taskbar that offers settings, such as your computer's date and time, as well as shortcuts to your most frequently accessed programs or files.

This chapter is an introduction to all the things you can do via the desktop. Along the way, you discover the Recycle Bin, where you place deleted files and folders, and the Frequently Used Programs area, which allows quick access to commonly used programs. You also find out how to work with application windows, create a desktop shortcut, and shut down your computer when you're done for the day.

Understand the Desktop

Think of the desktop as the place where you can open and work with all the windows that you use to get your work done. The desktop appears when you first turn on your computer. You can use various elements of the desktop to open or manage files, access settings for Windows, go online, and more. **Figure 3-1** shows the desktop and some of the elements on it, including the following:

➡ **The taskbar** is home to the Start menu, accessed by clicking the Start button. Currently open programs are listed here, and you can click on one to switch programs. Finally, you can work with various settings such as the volume control using icons displayed on the taskbar.

➤ The right side of the taskbar, which is called the **Notifications area,** contains many commonly used functions such as the computer date and time settings, the network connections icons, and the icon you click to safely remove hardware, such as a USB storage device, from your computer.

➤ **The Frequently Used Programs area** is a set of icons within the taskbar that you use to open frequently used programs. You can customize this area of the taskbar to contain any programs you want. See the section "Work with Frequently Used Programs" later in this chapter.

➤ **The Recycle Bin** holds recently deleted items. It will empty itself when it reaches its maximum size (which you can modify by right-clicking the Recycle Bin and choosing Properties), or you can do so manually. Check out the section "Empty the Recycle Bin" later in this chapter for more about this.

➤ **Desktop shortcuts** are icons that reside on the desktop and provide a shortcut to opening a software program or file. Your computer usually comes with some shortcuts, such as the Recycle Bin and a browser shortcut, but you can also add or delete shortcuts. Click a desktop shortcut to launch an associated program. See the "Create a Shortcut to a File or Folder" section later in this chapter.

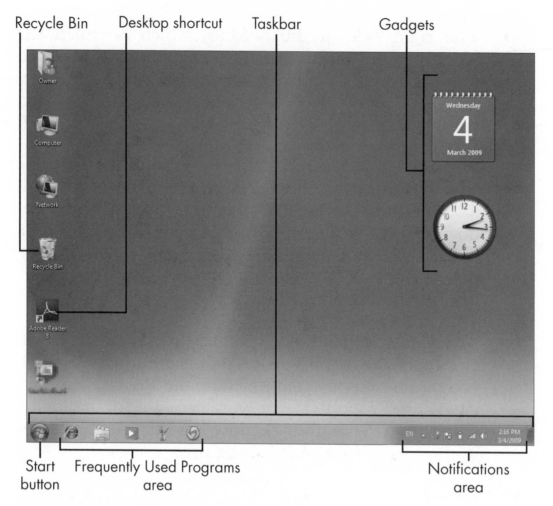

Recycle Bin   Desktop shortcut   Taskbar   Gadgets

Start button   Frequently Used Programs area   Notifications area

Figure 3-1

➼ **Gadgets** can be placed on the desktop. These are handy little tools including a stock ticker, a clock, and a calendar, but you can also download lots of other gadgets from the Windows Web site. Chapter 10 explains how to get started with gadgets.

The desktop is always there as you open program windows to get your work done. If you make a program window as big as it can be (*maximize* it), you won't see the desktop, but you can go back to the desktop at any time by shrinking a window (*minimizing* it) or closing windows. You can also press Alt+Tab simultaneously and choose the desktop from the open programs' icons in the window that appears.

Work with the Start Menu

1. Press the Windows key on your keyboard or click the Start button on the desktop to display the Start menu (see **Figure 3-2**).

2. From the Start menu, you can do any of the following:

- Click All Programs to display a list of all programs on your computer. You can click any program in the list to open it.

- Click any category on the right of the Start menu to display a Windows Explorer window with related folders and files (see **Figure 3-3**).

- Click either frequently used programs at the left of the Start menu or click the arrow to the right of an application to display a list of recently used files and click on a file to open it in that application.

- Click the Power button icon to close all programs and turn off Windows.

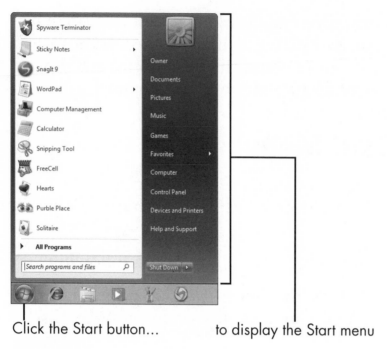

Click the Start button...   to display the Start menu

Figure 3-2

Files in the Pictures folder

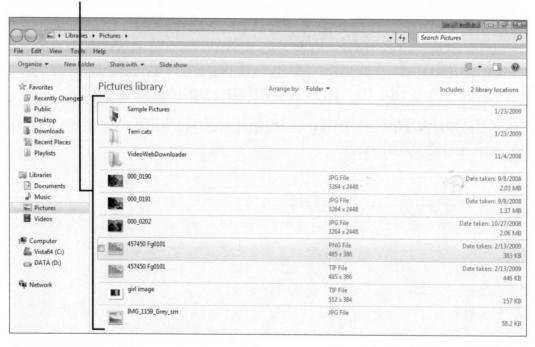

Figure 3-3

66

- Click the arrow next to the Power button to display a menu of choices for putting your computer in sleep or hibernate mode (see the next tip for more about these settings), for restarting your computer; or for logging off or logging in as a different user.

3. When you move your cursor away from the Start menu, it disappears.

 Putting your computer in sleep mode is like pausing your computer without closing open documents and programs. Sleep still uses a bit of power and allows you to quickly get back to work after only a few seconds. Hibernate mode is mainly for laptops because it saves your battery life. When you choose Hibernate, open documents and program settings are saved to your hard drive and your computer switches off. It takes longer to boot up your computer from Hibernate and have the Windows desktop display, but it saves more power than Sleep.

 Open the Start menu, right-click in a blank area, and click Properties to display the Taskbar and Start Menu Properties dialog box, where you can customize the Start menu behavior. For example, you can modify the functionality of the Power button and choose whether to list recently opened programs and files in the Start menu.

 If you open the Start menu and right-click in a blank area of the menu, a shortcut menu pops up. Choose Properties to display the Taskbar and Start Menu Properties dialog box, where you can customize the Start menu behavior. If you would rather use the look and feel of the Start menu in older versions of Windows, select Classic Start Menu in the Taskbar and Start Menu Properties dialog box and then click OK.

(Note that this book deals only with the Windows 7 Start menu features.)

Work with Frequently Used Programs

1. If you have programs you use often, you can pin them to the Frequently Used Programs area, which is the area of the taskbar just to the right of the Start button (see **Figure 3-4**). When you first open Windows, this area may include icons for programs such as Internet Explorer and Windows Media Player or a shortcut to open Windows Explorer.

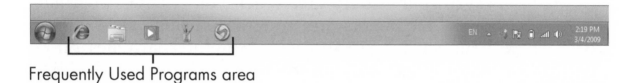

Frequently Used Programs area

Figure 3-4

2. To open any of these items, click its icon and the window for that program opens (see **Figure 3-5**).

Figure 3-5

3. To close an item you've opened, click the Close button in the top-right corner of the window (with an "X" on it).

To display additional items in the taskbar, right-click that application in the Start menu or on the desktop and then choose Pin to Taskbar. You can also drag a desktop icon to the taskbar. (If you want help creating a desktop shortcut, see the task, "Create a Shortcut to a File or Folder," later in this chapter.)

You can add other functions to the taskbar. Right-click on a blank area of the taskbar and choose Properties. Click the Toolbars tab to display it. Click the check box for any of the additional items listed there, such as a browser Address bar or links.

Arrange Icons on the Desktop

1. Right-click the desktop and choose View in the resulting shortcut menu; be sure that Auto Arrange Icons isn't selected, as shown in **Figure 3-6.** (If it is selected, deselect it before proceeding to the next step.)

Verify that Auto Arrange Icons isn't selected

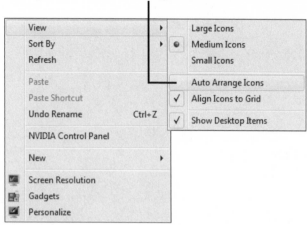

Figure 3-6

2. Right-click the Windows 7 desktop. In the resulting shortcut menu, choose Sort By, and then click the criteria for sorting your desktop shortcuts (see **Figure 3-7**).

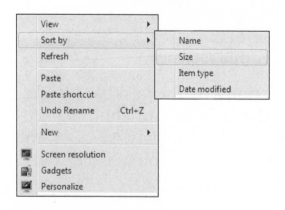

Figure 3-7

70

3. You can also click any icon and drag it to another location on the desktop — for example, to separate it from other desktop icons so you can find it easily.

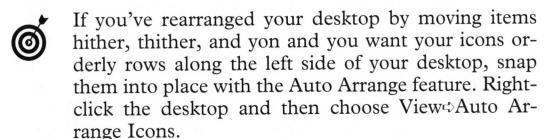 If you've rearranged your desktop by moving items hither, thither, and yon and you want your icons or- derly rows along the left side of your desktop, snap them into place with the Auto Arrange feature. Right- click the desktop and then choose View⇨Auto Ar- range Icons.

Use the shortcut menu in Step 1 and choose Large Icons, Medium Icons, or Small Icons in the View sub- menu to change the size of desktop icons.

Empty the Recycle Bin

1. When you throw away junk mail, it's still in the house — it's just in the trash bin instead of on your desk. That's the idea behind the Windows Recycle Bin. Your old files sit there, and you can retrieve them until you empty it or until it reaches its size limit and Windows dumps a few files. Right-click the Recycle Bin icon on the Windows 7 desktop and choose Empty Recycle Bin from the menu that appears (see **Figure 3-8**).

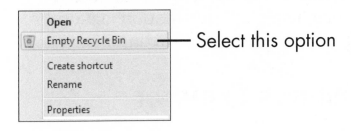

Select this option

Figure 3-8

71

2. In the confirmation dialog box that appears (see **Figure 3-9**), click Yes. A progress dialog box appears indicating the contents are being deleted. **Remember:** After you empty the Recycle Bin, all files in it are unavailable to you.

 Up until the moment you permanently delete items by performing the preceding steps, you can retrieve items from the Recycle Bin by right-clicking the desktop icon and choosing Open. Select the item you want to retrieve and then click the Restore This Item link near the top of the Recycle Bin window.

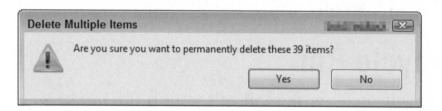

Figure 3-9

 You can modify the Recycle Bin properties by right-clicking it and choosing Properties. In the dialog box that appears, you can change the maximum size for the Recycle Bin and whether to immediately delete files you move to the Recycle Bin. You can also deselect the option of having a confirmation dialog box appear when you delete Recycle Bin contents.

Find a File with Windows Explorer

1. Windows Explorer is a program you can use to find a file or folder by navigating through an outline of folders and subfolders. It's a great way to look for files on your computer. Right-click the Start menu button and choose

Open Windows Explorer, or click the Windows Explorer button on the taskbar (it looks like a set of folders).

2. In the resulting Windows Explorer window (shown in **Figure 3-10**), double-click a folder in the main window or in the list along the left side to open the folder.

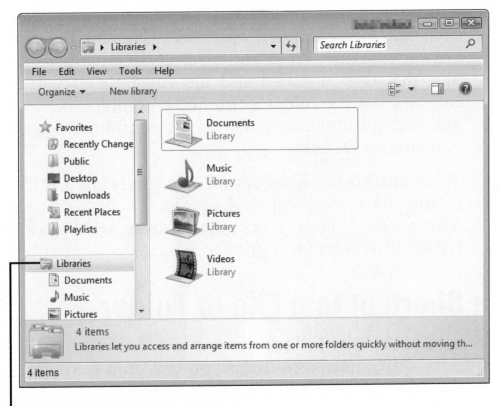

Double-click a folder to open it

Figure 3-10

3. The folder's contents are displayed. If necessary, open a series of folders in this manner until you locate the file you want.

4. When you find the file you want, double-click it to open it.

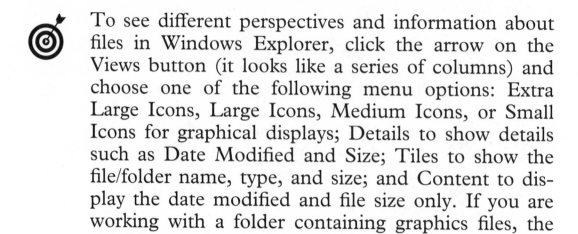 To see different perspectives and information about files in Windows Explorer, click the arrow on the Views button (it looks like a series of columns) and choose one of the following menu options: Extra Large Icons, Large Icons, Medium Icons, or Small Icons for graphical displays; Details to show details such as Date Modified and Size; Tiles to show the file/folder name, type, and size; and Content to display the date modified and file size only. If you are working with a folder containing graphics files, the graphics automatically display as thumbnails unless you choose Details.

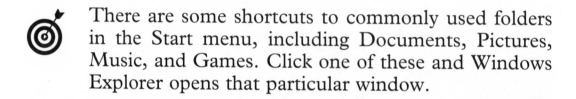 There are some shortcuts to commonly used folders in the Start menu, including Documents, Pictures, Music, and Games. Click one of these and Windows Explorer opens that particular window.

Create a Shortcut to a File or Folder

1. Shortcuts are handy little icons you can put on the desktop for quick access to items you use on a frequent basis. (See this chapter's first section, "Understand the Desktop," for an introduction to shortcuts.) To create a new shortcut, first choose Start⇨All Programs and locate the program in the list of programs that appears.

2. Right-click an item, FreeCell for example, and choose Send To⇨Desktop (Create Shortcut), as shown in **Figure 3-11**.

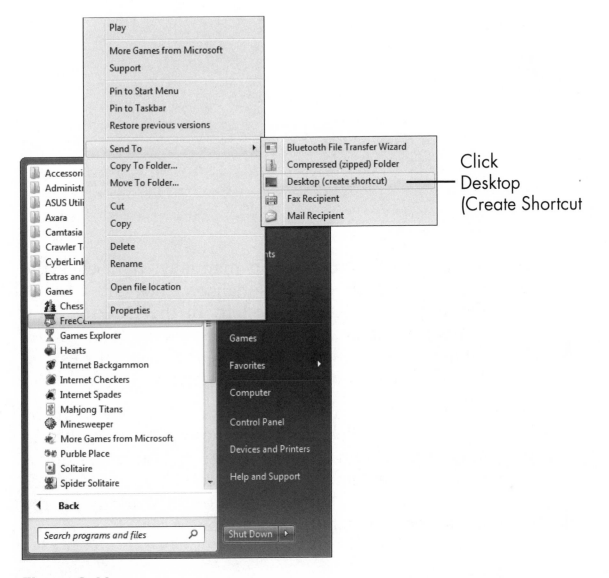

Figure 3-11

3. The shortcut appears on the desktop (see **Figure 3-12**). Double-click the icon to open the application.

> Occasionally, Windows 7 offers to delete desktop icons that you haven't used in a long time. Let it. The desktop should be reserved for frequently used programs, files, and folders. You can always re-create shortcuts easily if you need them again.

Double-click to use the new shortcut

Figure 3-12

 To clean up your desktop manually, right-click the desktop and choose Personalize. Click the Change Desktop Icons link to the left. In the Desktop Icon Setting dialog box that appears, click the Restore Default button, which returns to the original desktop shortcuts set up on your computer.

 You can create a shortcut for a brand-new item by right-clicking the desktop, choosing New, and then choosing an item to place there, such as a text document, bitmap image, or contact. Then double-click the shortcut that appears and begin working on the file in the associated application.

Start a Program

1. Before you can use a program, you have to start it (also called *launching* a program). Launch an application by using any of the following four methods:

   • Choose Start⇨All Programs. Locate the program name on the All Programs list that appears and click it. Clicking an item with a folder icon displays a list of programs within it; just click the program on that sublist to open it (as shown in **Figure 3-13**).

Click a folder to display the programs within

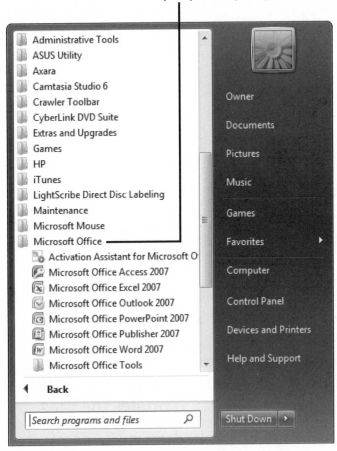

Figure 3-13

- Double-click a program shortcut icon on the desktop (see **Figure 3-14**).

- Click an item on the taskbar. The taskbar should display by default; if it doesn't, press the Windows key (on your keyboard) to display it, and then click an icon on the taskbar (refer to **Figure 3-14**), just to the right of the Start button.

- If you used the program recently and saved a document, choose it from the list of recently used programs displayed when you first open the Start menu. Then click a document created in that program from the list that displays.

Double-click a program shortcut . . .

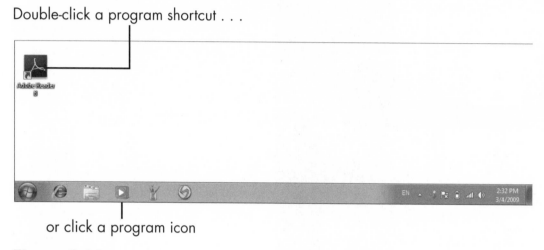

or click a program icon

Figure 3-14

2. When the application opens, if it's a game, play it; if it's a spreadsheet, enter numbers into it; if it's your e-mail program, start deleting junk mail. . . . You get the idea.

 Not every program that's installed on your computer appears as a desktop shortcut or taskbar icon. To add a program to the taskbar or to add a desktop shortcut, see Chapter 3.

Resize Windows

1. When you open an application window, it can be maximized to fill the whole screen, restored down to a smaller window, or minimized to an icon on the taskbar. With an application open and maximized, click the Restore Down button (the icon showing two overlapping windows) in the top-right corner of the program window (see **Figure 3-15**). The window reduces in size.

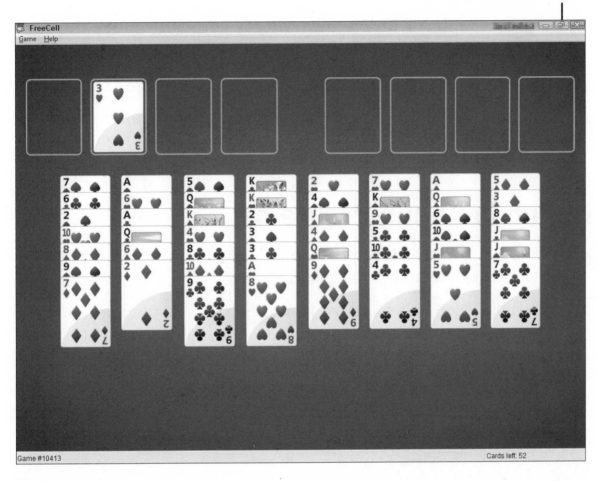

Figure 3-15

2. To enlarge a window that has been restored down to again fill the screen, click the Maximize button. (**Note:** This button is in the same location as the Restore Down button; this button changes it's name to one or the other, depending on whether you have the screen reduced in size or maximized. A ScreenTip identifies the button when you rest your mouse pointer on it.)

3. Click the Minimize button (it's to the left of the Restore Down/Maximize button and looks like a small bar) to minimize the window to an icon on the taskbar. To open

the window again, just click the taskbar icon.

 With a window maximized, you can't move the window. If you reduce a window in size, you can then click and hold the title bar to drag the window around the desktop, which is one way to view more than one window on your screen at the same time. You can also click and drag the corners of a reduced window to resize it to any size you want.

Switch between Programs

1. Open two or more programs. The last program that you open is the active program.

2. Press Alt+Tab to move from one open application window to another.

3. Press and hold Alt+Tab to open a small box, as shown in **Figure 3-16,** revealing all opened programs.

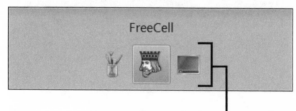

Press the Tab key to select another
open program in this list

Figure 3-16

4. Release the Tab key but keep Alt pressed down. Press Tab to cycle through the icons representing open programs.

5. Release the Alt key, and Windows 7 switches to

whichever program is selected. To switch back to the last program that was active, simply press Alt+Tab, and that program becomes the active program once again.

 All open programs also appear as items on the Windows 7 taskbar. Just click any running program on the taskbar to display that window and make it the active program. If the taskbar isn't visible, press the Windows key on your keyboard to display it.

Close a Program

1. With an application open, first save any open documents (typically you can choose File⇨Save to do this, though in recent Microsoft Office products you click the application button and choose Save As) and then close the application by using one of these methods:

   • Click the Close button in the upper-right corner of the window.

   • Click Alt+F4 to close an active open window.

   • Choose File (or application button)⇨Exit (see **Figure 3-17**).

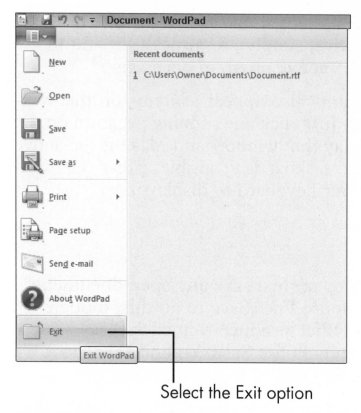

Select the Exit option

Figure 3-17

2. The application closes. If you haven't saved changes in any open documents before trying to close the application, you see a dialog box asking whether you want to save the document(s) (see **Figure 3-18**). Click Save or Don't Save, depending on whether you want to save your changes.

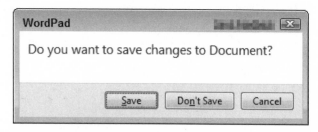

Figure 3-18

To save a document before closing an application, choose File⇨Save and use settings in the Save dialog box (that appears) to name the file and also specify which folder to save it to.

Note that choosing File⇨Exit closes all open documents in an application. Choose File⇨Close to close only the currently active document and keep the application and any other open documents open.

You don't have to close an application to open or switch to another. To switch between open applications, press Alt+Tab and use the arrow keys to move to the application (or document if multiple documents are open in an application) in which you want to work.

Chapter 4

Setting Up Your Display

You chose your designer Day Planner, paper clip holder, and solid maple inbox for your real-world desktop, right? Why shouldn't the Windows desktop give you the same flexibility to make things look the way you like? After all, this is the main work area of Windows, a space that you traverse many, many times in a typical day. Take it from somebody who spends many hours in front of a computer:

Customizing your desktop pays off in increased productivity as well as decreased eyestrain.

To customize your desktop, you can do the following:

➤ Set up Windows to display images and colors.

➤ Use screen saver settings to switch from everyday work stuff to a pretty animation when you've stopped working for a time.

➤ You can modify your *screen resolution* setting, which controls how sharp and detailed a picture your screen displays. (See Chapter 5 for more about settings that help those with visual challenges.)

➤ Modify Windows transparency. Windows Aero Glass is an effect that makes the borders of your windows transparent so you can see other windows layered underneath the active window. You might love it, or hate it, but you should know how to turn the effect on or off.

Customize Windows' Appearance

When you take your computer out of the box, Windows comes with certain preset, or default, settings such as the appearance of the desktop and a color scheme for items you see on your screen. Here are some of the things you can change about the Windows environment and why you might want to change them:

➤ As you work with your computer, you might find that changing the appearance of various elements on your screen not only makes it more pleasant to look at, but also helps you see the text and images more easily. You can change the graphic that's shown as the desktop background, even displaying your own picture there.

➤ You can adjust your screen resolution to not only affect the crispness of images on your screen but also to display items larger on your screen, which could help you if you have visual challenges. (See Chapter 5 for more about Windows features that help people with visual, hearing, or dexterity challenges.)

➤ Windows has built-in *themes* that you can apply quickly. Themes save sets of elements that include menu appearance, background colors or patterns, screen savers, and even mouse cursors and system sounds. If you choose a theme and then modify the way your computer looks in some way — for example, by changing the color scheme — that change overrides the setting in the theme you last applied.

➤ Screen savers are animations that appear after your computer has remained inactive for a time. In the early days of personal computers, screen savers helped to keep your monitor from burning out from constant use. Today, people use screen savers to automatically conceal what they're doing from passersby or just to enjoy the pretty picture.

Set Your Screen's Resolution

1. Changing screen resolution can make items on-screen easier to see. Choose Start⇨Control Panel⇨Appearance and Personalization and click the Adjust Screen Resolution link.

2. In the resulting Screen Resolution window, click the arrow to the right of the Resolution field.

3. Use the slider (as shown in **Figure 4-1**) to select a higher or lower resolution. You can also change the orientation of your display by making a choice in the Orientation drop-down list.

4. Click OK to accept the new screen resolution and then click the Close button to close the window.

 Higher resolutions, such as 1400 x 1250, produce smaller, crisper images. Lower resolutions, such as 800 x 600, produce larger, somewhat jagged images. The upside of higher resolution is that more fits on your screen; the downside is that words and graphics can be hard to see.

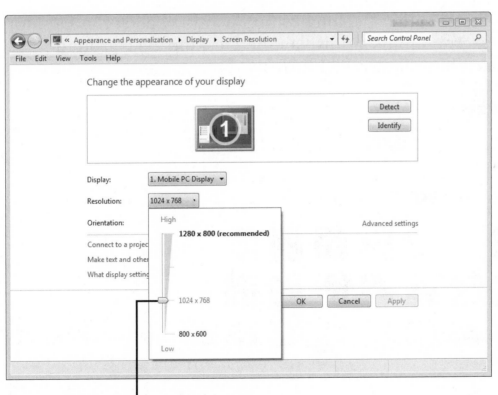

Click and drag the Resolution slider

Figure 4-1

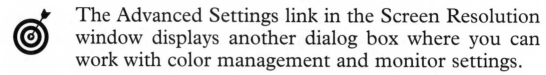 The Advanced Settings link in the Screen Resolution window displays another dialog box where you can work with color management and monitor settings.

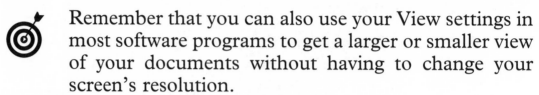 Remember that you can also use your View settings in most software programs to get a larger or smaller view of your documents without having to change your screen's resolution.

Change the Desktop Background

1. You can display a picture or color that appeals to you on your desktop. Right-click the desktop and choose Personalize from the shortcut menu.

2. In the resulting Personalization window, click the Desktop Background link to display the Desktop Background dialog box, shown in **Figure 4-2.**

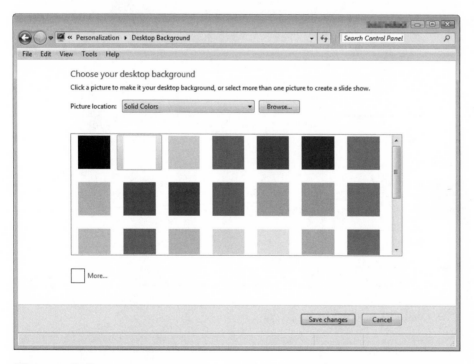

Figure 4-2

3. Select a category of desktop background options from the Picture Location list box (see **Figure 4-3**) and then click the image from the background preview list that you want to use. The background is previewed on your desktop.

4. Click Save Changes to apply the settings and close the dialog box, and then close the Personalization window.

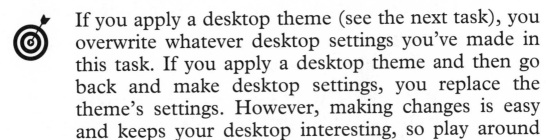 If you apply a desktop theme (see the next task), you overwrite whatever desktop settings you've made in this task. If you apply a desktop theme and then go back and make desktop settings, you replace the theme's settings. However, making changes is easy and keeps your desktop interesting, so play around with themes and desktop backgrounds all you like!

Select a location   Click a picture

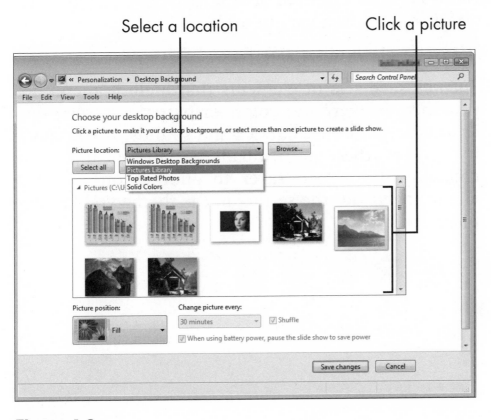

Figure 4-3

Choose a Desktop Theme

1. Themes apply several color and image settings at once. Right-click the desktop and choose Personalize. The Personalization window opens.

2. In the resulting Personalization window, shown in **Figure 4-4,** select a theme. Your options include the following:

    *   **My Themes** uses whatever settings you have and saves them with that name.

    *   **Windows Themes** offers up themes related to Nature, Landscapes, Light Auras, and your country of residence.

    *   **Ease of Access Themes** offer a variety of easy to read contrast settings in a variety of themes.

3. Click Close to close the dialog box.

 Themes save sets of elements that include menu appearance, background colors or patterns, screen savers, and even mouse cursors and sounds. If you modify any of these individually — for example, by changing the screen saver to another one — that change overrides the setting in the theme you last applied.

Select a desktop theme

Figure 4-4

 You can save custom themes. Simply apply a theme, make any changes to it you like using the various Appearance and Personalization settings options, and then in the Personalization dialog box, click Save Theme. In the resulting dialog box give your new theme a name and click Save. It will now appear on the Theme list.

Set Up a Screen Saver

1. If you want an animated sequence to appear when your computer is not in use for a period of time, set up a screen saver. Right-click the desktop and choose Personalize. In the resulting Personalization window, click the Screen Saver button to display the Screen Saver Settings dialog box, as shown in **Figure 4-5.**

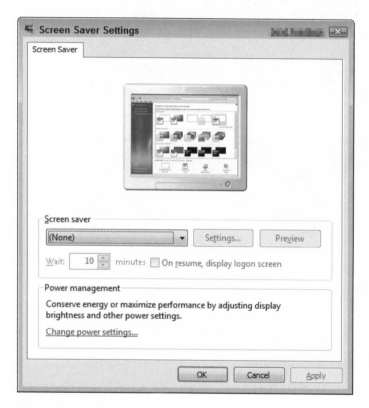

Figure 4-5

2. From the Screen Saver drop-down list, choose a screen saver.

3. Use the arrows in the Wait *xx* Minutes text box to set the number of inactivity minutes that Windows 7 waits before displaying the screen saver.

4. Click the Preview button to take a peek at your screen saver of choice (see **Figure 4-6**). When you're happy with your settings, click to stop the preview, and then click OK.

5. Click the Close button in the Personalization window to close it.

Figure 4-6

 Some screen savers allow you to modify their settings: for example, how fast they display or how many lines they draw on-screen. To customize this, click the Settings button when in the Screen Saver Settings dialog box.

Change the Color and Appearance of Windows

1. You can modify the appearance of elements on your screen one by one. Right-click the desktop and choose Personalize.

2. In the resulting Personalization window, click the Window Color button to display the Window Color and Appearance dialog box, as shown in **Figure 4-7.**

Figure 4-7

3. Select items one by one from the Item drop-down list. Make any changes you wish by using the Size, Color, and Font settings.

94

4. Click OK to accept the settings, and then click Save Changes to return to the Personalization window.

5. Click the Close button to close the Personalization window.

When customizing a color scheme, be aware that not all screen elements allow you to modify all settings. For example, setting an Application Background doesn't make the Font setting available — because it's just a background setting. Makes sense, huh?

Some colors are easier on the eyes than others. For example, green is more restful to look at than orange. Choose a color scheme that is pleasant to look at and easy on the eyes!

Modify Windows Transparency

1. You can apply a Windows Aero theme to get a transparent effect on windows you display. Choose Start⇨ Control Panel⇨Appearance and Personalization. In the Appearance and Personalization window that appears (see **Figure 4-8**), click Personalization.

2. In the resulting Personalization window (see **Figure 4-9**) click on a theme in the Aero Themes section of My Themes.

3. Click the Close button to close the Personalization window and see the results.

Click the Personalization link

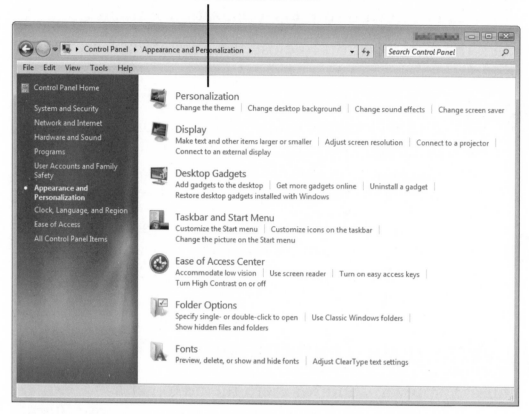

Figure 4-8

 You have to have a graphics card that supports Windows Aero to see the effect. If nothing happens when you apply an Aero effect, click the Troubleshoot Problems with Transparency and Other Aero Effects link at the bottom of the Personalization window to have Windows search for the cause.

Select a theme from the Aero Themes section

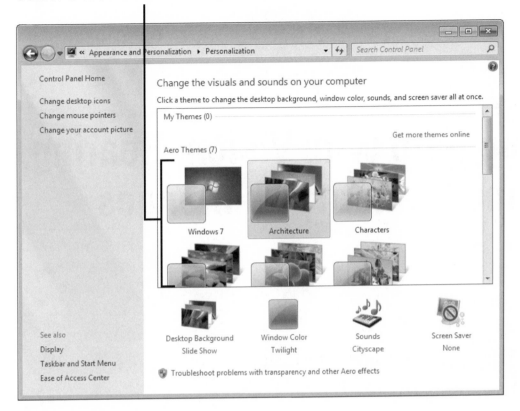

Figure 4-9

Chapter 5

Getting Help with Vision, Hearing, and Dexterity Challenges

People don't always know right off the bat how to get along when they meet someone new. Similarly, sometimes Windows has to be taught how to behave. For example, it doesn't know right off the bat that somebody using it has a vision challenge that requires special help, or that a user prefers a certain mouse cursor or has difficulty using a keyboard.

Somebody taught you manners, but Windows depends on you to make settings that customize its behavior. This is good news for you because the ability to customize Windows gives you a lot of flexibility in how you interact with it.

Here's what you can do to customize Windows:

➤ Control features that help visually challenged users to work with a computer, such as setting a higher contrast, using a Narrator to read the on-screen text aloud, or increasing the size of text on-screen.

➤ Work with the Speech Recognition feature that allows you to input data into a document using speech rather than a keyboard or mouse.

➤ Modify the mouse functionality for left-handed use, change the cursor to sport a certain look, or make viewing the cursor as it moves around your screen easier.

➤ Work with keyboard settings that make input easier for those who are challenged by physical conditions, such as carpal tunnel syndrome or arthritis.

Use Tools for the Visually Challenged

1. You can set up Windows to use higher screen contrast to make things easier to see, read descriptions to you rather than make you read text, and more. Choose Start⇨ Control Panel.

2. In the Control Panel window, click the Optimize Visual Display link under the Ease of Access tools.

3. In the resulting Make the Computer Easier to See dialog box (as shown in **Figure 5-1**), select the check boxes for features you want to use:

- **High Contrast:** Turn on higher contrast when left Alt+left Shift+Print Screen is pressed. High contrast is a color scheme that makes your screen easier to read. You can also choose to have a warning message display when you turn this setting on, or have a sound play when it's turned off or on.

- **Hear Text and Descriptions Read Aloud:** You can turn on a Narrator feature that will read on-screen text or an Audio Description feature to describe what's happening in video programs.

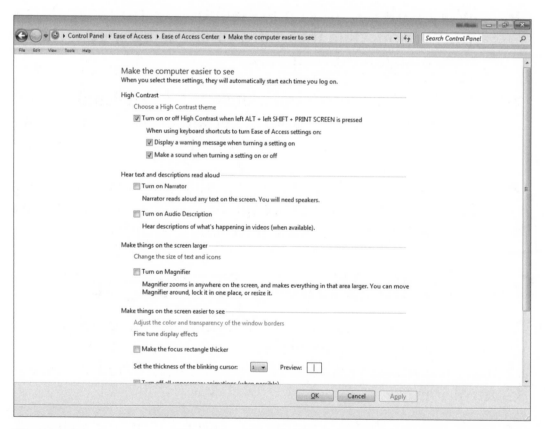

Figure 5-1

- **Make Things on the Screen Larger:** If you click Turn on Magnifier, you have two cursors on-screen. One cursor appears in the Magnifier window where everything is shown enlarged, and one appears in whatever is showing on your computer (for example, your desktop or an open application). You can maneuver either cursor to work in your document. (They're both active, so it does take some getting used to.)

- **Make Things On the Screen Easier to See:** Here's where you make settings that adjust on-screen contrast to make things easier to see, enlarge the size of the blinking mouse cursor (see **Figure 5-2**), and get rid of distracting animations and backgrounds.

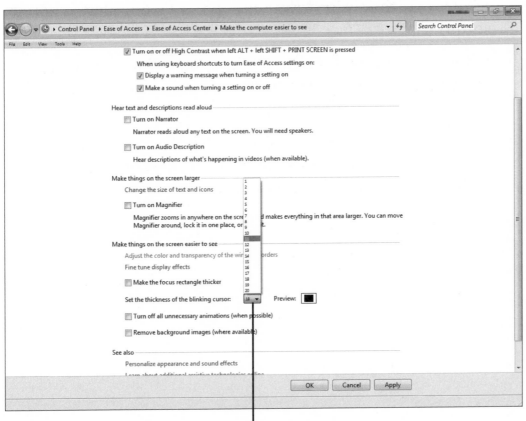

Set the size of the mouse cursor

Figure 5-2

4. When you finish making settings, click OK to apply them and then click the Close button to close the dialog box.

Replace Sounds with Visual Cues

1. Sometimes Windows alerts you to events with sounds. If you have hearing challenges, you might prefer to get visual cues. Choose Start⇨Control Panel⇨Ease of Access and then click the Replace Sounds with Visual Cues link.

2. In the resulting Use Text or Visual Alternatives for Sounds dialog box (see **Figure 5-3**), make any of the following settings:

- Turn on Visual Notifications for Sounds (Sound Sentry) so that Windows will give a visual alert when a sound plays.

- Choose a setting for visual warnings. These warnings essentially flash a portion of your screen to alert you to an event.

- To control text captions for any spoken words, select Turn on Text Captions for Spoken Dialog. **Note:** This isn't always available with every application you use.

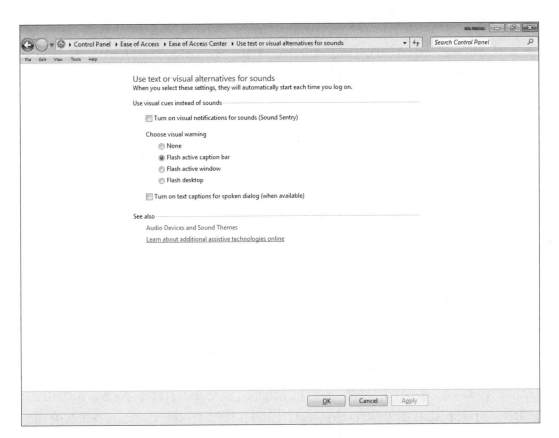

Figure 5-3

3. To save the new settings, click OK, and then click the Close button to close the dialog box.

 Visual cues are useful if you are hard of hearing and don't always pick up system sounds alerting you to error messages or a device disconnect. After the setting is turned on, it is active until you go back to the Use Text or Visual Alternatives for Sounds dialog box and turn it off.

 This may seem obvious, but if you are hard of hearing you may want to simply increase the volume for your speakers. You can do this by using the volume adjustment in a program such as Windows Media Player (see Chapter 14) or by modifying your system volume

103

by choosing Hardware and Sound in the Control Panel and then clicking the Adjust System Volume link.

Make Text Larger or Smaller

1. Choose Start➪Control Panel➪Appearance and Personalization. Click Make Text and Other Items Larger or Smaller in the resulting window.

2. In the resulting Display window (see **Figure 5-4**), click the radio button for the size of text you prefer. Smaller is the default, but you can expand text size to 125 percent with the Medium setting and 150 percent with the Larger setting.

3. Click Apply and then click the Close button to close the dialog box. You'll see the results (see **Figure 5-5,** which shows the Larger setting applied) the next time you log in to Windows.

Make your text size selection

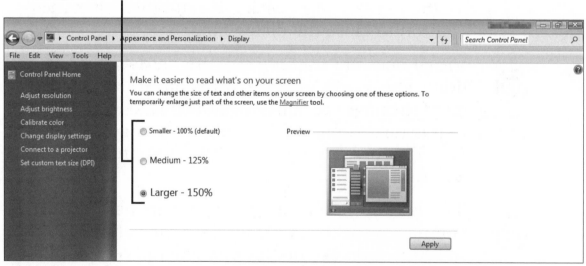

Figure 5-4

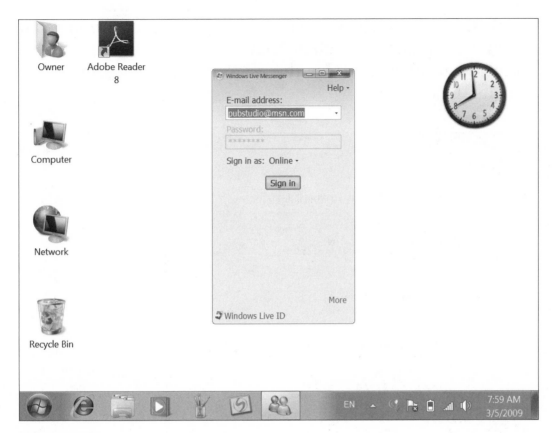

Owner

Adobe Reader 8

Computer

Network

Recycle Bin

Windows Live Messenger

Help ▾

E-mail address:
pubstudio@msn.com

Password:
****

Sign in as: Online ▾

Sign in

More

Windows Live ID

EN

7:59 AM
3/5/2009

Figure 5-5

Set Up Speech Recognition

1. If you have dexterity challenges from a condition such as arthritis, you might prefer to speak commands, using a technology called speech recognition, rather than type them. Attach a desktop microphone or headset to your computer and choose Start➪Control Panel➪Ease of Access➪Start Speech Recognition.

2. The Welcome to Speech Recognition message appears; click Next to continue. (***Note:*** If you've used Speech Recognition before, this message will not appear.)

3. In the resulting Microphone Setup Wizard dialog box

(shown in **Figure 5-6**), select the type of microphone that you're using and then click Next. The next screen tells you how to place and use the microphone for optimum results. Click Next.

Figure 5-6

4. In the following dialog box (see **Figure 5-7**), read the sample sentence aloud. When you're done, click Next. A dialog box appears telling you that your microphone is now set up. Click Next.

 During the Speech Recognition setup procedure, you are given the option of printing out commonly used commands. It's a good idea to do this, as speech commands aren't always second nature!

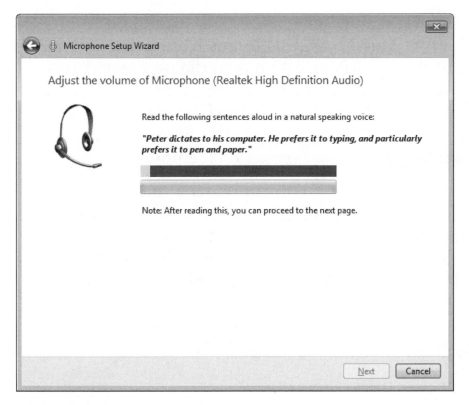

Realtek High Definition Audio)

Figure 5-7

5. In the resulting dialog box, choose whether to enable or disable document review. Document review allows Windows to review your documents and e-mail to help it recognize your speech patterns. Click Next.

6. In the resulting dialog box, choose either manual activation mode, where you can use a mouse, pen, or keyboard to turn the feature on, or voice activation, which is useful if you have difficulty manipulating devices because of arthritis or a hand injury. Click Next.

7. In the resulting screen, if you wish to view and/or print a list of speech recognition commands, click the View Reference Sheet button and read about or print reference information, and then click the Close button to close that window. Click Next to proceed.

8. In the resulting dialog box, either click Run Speech Recognition at Startup to disable this feature or leave the default setting. Click Next. The final dialog box informs you that you can now control the computer by voice, and offers you a Start Tutorial button to help you practice voice commands. Click that button, or click Skip Tutorial to skip the tutorial and leave the Speech Recognition set up.

9. The Speech Recognition control panel appears (see **Figure 5-8**). Say, "Start listening" to activate the feature if you used voice activation in Step 6, or click the Start Speech Recognition link if you chose manual activation in Step 6. You can now begin using spoken commands to work with your computer.

The Speech Recognition control panel

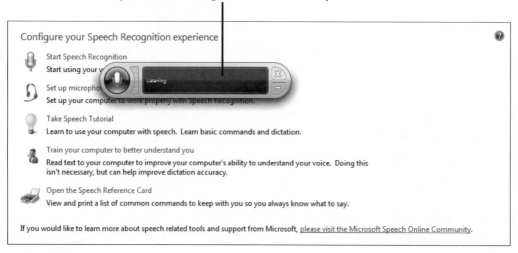

Configure your Speech Recognition experience

Start Speech Recognition
Start using your v

Set up micropho
Set up your computer to work properly with Speech Recognition.

Take Speech Tutorial
Learn to use your computer with speech. Learn basic commands and dictation.

Train your computer to better understand you
Read text to your computer to improve your computer's ability to understand your voice. Doing this isn't necessary, but can help improve dictation accuracy.

Open the Speech Reference Card
View and print a list of common commands to keep with you so you always know what to say.

If you would like to learn more about speech related tools and support from Microsoft, please visit the Microsoft Speech Online Community.

Figure 5-8

 To stop Speech Recognition, click the Close button on the Control Panel. To start the Speech Recognition feature again, choose Start⇨Control Panel⇨Ease of Access and then click the Start Speech Recognition link. To learn more about Speech Recognition commands, click the Take Speech Tutorial link in the Speech Recognition Options window accessed from the Ease of Access window of the Control Panel.

Modify How Your Keyboard Works

1. If your hands are a bit stiff with age or you have carpal tunnel problems, you might look into changing how your keyboard works. Choose Start⇨Control Panel⇨Ease of Access and then click the Change How Your Keyboard Works link.

2. In the resulting Make the Keyboard Easier to Use dialog box (see **Figure 5-9**), make any of these settings:

- **Turn on Mouse Keys** to control your mouse by keyboard commands. If you turn on this setting, click the Set Up Mouse Keys link to specify settings for this feature.

- Select the **Turn on Sticky Keys** feature to enable keystroke combinations to be pressed one at a time, rather than in combination.

- **Turn on Toggle Keys.** You can set up Windows to play a sound when you press Caps Lock, Num Lock, or Scroll Lock (which I do all the time by mistake!).

- If you sometimes press a key very lightly or press it so hard it activates twice, you can use the **Turn on Filter Keys** setting to adjust repeat rates to adjust for that. Use the Set Up Filter Keys link to fine-tune settings if you make this choice.

- To have Windows highlight keyboard shortcuts and access keys with an underline wherever these shortcuts appear, click that setting.

- If you want to avoid having windows shift automatically when you move them to the edge of your screen, use the **Make It Easier to Manage Windows** setting.

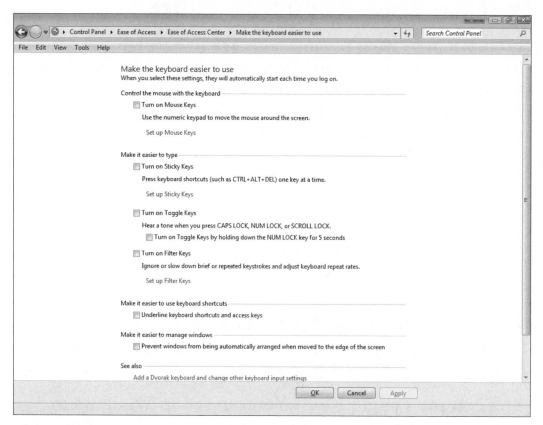

Figure 5-9

3. To save the new settings, click OK, and then click the Close button to close the Ease of Access Center.

 You can click the Learn about Additional Assistive Technologies Online link to go the Microsoft Web site and discover add-on and third party programs that might help you if you have a visual, hearing, or input-related disability.

Keyboards all have their own unique feel. If your keyboard isn't responsive and you have a keyboard-challenging condition, you might also try different keyboards to see if one works better for you than another.

Use the On-screen Keyboard Feature

1. Clicking keys with your mouse may be easier for some than using a regular keyboard. To use the on-screen keyboard, choose Start⇨Control Panel⇨Ease of Access category.

2. In the resulting window, click the Ease of Access Center link to open the Ease of Access Center dialog box (see **Figure 5-10**), click Start On-Screen Keyboard. The on-screen keyboard appears (see **Figure 5-11**).

3. Open a document in any application where you can enter text, and then click the keys on the on-screen keyboard to make entries.

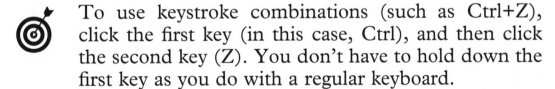 To use keystroke combinations (such as Ctrl+Z), click the first key (in this case, Ctrl), and then click the second key (Z). You don't have to hold down the first key as you do with a regular keyboard.

4. To change settings, such as how you select keys (Typing Mode) or the font used to label keys (Font), click the Options key on the on-screen keyboard and then choose one of the four options shown in the Options dialog box and click OK.

111

Click this link

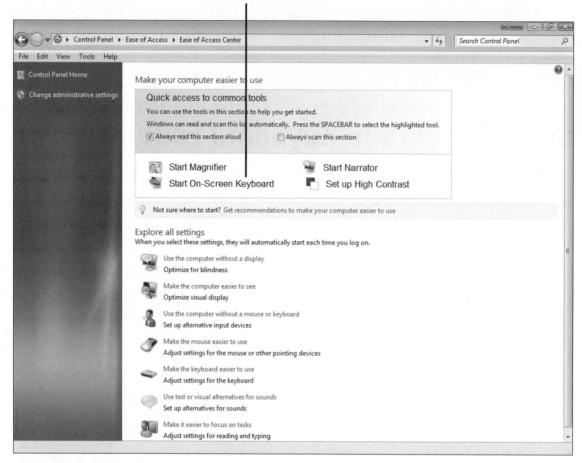

Figure 5-10

5. Click the Close button on the on-screen keyboard to stop using it.

 You can set up the Hover typing mode to activate a key after you hover your mouse over it for a predefined period of time (*x* number of seconds). If you have arthritis or some other condition that makes clicking your mouse difficult, this option can help you enter text. Click the Hover over Keys item in the Options dialog box and use the slider to set how long you have to hover before activating the key.

112

Figure 5-11

Set Up Keyboard Repeat Rates

1. Adjusting your keyboard settings might make it easier for you to type, and it can be helpful to people with dexterity challenges. To see your options, choose Start➪Control Panel➪All Control Panel Items. In the resulting window, click the Keyboard link.

2. In the Keyboard Properties dialog box that appears, click the Speed tab (see **Figure 5-12**) and drag the sliders to adjust the two Character Repeat settings, which do the following:

   • **Repeat Delay:** Affects the amount of time it takes before a typed character is typed again when you hold down a key.

   • **Repeat Rate:** Adjusts how quickly a character repeats when you hold down a key after the first repeat character appears.

   > If you want to see how the Character Repeat settings work in action, click in the text box below the two settings and hold down a key to see a demonstration.

3. Drag the slider in the Cursor Blink Rate section. This affects cursors, such as the insertion line that appears in text.

113

Figure 5-12

4. Click OK to save and apply changes and close the dialog box. Click the Close button to close the Control Panel window.

 If you have trouble with motion (for example, because of arthritis or carpal tunnel syndrome), you might find that you can adjust these settings to make it easier for you to get your work done. For example, if you can't pick up your finger quickly from a key, a slower repeat rate might save you from typing more instances of a character than you'd intended.

Customize Mouse Behavior

1. To avoid having to click your mouse too often, instead of moving your mouse with your hand, you can use your

keyboard to move the cursor; or, you can cause a window to activate by hovering your mouse over it rather than clicking. Choose Start➪Control Panel➪Ease of Access and then click the Change How Your Mouse Works link. The Make the Mouse Easier to Use dialog box opens (see **Figure 5-13**).

2. To use the numeric keypad to move your mouse cursor on your screen, choose the Turn on Mouse Keys setting. If you turn this feature on, click Set Up Mouse Keys to fine-tune its behavior.

3. Select the Activate a Window by Hovering Over It with The Mouse check box to enable this (pretty self-explanatory!) feature.

4. Click OK to save the new settings and then click the Close button to close the Ease of Access Center.

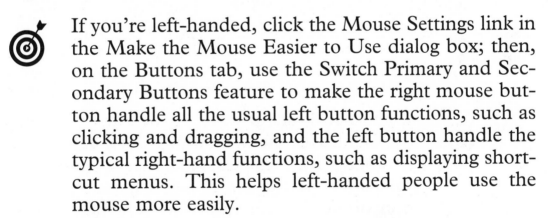 If you're left-handed, click the Mouse Settings link in the Make the Mouse Easier to Use dialog box; then, on the Buttons tab, use the Switch Primary and Secondary Buttons feature to make the right mouse button handle all the usual left button functions, such as clicking and dragging, and the left button handle the typical right-hand functions, such as displaying shortcut menus. This helps left-handed people use the mouse more easily.

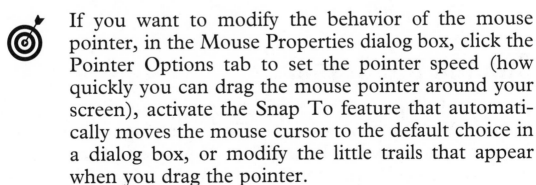 If you want to modify the behavior of the mouse pointer, in the Mouse Properties dialog box, click the Pointer Options tab to set the pointer speed (how quickly you can drag the mouse pointer around your screen), activate the Snap To feature that automatically moves the mouse cursor to the default choice in a dialog box, or modify the little trails that appear when you drag the pointer.

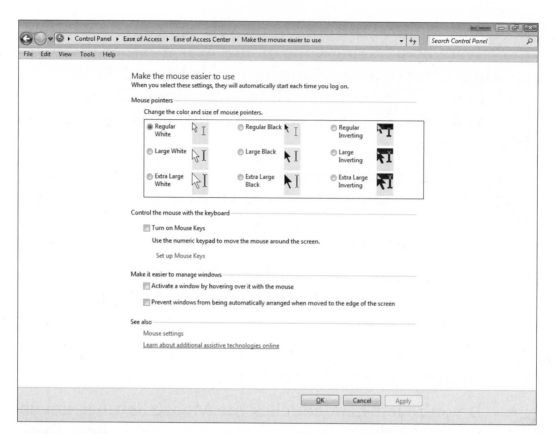

Figure 5-13

 If you have difficulty seeing the cursor on-screen, experiment with the Windows 7 color schemes to see if another setting makes your cursor stand out better against the background. See Chapter 4 for information on setting up the color scheme for your computer.

Change the Cursor

1. Having trouble finding the mouse cursor on your screen? You might want to enlarge it or change its shape. Choose Start⟿Control Panel⟿Ease of Access⟿Change How Your Mouse Works. In the resulting Make the Mouse Easier to

Use dialog box, click the Mouse Settings link.

2. In the resulting Mouse Properties dialog box, on the Pointers tab, as shown in **Figure 5-14,** click to select a pointer such as Normal Select and then click the Browse button. (Note that this dialog box may have slightly different tabs depending on your mouse's model features.) In the Browse dialog box that appears, click on an alternate cursor and then click Open.

Figure 5-14

3. Click Apply to use the new pointer setting and then click the Close button to close the Mouse Properties dialog box.

 Be careful not to change the cursor to another standard cursor (for example, changing the Normal Select cursor to the Busy hourglass cursor). This could prove slightly confusing for you and completely baffling to anybody else who works on your computer. If you make a choice and decide it was a mistake, click the Use Default button on Pointers tab in the Mouse Properties dialog box to return a selected cursor to its default choice.

 You can also choose the color and size of mouse pointers in the Make the Mouse Easier to Use dialog box. A large white or extra large black cursor might be more visible to you, depending on the color scheme you have applied to Windows Vista.

Chapter 6

Setting Up Printers and Scanners

Acomputer is a great storehouse for data, images, and other digital information, but sometimes you need ways to turn printed documents into electronic files you can work with on your computer or to print *hard copies* (a fancy term for paper printouts) of electronic documents and images. Here are a few key ways to do just that:

119

➽ **Printers** allow you to create hard copies of your files on paper, transparencies, or whatever stock your printer can accommodate. To use a printer, you have to have software installed — a *printer driver* — and use certain settings to tell your computer how to find the printer and what to print.

➽ You use a **scanner** to create electronic files — pictures, essentially — from hard copies of newspaper clippings, your birth certificate or driver's license, pictures, or whatever will fit into/onto your scanner. You can then work with the files, send them to others as an e-mail attachment, or print them. Scanners also require that you install a driver that comes with your machine.

Install a Printer

1. Read the instructions that came with the printer.
Some printers require that you install software before connecting them, but others can be connected right away.

2. Turn on your computer and then follow the option that fits your needs:

• If your printer is a Plug and Play device, connect it and power it on; Windows installs what it needs automatically.

• Insert the disk (or disc) that came with the device and follow the on-screen instructions.

• Choose Start➪Devices and Printers.

• If you have a wireless printer, choose Start➪Devices and Printers and click the Add a Printer link in the window that appears. Choose the Add a Network,

Wireless, or Bluetooth Printer option and follow the instructions provided.

3. If you choose the third option in Step 2, in the Devices and Printers window that appears click the Add a Printer link near the top.

4. In the resulting wizard window (the Add Printer dialog box, shown in **Figure 6-1**), click the Add a Local Printer option and click Next.

5. In the Choose a Printer Port dialog box, shown in **Figure 6-2,** click the down arrow on the Use an Existing Port field and select a port, or just use the recommended port setting that Windows selects for you. Click Next.

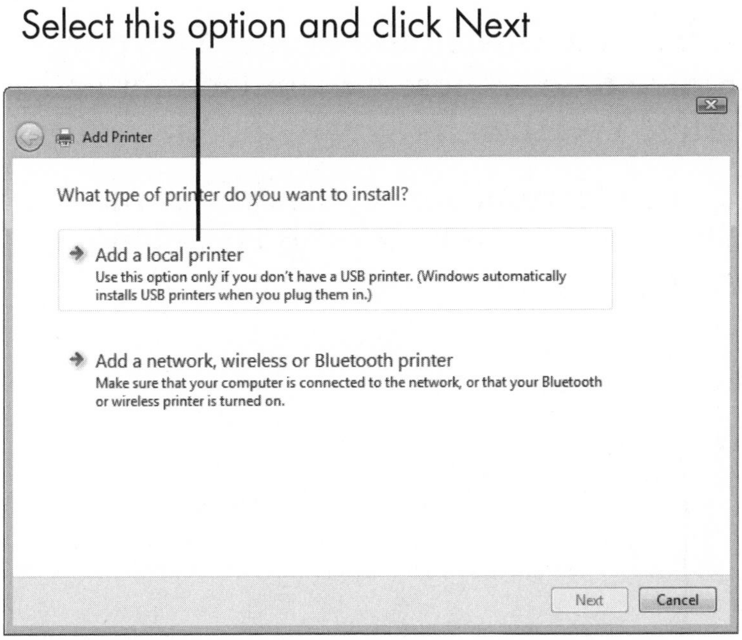

Select this option and click Next

Figure 6-1

Select a printer port

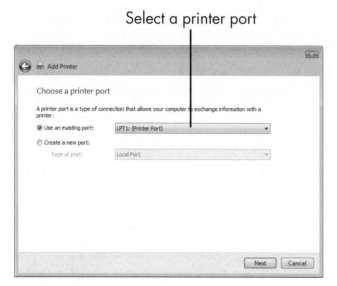

Figure 6-2

6. In the next wizard window (Install the Printer Driver dialog box; see **Figure 6-3**), choose a manufacturer and then choose a printer. You then have two options:

- If you have the manufacturer's disc, insert it in the appropriate CD drive now and click the Have Disk button. Click Next.

Choose a manufacturer   Then choose a printer

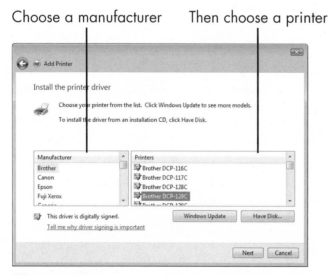

Figure 6-3

- If you don't have the manufacturer's disc, click the Windows Update button to see a list of printer drivers that you can download from the Microsoft Web site. Click Next.

7. In the resulting Type a Printer Name dialog box (see **Figure 6-4**), enter a printer name. Click Next.

Enter a name for your printer

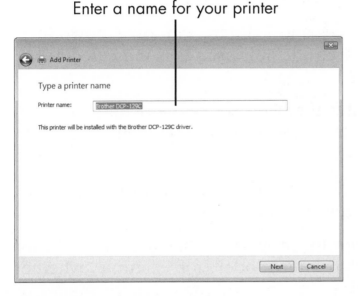

Figure 6-4

8. In the resulting dialog box, click Finish to complete the Add Printer Wizard.

 If your computer is on a network and you choose the fourth option in Step 2, you get additional dialog boxes in the wizard, including one right after you name the printer, which allows you to share the printer on your network. Select the Do Not Share This Printer option to stop others from using the printer, or select the Share Name option and enter a printer name to share the printer on your network. This means that others can see and select this printer to print to.

Set a Default Printer

1. You can set up a default printer that will be used every time you print so you don't have to select a printer each time. Choose Start⇨Devices and Printers.

2. In the resulting Devices and Printers window (shown in **Figure 6-5**), the current default printer is indicated by a check mark.

3. Right-click any printer that isn't set as the default and choose Set as Default Printer from the shortcut menu, as shown in **Figure 6-6.**

4. Click the Close button in the Devices and Printers window to save the new settings.

 To modify printing properties that are available for your particular printer model (for example, whether the printer prints in draft or high-quality mode, or whether it uses color or only black and white), right-click a printer in the Devices and Printers window (refer to **Figure 6-6**) and choose Printing Preferences. This same dialog box is available from most common Windows-based software programs, such as Microsoft Word or Excel, by clicking the Properties button in the Print dialog box.

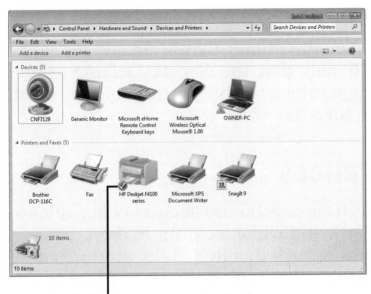

The default printer is checked

Figure 6-5

Choose Set As Default Printer

Figure 6-6

125

If you right-click the printer that is already set as the default, you'll find that the Set as Default Printer command will not be available on the shortcut menu mentioned in Step 3.

Set Printer Preferences

1. Your printer might have capabilities such as being able to print in color or black and white, or print in draft quality (which uses less ink) or high quality (which produces a darker, crisper image). To modify these settings for all documents you print, choose Start⇨Devices and Printers (in the Hardware and Sound group).

2. In the resulting Devices and Printers window, any printers you have installed are listed. Right-click a printer and then choose Printing Preferences.

3. In the Printing Preferences dialog box that appears (shown in **Figure 6-7**), click any of the tabs to display various settings, such as Color (see **Figure 6-8**). Note that different printers might display different choices and different tabs in this dialog box, but common settings include

   • **Color/Grayscale:** If you have a color printer, you have the option of printing in color. The grayscale option uses only black ink. When printing a draft of a color document, you can save colored ink by printing in grayscale, for example.

   • **Quality:** If you want, you can print in fast or draft quality (these settings may have different names depending on your manufacturer) to save ink, or you can print in a higher or best quality for your finished documents. Some printers offer a dpi setting for quality — the higher the dpi setting, the better the quality.

- **Paper Source:** If you have a printer with more than one paper tray, you can select which tray to use for printing. For example, you might have 8½ x 11 paper (letter sized) in one tray and 8½ x 14 (legal sized) in another.

- **Paper Size:** Choose the size of paper or envelope you're printing to. In many cases, this option displays a preview that shows you which way to insert the paper. A preview can be especially handy if you're printing to envelopes and need help figuring out how to insert them in your printer.

Click a tab to see different settings

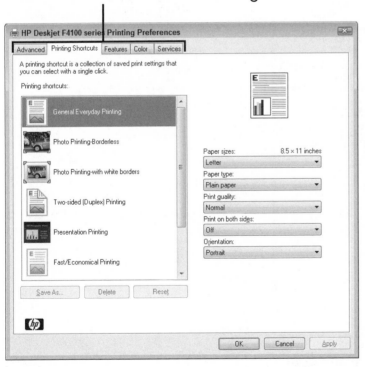

Figure 6-7

127

4. Click the OK button to close the dialog box and save settings and then click the Close button to close other open Control Panel windows.

 Also, the settings in the Printing Preferences dialog box may differ slightly depending on your printer model; color printers offer different options from black and white printers, for example.

 Whatever settings you make using the procedure in this task are your default settings for all printing you do. However, when you're printing a document from within a program such as Works word processor, the Print dialog box you display gives you the opportunity to change the printer settings for that document only. See Chapter 11 for information about printing a document.

Click OK to save settings

Figure 6-8

128

View Currently Installed Printers

1. Over time you might install multiple printers, in which case you may want to remind yourself of the capabilities of each or view the documents you have sent to be printed. To view the printers you have installed and view any documents currently in line for printing, choose Start⇨View Devices and Printers.

2. In the resulting Devices and Printers window (see **Figure 6-9**), a list of installed printers and fax machines appears. If a printer has documents in its print queue, the number of documents is listed at the bottom of the window. If you want more detail about the documents or want to cancel a print job, select the printer and click the See What's Printing button at the top of the window. In the window that appears, click a document and choose Document⇨Cancel to stop the printing, if you want. Click the Close button to return to the Devices and Printers window.

The number of documents in queue to print

Figure 6-9

3. You can right-click any printer and then choose Properties (see **Figure 6-10**) to see details about it, such as which port it's plugged into or whether it can print color copies.

Figure 6-10

4. Click the Close button (the red X in the upper right) to close the Devices and Printers window.

Remove a Printer

1. Over time, you might upgrade to a new printer and chuck the old one. When you do, you might want to also remove the older printer driver from your computer so your Printers window isn't cluttered with printers you don't need anymore. To remove a printer, choose Start⇨ Devices and Printers (in the Hardware and Sound group).

2. In the resulting Devices and Printers window (see **Figure 6-11**), right-click a printer and choose Remove Device. (Note you can also select the printer and click the Remove Device button at the top of the window.)

3. In the Printers dialog box that appears, click Yes; the Devices and Printers window closes, and your printer is removed from the printer list.

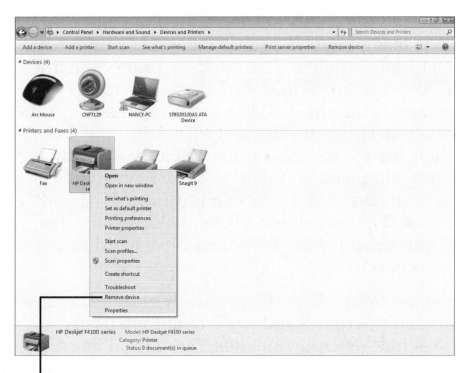

Click Remove Device

Figure 6-11

 If you remove a printer, it's removed from the list of installed printers, and if it was the default printer, Windows makes another printer you have installed the default printer. You can no longer print to it unless you install it again. See the task, "Install a Printer," if you decide you want to print to that printer again.

131

Install a Scanner

1. Before you can scan documents into your computer with a scanner, you need to install the scanner driver so your scanner and computer can communicate. Start by connecting the scanner to your computer's USB port (see your scanner manual for information about how it connects to your computer).

2. Turn the scanner on. Some scanners use Plug and Play, a technology that Windows uses to recognize equipment and automatically install and set it up. If your scanner is Plug and Play enabled, Windows 7 shows a Found New Hardware message in the Taskbar notification area (in the lower-right corner). Most Plug and Play devices will then automatically install, the message will change to verify the installation is complete, and that's all you have to do. If that doesn't happen, either you're not using a Plug and Play device or Windows doesn't have the driver for that device, so you should click the Found New Hardware message to proceed.

3. In the resulting Found New Hardware Wizard (this starts only if you don't permit Windows 7 to automatically connect to Windows Update), click Yes, This Time Only and then click Next.

4. If you have a CD for the scanner, insert it in your CD drive and click Next. Windows 7 searches for your scanner driver software and installs it.

5. Choose Start⇨Control Panel. In the Search box type **scanners**. Windows returns a set of links. Click on the View Scanners and Cameras link. In the resulting Scanners and Cameras window, click the Add Device button.

6. In the resulting Scanner and Camera Installation Wizard window, click Next. In the next screen of the wizard (see **Figure 6-12**), click a Manufacturer in the list on the left and then click a model in the list on the right.

Select a manufacturer   Then select a model

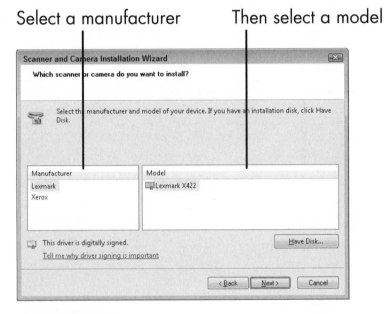

Figure 6-12

7. Follow the wizard directions based on the model of scanner you choose in Step 6 and whether you have a manufacturer's disc (a CD- or DVD-ROM). If you don't have a disc, Windows will help you download software from the Internet. When you reach the end of the wizard, click Finish to complete the installation.

Modify Scanner Settings

1. After you install a scanner, you might want to take a look at or change its default settings. To do so, choose Start⇨Control Panel. Type **scanners** in the Control Panel search field and press Enter.

2. In the resulting Control Panel window, click View Scanners and Cameras.

3. In the resulting Scanners and Cameras dialog box, a list of installed scanners appears (see **Figure 6-13**). Click any scanner in the Scanners and Cameras area, and then click the Scan Profiles button.

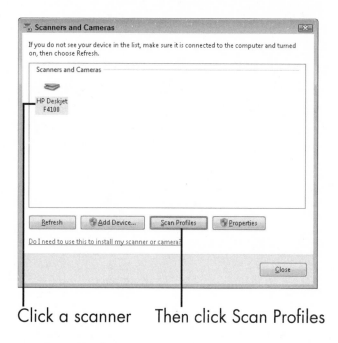

Click a scanner   Then click Scan Profiles

Figure 6-13

4. In the resulting Profiles dialog box, select a scanner and click Edit. In the Edit Default Profile dialog box (see **Figure 6-14**), review the settings, which may include (depending on your scanner model) color management for fine tuning the way colors are scanned and resolution settings that control how detailed a scan is performed (the higher the resolution, the crisper and cleaner your electronic document, but the more time it may take to scan).

134

5. Click Save Profile to return to the Properties dialog box and then click the Close button twice to close the Scan Profiles and Scanners and Cameras windows.

 When you're ready to run a scan, place the item to be scanned in your scanner. Depending on your model, the item may be placed on a flat "bed" with a hinged cover or fed through a tray. Check your scanner's manual for the specific procedure to initiate a scan (for example, pressing a Scan or Start button). After you begin the scan, your computer automatically detects it and displays a dialog box showing you the scan progress and allowing you to view and save the scanned item.

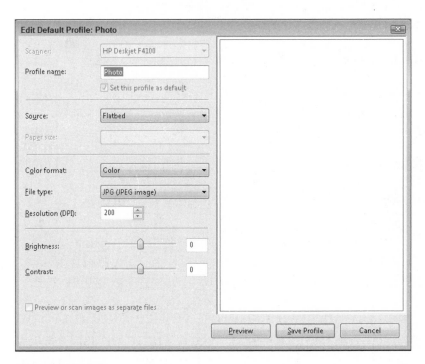

Figure 6-14

135

Chapter 7

Getting Help

With so many Windows features, you're bound to run into something that doesn't work right or isn't easy to figure out (or that this book doesn't cover). That's when you need to call on the resources that Microsoft provides to help you out.

Through the Help and Support Center, you can get help in various ways, including the following:

➡ **Access information that's stored in the Help system database.** Logically enough, a database contains data; in this case, it contains information about Windows 7 organized by topics such as Printers or Using Your Mouse. Drill down from one topic to another or by using a powerful search mechanism to search by keywords such as "e-mail." There's even a troubleshooting feature that helps you pin down your problem.

➡ **Get help from your fellow Windows users.** Tap into information exchanged by users in Windows Communities (sort of like the community bulletin board in your local community center) or by using a little feature called *Remote Assistance,* which allows you to let another user take over your computer from a distance (via the Internet) and figure out your problem for you.

➡ **Open your wallet and pay for it.** Microsoft offers some help for free (for example, help for installing its software that you paid good money for), but some help comes at a price. When you can't find help anywhere else, you may want to consider forking over a few hard-earned bucks for this option.

Explore the Help Table of Contents

1. Your first stop in searching for help is likely to be the built-in help database. One of the simplest ways to find what you need here is to use the Table of Contents, which is similar to a book's Table of Contents. Choose Start⇨Help and Support to open Windows Help and Support, shown in **Figure 7-1.** ***Note:*** If your copy of

137

Windows came built into your computer, some computer manufacturers (such as Hewlett-Packard) customize this center to add information that's specific to your computer system.

2. Click the Browse Help Topics link to display a list of topics. Click any of the topics to see a list of subtopics. Eventually, you get down to the deepest level of detailed subtopics, as shown in **Figure 7-2.**

3. Click a subtopic to read its contents. Some subtopics contain blue links that lead to related topics or perform an action such as opening a dialog box. Green links display a definition or explanation of a term when clicked.

4. When you finish reading a help topic, click the Close button to close the Windows Help and Support window.

You can click the Print icon in the set of tools at the top right of the Windows Help and Support window to print any displayed topic. You can also click the Minimize button in the title bar to minimize the window and keep it available while you work on your computer.

Windows will automatically get the most up-to-date help information if you are connected to the Internet when you open Help and Support. If you are not connected, you can still browse the database of help information installed with Windows 7. See Chapter 16 for help with connecting to the Internet.

Click this link

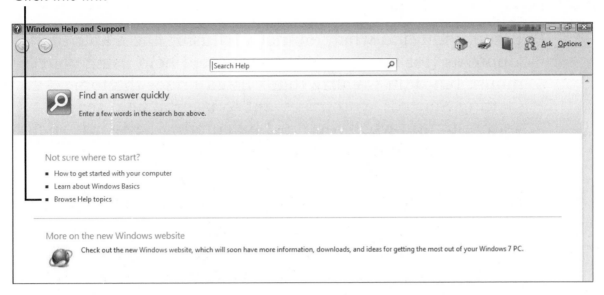

Figure 7-1

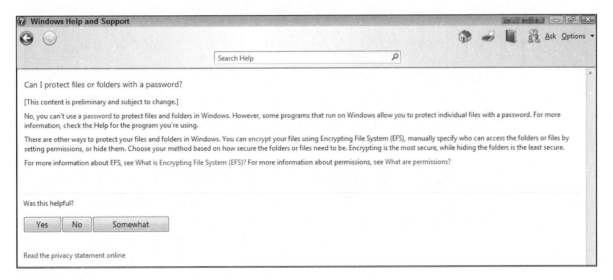

Figure 7-2

Search for Help

1. If you don't find what you need by using the Table of Contents (for instance, say you wanted help using your mouse but didn't realize that's listed under the topic Getting Started), you may want to use the help search feature to find what you need by entering keywords such as *mouse* or *input.* Start by opening the Windows Help and Support window.

2. Enter a search term in the Search Help box and then click the Search Help button. Search results, such as those shown in **Figure 7-3,** appear. Windows will search online help by default, if you are connected to the Internet. If you wish to only use offline help, click the Online Help link in the bottom-right corner and choose Get Offline Help.

3. Explore topics by clicking various links in the search results. These links offer a few different types of help:

   • Procedures, such as Make the mouse easier to use.

   • Troubleshooting help items are phrased as statements, such as I can't hear any text read aloud with Narrator. Clicking one of these takes you to a troubleshooter wizard.

   • Some items provide general information rather than procedures, such as Tips for Searching the Internet. (See **Figure 7-4.**)

4. If you have no luck, enter a different search term in the Search Help text box and start again.

 If you don't find what you need with Search, consider clicking the Browse Help button in the top right of the Windows Help and Support window (it sports a little blue icon in the shape of a book) to display a list

140

of major topics. Those topics may also give you some ideas for good search terms to continue your search.

Enter a search term here

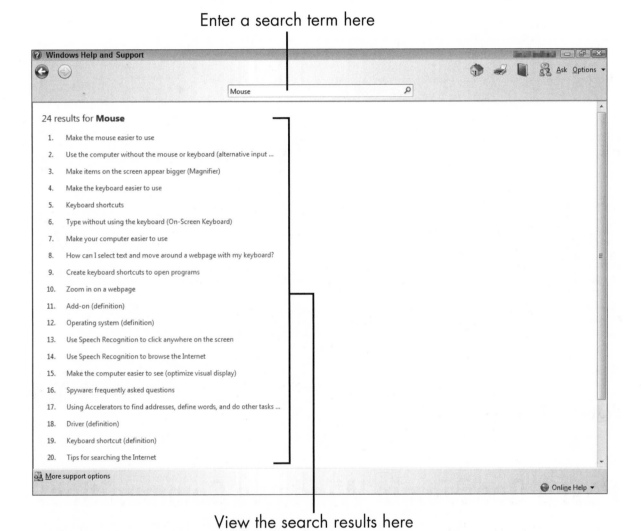

View the search results here

Figure 7-3

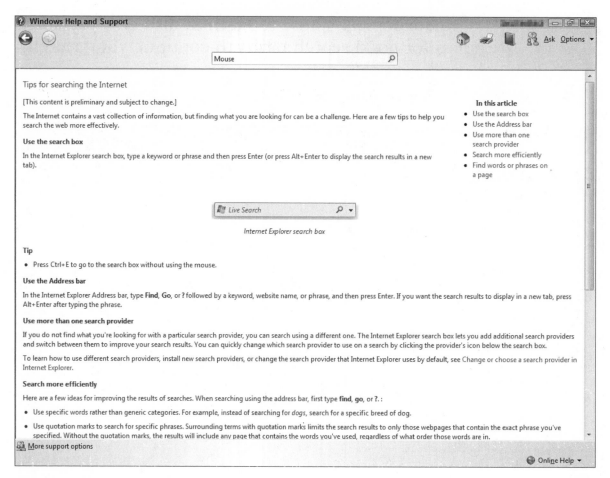

Figure 7-4

Post a Question in Windows Communities

1. If you want to see how other Windows users have solved a problem, you can visit Windows Communities and read posted messages, or even post one yourself and see if others can help you out. Open the Windows Help and Support window. Click the Ask button in the top-right corner. In the Ask a Person for Help section of the page, click the Microsoft Answers link.

2. In the Microsoft Answers page that opens in your

browser, click the topic on the left that relates to your problem or question (see **Figure 7-5**).

Click a topic link

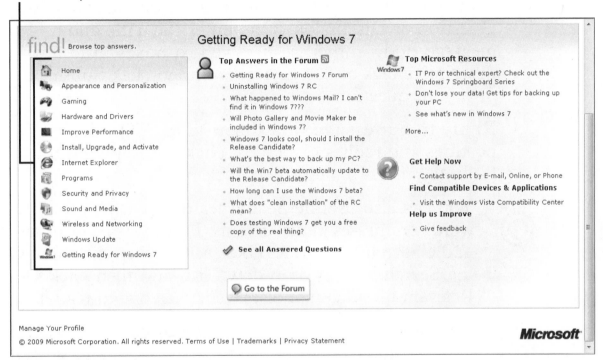

Figure 7-5

3. Click the Go to the Forum button which displays discussion summaries and indicates the number of discussion messages (see **Figure 7-6**).

4. Click on the discussion title to display the threads (series of related postings) contained in it.

5. Click on a thread title to open it and scroll through the original posting and replies to it.

• **Post a new message.** To post a message, you have to sign into Microsoft TechNet using a Windows Live ID (which you can get for free by going to www.

143

windowslive.com). Next, select the discussion group to participate in, and then click the Ask a Question button. If you have never participated in a discussion, you will be asked to create a profile. Enter a display name and click the Accept button. In the Start a New Question or Discussion form, enter the Title and message Body in their respective text boxes. Add any descriptive tags or categories, and then click Submit to post your question.

- **Reply to a message in a discussion.** With the list of postings and replies displayed, click the Reply button, fill in the message, and then click Post.

You can also use the Search feature to search for key-words or phrases in discussions. Enter a word or phrase in the Search Forums text box, select where to search in the Search Forum drop-down list, and then click Go. Relevant messages are displayed; click one to read it.

It's a good idea to roam around a discussion for a bit before you post a question to see if it's been addressed before. If you post a question that's been answered several times before, you not only waste your time and the time of others, but you may find yourself the recipient of a bit of razzing by regulars to the discussion forum.

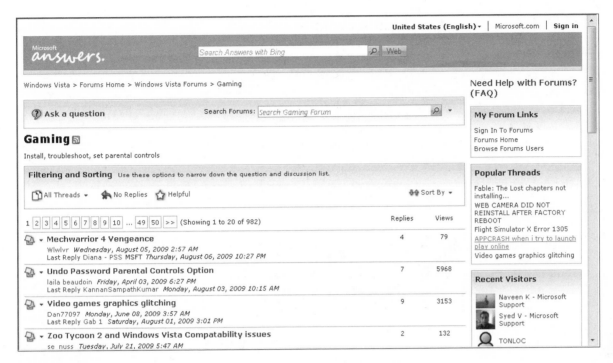

Figure 7-6

Access Windows Online Help

1. Enter **http://windows.microsoft.com/en-us/windows7/ help** in your browser address line and click the Go button.

2. In the Windows 7 Help & How-To window that appears (see **Figure 7-7**), use the links in the following sections to get help:

   - **Getting Started** includes topics such as installing Windows or hardware and personalizing your PC (see **Figure 7-8**).

   - **Top Solutions** takes you to the most-viewed troubleshooting topics that help you work with Windows features and settings.

Use these sections to get help

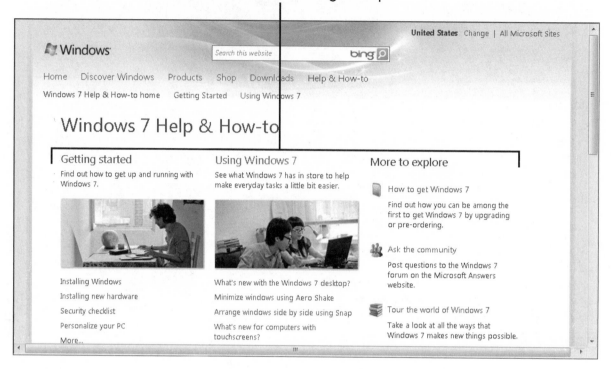

Figure 7-7

- **More to Explore** offers information on upgrading to Windows 7, a link to community forums, and how-to videos.

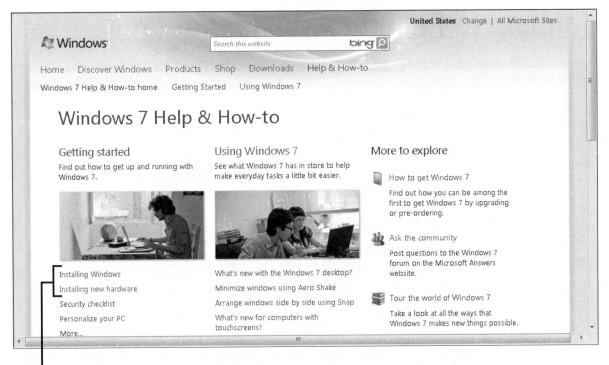

Getting Started offers help installing Windows and new hardware

Figure 7-8

3. Click the Close button to close the online help window in your browser, and then click the Close button to close Windows Help and Support.

 To set up Help and Support to always include Windows Online Help and Support when you search for help, click the Options button and choose Settings. Be sure the checkbox labeled Improve My Search Results by Using Online Help (recommended) is selected, and click OK to accept the change.

147

Connect to Remote Assistance

1. Remote Assistance can be a wonderful feature for new computer users because it allows you to permit somebody else to view or take control of your computer from their own computer no matter where they are. You can contact that person by phone or e-mail, for example, and ask for help. Then, you can send an invitation using Windows 7 Help. When that person accepts the invitation, you can give him or her permission to access your system. Be aware that by doing so you give the person access to all your files, so be sure this is somebody you trust. When that person is connected, he or she can either advise you about your problem or actually make changes to your computer to fix the problem for you. To use Remote Assistance, you and the other person first have to have Windows and an Internet connection.

2. Next, enable Remote Assistance by choosing Start⇨Control Panel⇨System and Security⇨Allow Remote Access. On the Remote tab of the System Properties dialog box that is displayed, select the Allow Remote Assistance Connections to This Computer check box, and then click OK.

3. Open the Windows Help and Support window.

4. Click the Ask button, and then click the Windows Remote Assistance link. On the window that appears, shown in **Figure 7-9,** click the Invite Someone You Trust to Help You link. If you have Windows Firewall or a third-party firewall active, you may have to disable that feature to allow remote access to your computer.

5. On the page that appears, you can choose to use your e-mail to invite somebody to help you. You have two options:

- Click the Save This Invitation as a File option and follow the instructions to save it as a file; then you can attach the file to a message using your Web-based e-mail program.

Click to invite a helper

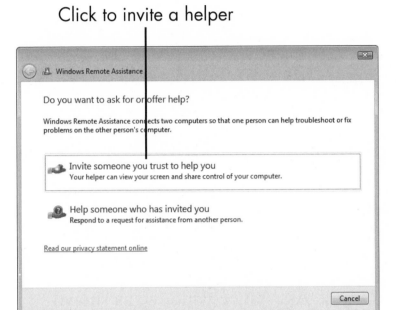

Figure 7-9

- Click the Use E-mail to Send an Invitation option to use a pre-configured e-mail program to send an e-mail (see **Figure 7-10**). Enter an address and additional message content, if you like, and send the e-mail.

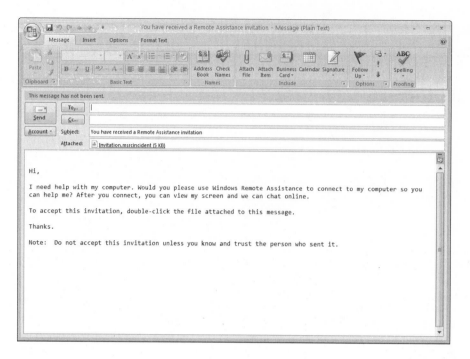

Figure 7-10

6. In the Windows Remote Assistance window, as shown in **Figure 7-11,** note the provided password. When an incoming connection is made, use the tools there to adjust settings, chat, send a file, or pause, cancel, or stop sharing.

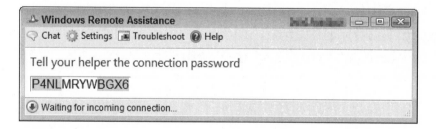

Figure 7-11

7. When you're finished, click the Close button to close the Windows Remote Assistance window.

Setting a time limit to not more than a few hours is a good idea. After all, you don't want somebody trying to log in to your computer unexpectedly two weeks from now when you've already solved the problem some other way. You can make these timing settings in the Remote Assistance settings in the System Properties dialog box.

 Remember that it's up to you to let the recipient know the password — it isn't included in your e-mail unless you add it. Although using a password used to be optional in Windows XP, it's mandatory in Windows 7.

Change Windows Help and Support Display Options

1. If you're having trouble reading help topics, get some help with modifying text size. Open the Windows Help and Support window.

2. Choose Options⇨Text Size and then choose one of the text size options: Largest, Larger, Medium (the default), Smaller, or Smallest (see **Figure 7-12**).

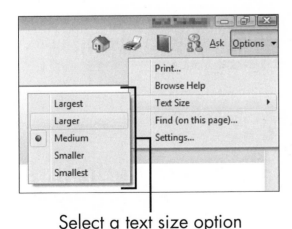

Select a text size option

Figure 7-12

3. Your new settings take effect immediately; click the Close button or navigate to another area of the Windows Help and Support window.

   If you don't like the colors in your Help and Support screen, you can change them by choosing a different color scheme in the Control Panel's Appearance and Personalization settings.

   Don't forget that you can reduce the size of the Help and Support window by clicking the Restore Down button in the upper-right corner of the window. This is especially useful with the Help window so you can display it side by side with an application or Control Panel window where you're trying to troubleshoot the described help topic.

Contact Microsoft Customer Support

1. Go to the Windows Help and Support window and click the Ask button in the upper-right corner. On the page that appears, shown in **Figure 7-13,** click the Contact Technical Support link to open the Customer Support Web site in your default browser.

2. In the Microsoft Help and Support window that appears, click a product to see what support options and information are offered (see **Figure 7-14**).

Click this link

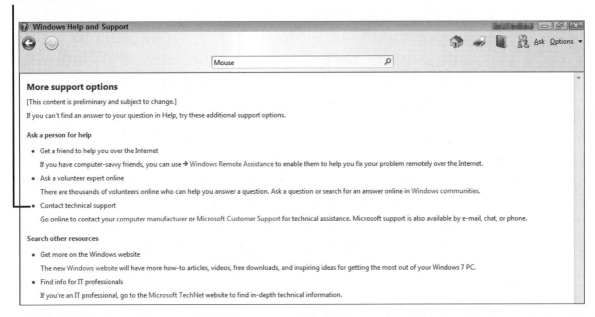

More support options

[This content is preliminary and subject to change.]

If you can't find an answer to your question in Help, try these additional support options.

Ask a person for help

• Get a friend to help you over the Internet

If you have computer-savvy friends, you can use → Windows Remote Assistance to enable them to help you fix your problem remotely over the Internet.

• Ask a volunteer expert online

There are thousands of volunteers online who can help you answer a question. Ask a question or search for an answer online in Windows communities.

• Contact technical support

Go online to contact your computer manufacturer or Microsoft Customer Support for technical assistance. Microsoft support is also available by e-mail, chat, or phone.

Search other resources

• Get more on the Windows website

The new Windows website will have more how-to articles, videos, free downloads, and inspiring ideas for getting the most out of your Windows 7 PC.

• Find info for IT professionals

If you're an IT professional, go to the Microsoft TechNet website to find in-depth technical information.

Figure 7-13

3. Click on various links for help topics. If you need help solving problems, click a Solution Center link along the left side of the product window.

4. Click Support Option links along the bottom left to contact Microsoft or to search for online help topics.

5. Use the Top Issues or Latest News links to find out what problems others are experiencing and how they've solved them or news from Microsoft about how to fix problems or download updates.

6. Click the Close button to close the Internet Explorer browser.

 Typically, you can call support for two free help sessions or unlimited installation support by submitting a request via e-mail support or by calling 1-800-936-3500. There is the option of Premier Third Tier Support, but this is for what Microsoft refers to as *non-mission-critical* issues. This program is geared towards corporations, and it gives customers access to Microsoft experts to solve their problems. If Windows 7 came preinstalled on your computer, you may be able to contact your manufacturer for support questions.

 To find out about specific support options in your country, click the Understand Your Support Options link in the Help and Support home page. Click Support Options on the page that appears, then select your country and press Enter. Use the product finder feature to drill down to the specific help available to you.

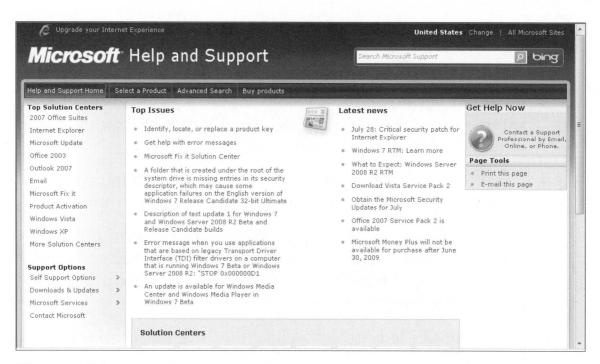

Figure 7-14

Part II

Having Fun and Getting Things Done with Software

The 5th Wave   By Rich Tennant

"Can't I just give you riches or something?"

Chapter 8

Working with Software Programs

You may think of Windows 7 as a set of useful accessories, such as games, a calculator, and a paint program for playing around with images, but Windows 7 is first and foremost an operating system. Windows 7's main purpose is to enable you to run and manage other software programs, from programs that manage your finances to a great animated game of bingo. By using the best methods for accessing and running programs with Windows 7, you save time; setting up Windows 7 in the way that works best for you can make your life easier.

In this chapter, you explore several simple and very handy techniques for launching and moving information between applications. You go through step-by-step procedures ranging from setting program defaults to removing programs when you no longer need them.

Launch a Program

1. Launch a program by using any of the following four methods:

- Choose Start⇨All Programs. Locate the program name on the All Programs list that appears and click it. Clicking an item with a folder icon displays a list of programs within it; just click the program on that sublist to open it (as shown in **Figure 8-1**).

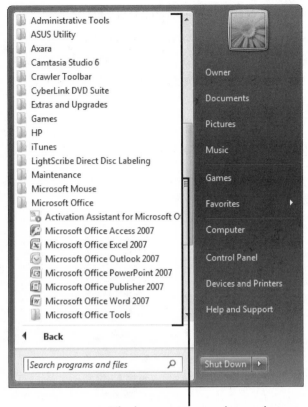

Click an item to launch it
or click a folder to see its sublist

Figure 8-1

- Double-click a program shortcut icon on the desktop (see **Figure 8-2**).

- Click an item on the taskbar. The taskbar should display by default; if it doesn't, press the Windows logo key (on your keyboard) to display it, and then click an icon on the taskbar (as shown in **Figure 8-2**), just to the right of the Start button. See Chapter 3 for more about working with the taskbar.

- If you used the program recently and saved a document, choose it from the list of recently used programs displayed when you first open the Start menu. Then click a document created in that program from the list that displays. (See Chapter 9 for information about displaying recently used files on the Start menu.)

Double-click a program's shortcut icon to launch it...

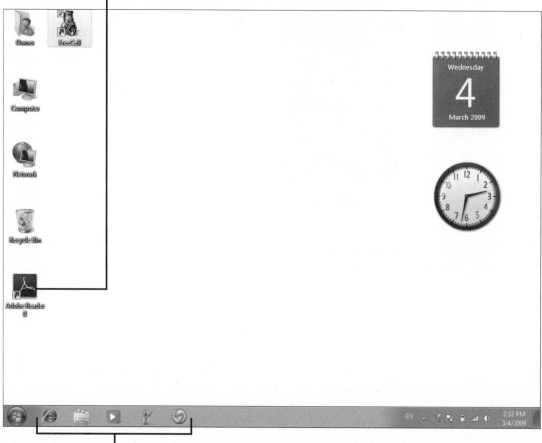

Or click an icon on the Taskbar

Figure 8-2

2. When the application opens, if it's a game, play it; if it's a spreadsheet, enter numbers into it; if it's your e-mail program, start deleting junk mail . . . you get the idea.

Not every program that's installed on your computer appears as a desktop shortcut or taskbar icon. To add a program to the taskbar or to add a desktop shortcut, see Chapter 3.

Move Information between Programs

1. Open documents in two programs (see the next section for more about opening applications). Right-click the taskbar on the Windows desktop and choose Show Windows Side by Side (see **Figure 8-3**).

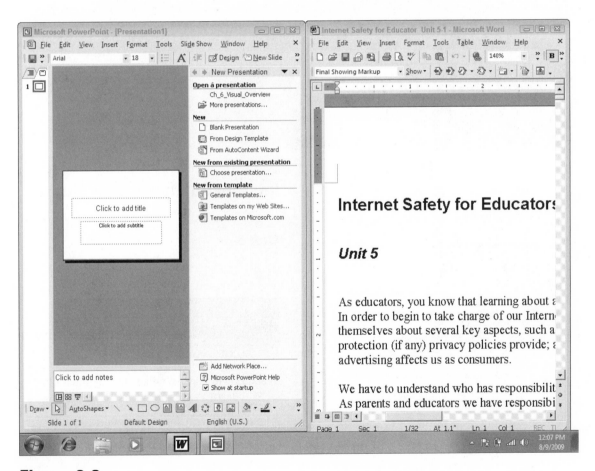

Figure 8-3

2. If you don't need one of the active programs displayed, click the Minimize button so just the programs you're working with appear.

3. Select the information that you want to move (for example text, numbers, or a graphical object in a document), and drag it to the other application document (see **Figure 8-4**).

4. Release your mouse, and the information is copied to the document in the destination window.

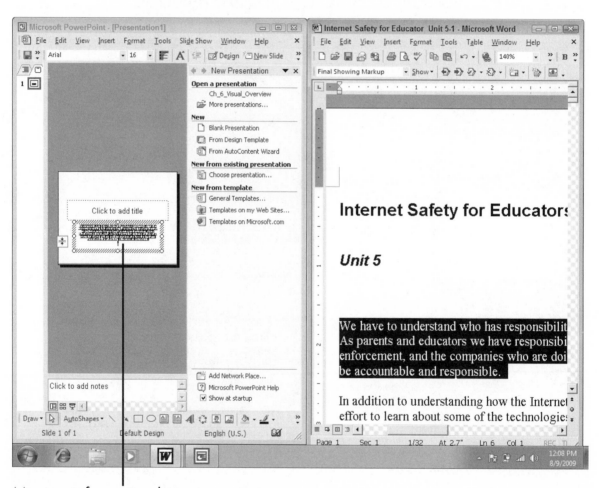

Moving information between programs

Figure 8-4

162

You can also use simple cut-and-paste or copy-and-paste operations to take information from one application and move it or place a copy of it into a document in another application. To do this, first click and drag over the information in a document, and then press Ctrl+X to cut or Ctrl+C to copy the item. Click in the destination document where you want to place the item and press Ctrl+V. In addition, some applications have Export or Send To commands to send the contents of a document to another application. For example, Microsoft Word has a Send To⇨Microsoft Office PowerPoint command to quickly send a Word document to be the basis of a PowerPoint presentation outline.

 Remember, this won't work between every type of program. For example, you can't click and drag an open picture in Paint into the Windows Calendar. It will most dependably work when dragging text or objects from one Office 2010 or other standard word-processing, presentation, database, or spreadsheet programs to another.

Start a Program Automatically

1. If you use a program often, you may want to set it to start every time you start your computer. Click Start⇨All Programs.

2. Right-click the Startup folder and click Open (see **Figure 8-5**).

3. Right-click Start and choose Open Windows Explorer. In the window that appears, locate and open the folder where the program you want to start when you start

163

Windows is located. Click to select it.

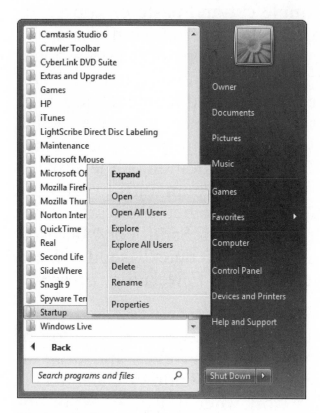

Figure 8-5

4. Drag the item to the Startup window you opened in Step 2. The program appears in the Startup folder (see **Figure 8-6**).

5. When you finish moving programs into the Startup folder, click the Close button in the upper-right corner of both windows. The programs you moved will now open every time you start Windows 7.

 If you place too many programs in Startup, it may take a minute or two before you can get to work because you have to wait for programs to load. Don't overfill your Startup folder: Use it just for the programs you need most often.

You can remove an application from the Startup folder by right-clicking it and choosing Delete.

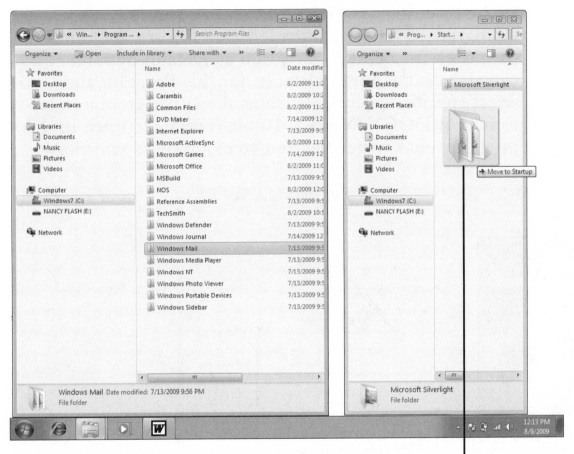

Moving the item to the Startup window

Figure 8-6

Set Program Defaults

1. To make working with files easier, you may want to control which programs are used to open files of different types. Choose Start⇨Control Panel⇨Programs.

2. In the resulting Programs window, shown in **Figure 8-7,** click the Set Your Default Programs link in the Default Programs section to see specifics about the programs that are set as defaults.

3. In the resulting Set Default Programs window, click a program in the list on the left (see **Figure 8-8**) and then click the Set This Program as Default option. You can also click Choose Defaults for this Program and select specific file types (such as the JPEG graphics file format or DOCX Word 2010 file format) to open in this program; click Save after you've made these selections

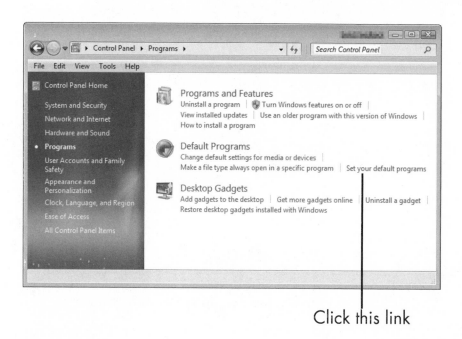

Click this link

Figure 8-7

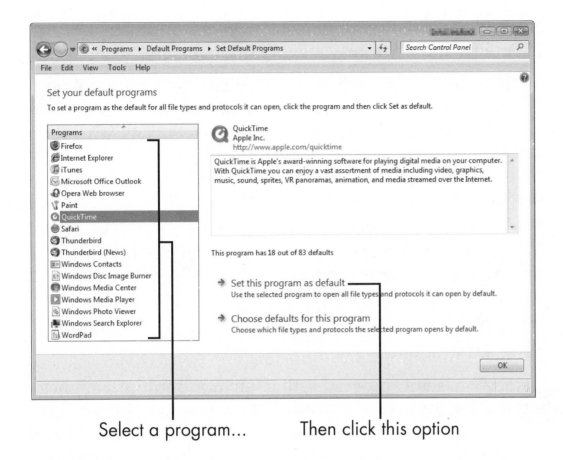

Select a program...   Then click this option

Figure 8-8

4. Click OK to save your settings.

 You can also choose which devices to use by default to play media such as movies or audio files by selecting Change Default Settings for Media or Devices in the Programs window you opened in Step 1 earlier.

Remove a Program

1. If you don't need a program, removing it may help your computer's performance, which can get bogged down when your hard drive is too cluttered. Choose

Start⇨Control Panel⇨Uninstall a Program (under the Programs and Features category).

2. In the resulting Uninstall or Change a Program window, shown in **Figure 8-9,** click a program and then click the Uninstall (or sometimes this is labeled Uninstall/Change) button that appears. Although some programs will display their own uninstall screen, in most cases, a confirmation dialog box appears (see **Figure 8-10**).

3. If you're sure that you want to remove the program, click Yes in the confirmation dialog box. A dialog box shows the progress of the procedure; it disappears when the program has been removed.

4. Click the Close button to close the Uninstall or Change a Program window.

 With some programs that include multiple applications, such as Microsoft Office, you get both an Uninstall and a Change option in Step 2 above. That's because you might want to remove only one program, not the whole shooting match. For example, you might decide that you have no earthly use for Access but can't let a day go by without using Excel and Word — so why not free up some hard drive space and send Access packing? If you want to modify a program in this way, click the Change button rather than the Uninstall button in Step 2 of this task. The dialog box that appears allows you to select the programs that you want to install or uninstall or even open the original installation screen from your software program.

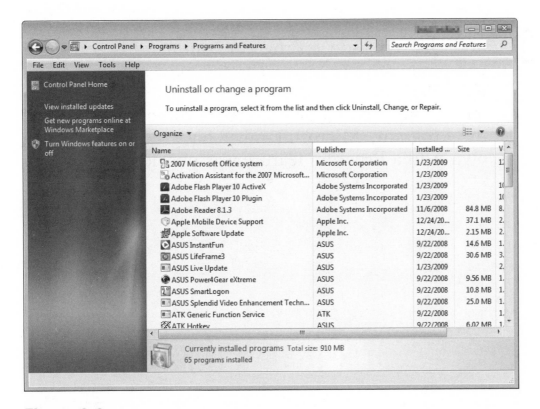

Figure 8-9

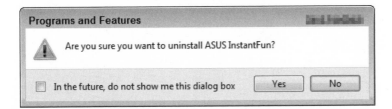

Figure 8-10

 Warning: If you click the Change or Uninstall button, some programs will simply be removed with no further input from you. Be really sure that you don't need a program before you remove it, or that you have the original software on disc (or disk) so you can reinstall it should you need it again.

169

If you used some earlier versions of Windows, you note that the Add a Program command is gone. Because all software created today allows you to put a CD/DVD into your drive or download it from the Internet and then follow on-screen directions to install the program, Microsoft must have decided that its own Add a Program feature was obsolete!

Chapter 9

Working with Files and Folders

171

Join me for a moment in the office of yesteryear. Notice all the metal filing cabinets and manila file folders holding paper rather than the sleek computer workstations and wireless Internet connections we use today.

Fast forward: You still organize the work you do every day in files and folders, but today, the metal and cardboard have been dropped in favor of electronic bits and bytes. *Files* are the individual documents that you save from within applications, such as Word and Excel, and you use folders and subfolders to organize several files into groups or categories, such as by project or by year.

In this chapter, you find out how to organize and work with files and folders, including

➤ **Finding your way around files and folders:** This includes tasks such as locating and opening files and folders.

➤ **Manipulating files and folders:** These tasks cover moving, renaming, deleting, and printing a file.

➤ **Squeezing a file's contents:** This involves creating a compressed folder to reduce a large file to a more manageable creature.

➤ **Backing up files and folders:** To avoid losing valuable data, you should know how to make backup copies of your files and folders on a recordable CD/DVD or flash drive (a small stick-shaped storage device that fits right into a USB port on your computer).

Understand How Windows Organizes Data

When you work in a software program, such as a word processor, you save your document as a file. Files can be saved to your computer hard drive, to removable storage media such as USB flash drives (which are about the size of a package of gum and you insert them into a USB port on your computer), or to recordable DVDs (small flat discs you insert into a disc drive on your computer).

You can organize files by placing them in folders. The Windows operating system helps you to organize files and folders in the following ways:

➤ **Take advantage of predefined folders:** Windows sets up some folders for you. For example, the first time you start Windows 7, you find folders for Documents, Pictures, Videos, and Music already set up on your computer. You can see them listed in Windows Explorer, shown in **Figure 9-1.** (See Chapter 3 for an explanation of Explorer.)

The Documents folder is a good place to store letters, presentations for your community group, household budgets, and so on. The Pictures folder is where you store picture files, which you may transfer from a digital camera or scanner, receive in an e-mail message from a friend or family member, or download from the Internet. Similarly, the Videos folder is a good place to put files from your camcorder, and the Music folder is where you place tunes you download or transfer from a music player.

Predefined folders help organize files

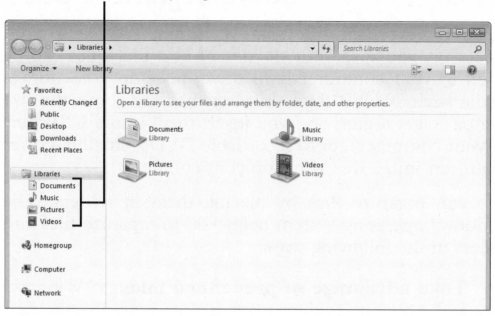

Figure 9-1

➡ **Create your own folders:** You can create any number of folders and give them a name that identifies the types of files you'll store there. For example, you might create a folder called *Digital Scrapbook* if you use your computer to create scrapbooks, or a folder called *Taxes* where you save e-mailed receipts for purchases and electronic tax filing information.

➡ **Place folders within folders to further organize files:** A folder you place within another folder is called a *subfolder.* For example, in your Documents folder, you might have a subfolder called *Holiday Card List* that contains your yearly holiday newsletter and address lists. In my Pictures folder, I organize the picture files by creating subfolders that begin with the year and then a description of the event or subject, such as *2008 Home Garden Project, 2010 Christmas, 2009 San Francisco Trip, 2010 Family Reunion, 2009 Pet Photos,* and so on. In **Figure 9-2,** you can see subfolders and files stored within the Pictures folder.

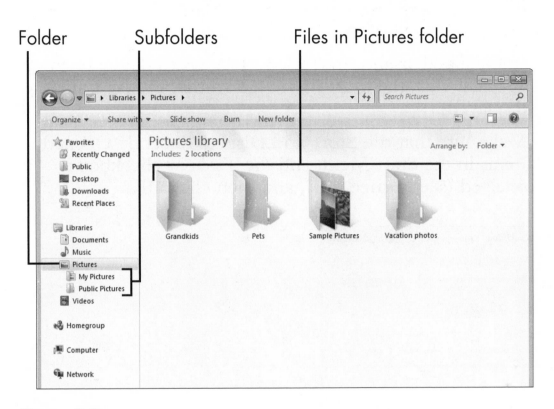

Folder   Subfolders   Files in Pictures folder

Figure 9-2

➡ **Move files and folders from one place to another:** Being able to move files and folders helps you if you decide it's time to reorganize information on your computer. For example, when you start using your computer, you might save all your documents to your Documents folder. That's okay for a while, but in time, you might have dozens of documents saved in that one folder. To make your files easier to locate, you can create subfolders by topic and move files into them.

175

Access Recently Used Items

1. If you worked on a file recently, Windows offers a shortcut to finding and opening it to work on again. Open the Start menu and right-click any blank area. From the resulting shortcut menu, choose Properties.

2. In the Taskbar and Start Menu Properties dialog box that appears, click the Start Menu tab (if that tab isn't already displayed).

3. Make sure that the Store and Display Recently Opened Items in the Start Menu and the Taskbar checkbox is selected (see **Figure 9-3**), and then click OK.

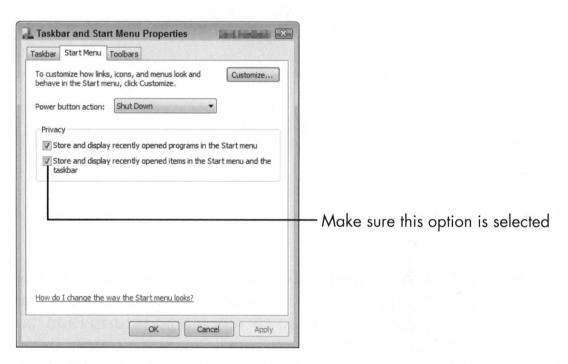

Make sure this option is selected

Figure 9-3

4. Open the Start menu and hover your mouse over any recently opened program listed on the left side that has an arrow and a submenu of recently opened items appears

176

to the right. Choose a file from the submenu (see **Figure 9-4**) to open it.

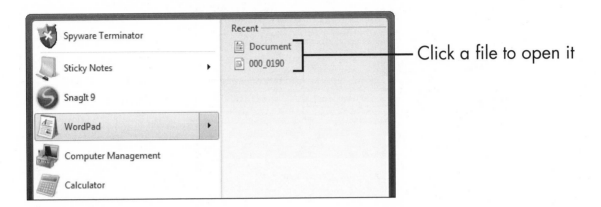

— Click a file to open it

Figure 9-4

 Recently opened programs should be displayed in the Start menu by default, but if they aren't, follow the directions in Step 1 to open the Taskbar and Start Menu Properties dialog box and make sure that the Store and Display Recently Opened Programs in the Start Menu checkbox is selected.

Locate Files and Folders in Your Computer

1. Can't remember what you named a folder or where on your computer or storage media you saved it? You can open the Computer window to locate it. Choose Start⇨Computer.

2. In the resulting Computer window (see **Figure 9-5**), double-click an item, such as a USB drive, a CD-ROM drive, or your computer hard drive, to open it.

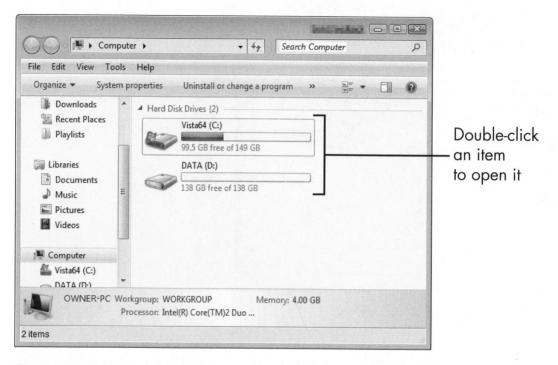

Double-click
an item
to open it

Figure 9-5

3. If the file or folder that you want is stored within another folder (see **Figure 9-6** for an example of the resulting window), double-click the folder or a series of folders until you locate it.

4. When you find the file you want, double-click it to open it in the application in which it was created.

Note the buttons on the top of the window in **Figure 9-6.** Use the commands in this area to perform common file and folder tasks, such as organizing, sharing, or opening files.

Depending on how you choose to display files and folders, you might see text listings, as shown in **Figure 9-6,** icons, or even thumbnail representations of file contents. Use the View menu in the Computer window to configure how to display files and folders.

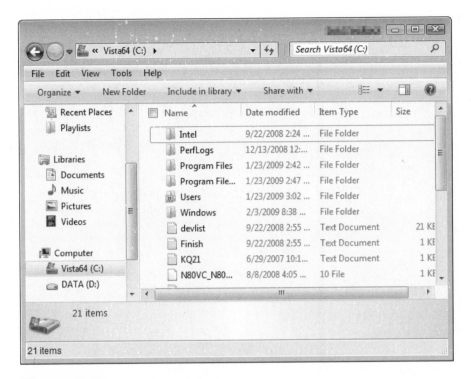

Figure 9-6

Search for a File

1. If you can't locate a file in the Computer window or in your Documents folder, you can perform a simple search for it. Open the Start menu and type a search term in the search box at the bottom.

2. A list of search results appears, divided by the location of the results (see **Figure 9-7**).

3. Click the See More Results link.

4. In the window that appears (see **Figure 9-8**), click an item to view it.

5. When you locate the file you want, you can double-click it to open it.

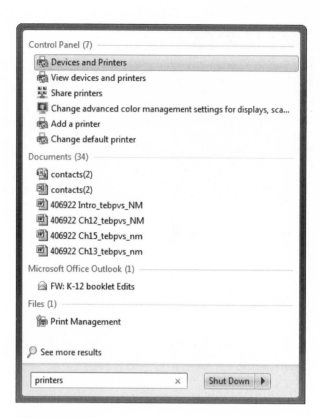

Control Panel (7)
- 🖨 Devices and Printers
- 🖨 View devices and printers
- 🖨 Share printers
- 🖥 Change advanced color management settings for displays, sca...
- 🖨 Add a printer
- 🖨 Change default printer

Documents (34)
- 📇 contacts(2)
- 📇 contacts(2)
- 📄 406922 Intro_tebpvs_NM
- 📄 406922 Ch12_tebpvs_NM
- 📄 406922 Ch15_tebpvs_nm
- 📄 406922 Ch13_tebpvs_nm

Microsoft Office Outlook (1)
- ✉ FW: K-12 booklet Edits

Files (1)
- 🖨 Print Management

🔍 See more results

| printers | ✕ | Shut Down ▶ |

Figure 9-7

 Search Folders was a new feature in Windows Vista that has carried over to Windows 7. To save the results of a search, you can click the Save Search button. In the Save As dialog box that appears, provide a filename and type, set the location to save it to, and then click Save. The search results are saved as a search folder on your computer in your user name folder.

 Choose the Folder and Search Options command from the Organize menu in the Search Results in Indexed Locations window shown in **Figure 9-8** to modify Search settings. Using the Search tab in the Folder Options dialog box that appears, indicate what locations to search, whether to find partial matches for search terms, and more.

180

Click an item to view it

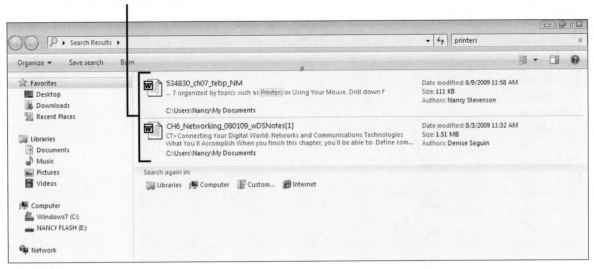

Figure 9-8

Move a File or Folder

1. Sometimes you save a file or folder in one place but in reorganizing your work decide you want to move the item to another location. To do so, right-click the Start menu button and choose Open Windows Explorer.

2. In the resulting Windows Explorer window, double-click a folder or series of folders to locate the file that you want to move (see **Figure 9-9**).

Figure 9-9

3. Take one of the following actions:

   • Click and drag the file to another folder in the Navigation pane on the left side of the window. If you right-click and drag, you are offered the options of moving or copying or creating a shortcut to the item when you place it via a shortcut menu that appears.

   • Right-click the file and choose Send To. Then choose from the options shown in the submenu that appears (as shown in **Figure 9-10**); these options may vary slightly depending on the type of file you choose and your installed software.

4. Click the Close button in the upper-right corner of the Windows Explorer window to close it.

182

If you change your mind about moving an item using the right-click-and-drag method, you can click Cancel on the shortcut menu that appears.

Figure 9-10

 If you want to create a copy of a file or folder in another location on your computer, right-click the item and choose Copy. Use Windows Explorer to navigate to the location where you want to place a copy, right-click, and choose Paste or press Ctrl+V.

Rename a File or Folder

1. You may want to change the name of a file or folder to update it or make it more easily identifiable from other

183

files or folders. Locate the file that you want to rename by using Windows Explorer. (Right-click Start and choose Open Windows Explorer, and then browse to find the file you want to rename.)

2. Right-click the file and choose Rename (see **Figure 9-11**).

Select Rename

Figure 9-11

3. The filename is now available for editing. Type a new name, and then click anywhere outside the filename to save the new name.

You can't rename a file to have the same name as another file located in the same folder. To give a file the same name as another, cut it from its current location, paste it into another folder, and then follow the procedure in this task. Or, open the file and save it to a new location with the same name, which creates a copy. Be careful, though: Two files with the same name can cause confusion when you search for files. If at all possible, use unique filenames.

Create a Shortcut to a File or Folder

1. You can place a shortcut to a file or folder you used recently on the desktop to make it quick and easy to open it. Locate the file or folder by using Windows Explorer. (Right-click Start and choose Open Windows Explorer, and then browse to find the file you want to make a shortcut to.)

2. In the resulting Windows Explorer window, right-click the file or folder that you want and select Send To⇨Desktop (Create Shortcut), as shown in **Figure 9-12**.

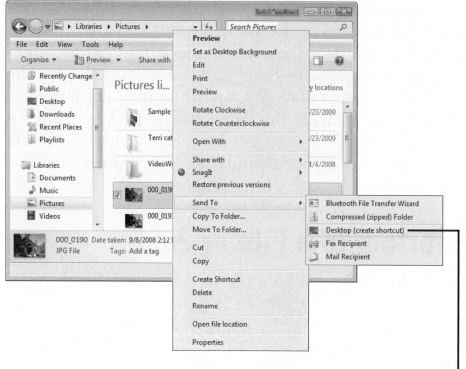

Select Desktop (Create Shortcut)

Figure 9-12

3. A shortcut appears on the desktop.

> 🎯 Once you have placed a shortcut on the desktop, to open the file in its originating application or to open a folder in Windows Explorer, simply double-click the desktop shortcut icon.

> 🎯 Instead of creating a shortcut and dragging it to the desktop, you can right-click a file or folder and choose Sent To⇨Desktop (Create Shortcut) to accomplish the same thing.

Delete a File or Folder

1. If you don't need a file or folder anymore, you can clear

186

up clutter on your computer by deleting it. Locate the file or folder by using Windows Explorer. (Right-click Start and choose Open Windows Explorer, and then browse to locate the file you want to delete.)

2. In the resulting Windows Explorer window, right-click the file or folder that you want to delete and then choose Delete (see **Figure 9-13**).

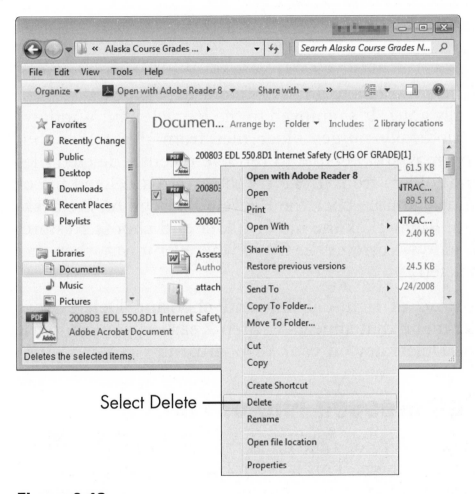

Figure 9-13

3. In the resulting dialog box (see **Figure 9-14**), click Yes to delete the file.

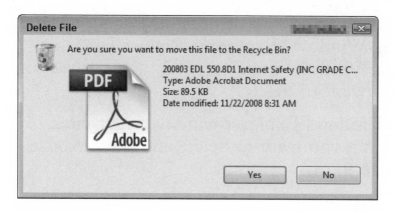

Figure 9-14

 When you delete a file or folder in Windows, it's not really gone. It's removed to the Recycle Bin. Windows periodically purges older files from this folder, but you may still be able to retrieve recently deleted files and folders from it. To try to restore a deleted file or folder, double-click the Recycle Bin icon on the desktop. Right-click the file or folder and choose Restore. Windows restores the file to wherever it was when you deleted it.

 Instead of right-clicking and choosing Delete from the menu that appears in Step 2 earlier, you can press the Delete key on your keyboard.

Create a Compressed File or Folder

1. To shrink the size of a file or all the files in a folder, you can compress them. This is often helpful when you're sending an item as an attachment to an e-mail message. Locate the files or folders that you want to compress by using Windows Explorer. (Right-click Start and choose Open Windows Explorer, and then browse to locate the file[s] or folder[s].)

2. In the resulting Windows Explorer window, you can do the following (as shown in **Figure 9-15**):

- **Select a series of files or folders:** Click a file or folder, press and hold Shift to select a series of items listed consecutively in the folder, and click the final item.

- **Select nonconsecutive items:** Press and hold the Ctrl key and click the items.

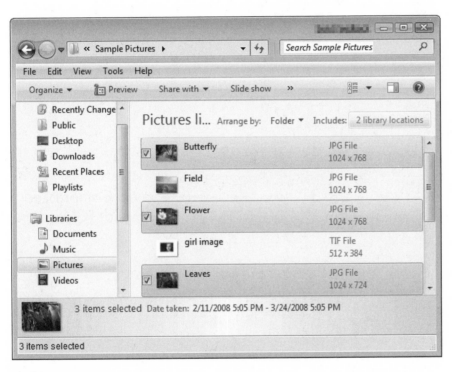

Figure 9-15

3. Right click the selected items. In the resulting shortcut menu (see **Figure 9-16**), choose Send To⇨Compressed (Zipped) Folder. A new compressed folder appears below the last selected file in the Windows Explorer list. The folder icon is named after the last file you selected in the series but can be renamed. Type a new name or click

189

outside the item to accept the default name.

 You may want to subsequently rename a compressed folder with a name other than the one that Windows automatically assigns to it. See the task "Rename a File or Folder," earlier in this chapter, to find out just how to do that.

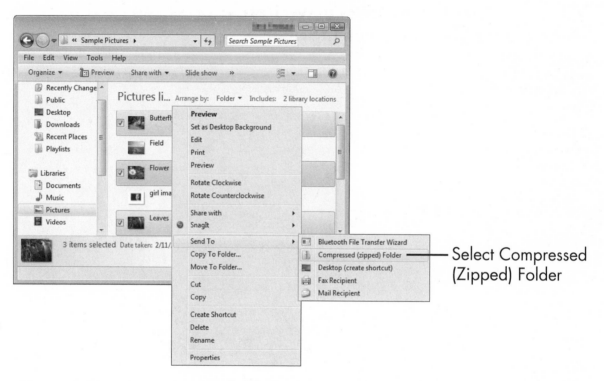

Select Compressed (Zipped) Folder

Figure 9-16

Add a File to Your Favorites List

1. The Favorites list in the Start menu offers another quick way to access frequently used items. Locate the files or folders that you want to make a Favorite by using Windows Explorer. (Right-click Start and choose Open Windows Explorer.)

2. In the resulting Windows Explorer window, click a file or folder and drag it to any of the Favorites folders in the ⎯n the left (see **Figure 9-17**).

⎯ur Favorites, choose Start⇨Favorites.

⎯bmenu (see **Figure 9-18**), click an item

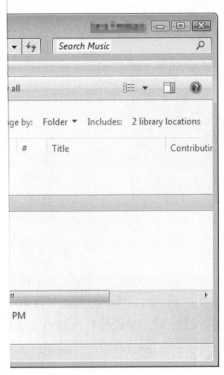

Adding a file to the Favorites list

Figure 9-17

Click an item to open it

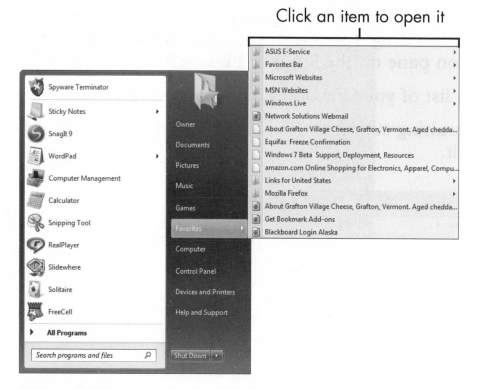

Figure 9-18

 If the Favorites item doesn't display on your Start menu, right-click the Start menu and choose Properties. On the Start Menu tab in the Taskbar and Start Menu Properties dialog box, click the Customize button. Make sure that Favorites Menu is selected, and then click OK twice to save the setting.

Back Up Files to a Read/Writable CD or DVD

1. You've put a lot of work into your files, so don't forget to back them up. If your computer is damaged or loses data, you'll have a copy safely tucked away. Place a blank writable CD-R/RW (read/writable) or DVD-R/

RW in your CD-RW or DVD-RW drive and then choose Start⇨Documents.

2. In the resulting Documents window (see **Figure 9-19**), select all the files that you want to copy to disc.

3. Right-click the files that you want and then choose Copy To Folder.

4. In the Copy Items dialog box that appears, click on the CD-R/RW or DVD-RW drive and click Copy.

5. Click the Close button to close the Document window.

If you want to back up the entire contents of a folder, such as the Document folder, you can just click the Documents folder itself in Step 2.

You can also back up to a network or another drive by using the Back Up Your Computer link in the Control Panel. Using Windows Backup, you can make settings to regularly back up to a local disk or CD-R/RW/DVD drive, or to a network. Backing up to a CD/DVD is a little different from burning a disc in that after you back up your files, only changes are saved each subsequent time a backup is run.

Figure 9-19

Chapter 10

Using the Desktop Gadget Gallery and Gadgets

Get ready to . . .

Windows 7 has a feature called the *Desktop Gadget Gallery.* The Gallery contains little applications, called *gadgets,* that you can display as icons on the desktop. Using gadgets, you can quickly access various handy features to check the time, organize your schedule with a calendar, feed online data direct to your desktop, and more. Here are some of the things you can do with the Windows gadgets that we cover in this chapter:

➤ **Work with images:** Slide Show is a continuous slide show of the photos in your Pictures folder.

➤ **Organize your time:** The Calendar gadget displayed on your desktop helps you keep track of the days, weeks, and months. The Clock gadget displays the time using an old style wall clock and allows you to make changes to your time zone.

➤ **Play with a puzzle:** A neat little Picture Puzzle allows you to play a game that's so tiny, even your boss won't notice you're not actually working.

➤ **Work with online data:** The Feed Headlines gadget allows you to grab data from online RSS feeds (a format used for syndication of news and other content), such as the latest news or other useful information. Stocks and Currency Conversion gadgets provide up-to-the-minute data on stocks and currency values.

➤ **Keep an eye on your system performance:** The CPU Meter provides up-to-date information about your computer processor speed and available memory.

Open the Gadget Gallery and Add Gadgets to the Desktop

1. Right-click the desktop and choose Gadgets to open the Gadget Gallery window, shown in **Figure 10-1.**

2. Click on any gadget and drag it to the desktop (see **Figure 10-2**).

Figure 10-1

Dragging a gadget to the desktop

Figure 10-2

3. Click the Close button to close the Gadget Gallery.

 Gadgets are hot, and people are creating more all the time. Click the Get More Gadgets Online link in the Gadget Gallery to scope out the latest gadgets and then download them.

 If you want to send a gadget away, just place your mouse over it and then click the Close button (marked with an X) that appears next to it. The gadget closes.

Just follow the steps above to display it on the desktop again at any time.

Check the Time

1. To display a clock on your desktop, right-click the desktop and choose Gadgets.

2. In the Gadget Gallery that appears, click on the clock and drag it to the desktop.

3. To make changes to the clock style or to change the time zone, place your mouse over the clock and click the settings button (it sports a little wrench symbol).

4. In the resulting Clock dialog box (see **Figure 10-3**), click the Next or Previous button to move through the various available clock styles.

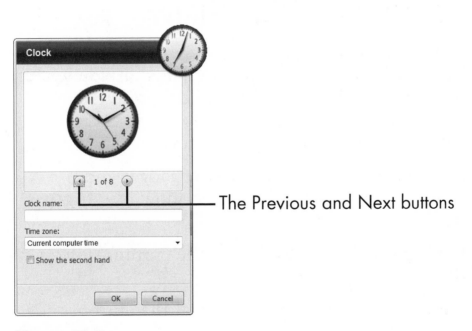

Clock

Clock name:

Time zone:
Current computer time

☐ Show the second hand

OK   Cancel

———The Previous and Next buttons

Figure 10-3

5. If you wish, you can enter a name for the clock in the Clock Name field. To change the time zone, click the arrow in the Time Zone field and choose your local time.

6. Click OK to save the clock settings.

You can display a second hand on your clock by clicking the Show the Second Hand checkbox in the Clock Settings dialog box.

If you are on the road and want to keep track of the local time and the time back home, you can display more than one clock by simply dragging the clock gadget to the desktop from the Gadget Gallery again. Make changes to the time zone settings and even use two different styles of clock to tell them apart at a glance.

Display a Continuous Slide Show

1. You can display a continuous slide show of the pictures in your Pictures folder to keep you entertained as you work or play on your computer. Add the Slide Show gadget to the desktop (see the earlier task "Open the Gadget Gallery and Add Gadgets to the Desktop").

2. Move your mouse over the Slide Show gadget and use the tools along the bottom of the slide show (see **Figure 10-4**) to do the following:

- Click the **View button** to display the current slide in Windows Photo Viewer.

- Click **Pause** to stop the slide show at the current slide.

- Click **Previous** to go to the previous slide.

- Click **Next** to go to the next slide.

3. The Slide Show gadget uses the Sample Pictures folder contents by default. Click the Settings button. In the resulting Slide Show dialog box (see **Figure 10-5**), change the picture folders to include in the slide show, modify the number of seconds to display each slide, or add a transition effect to use between slides.

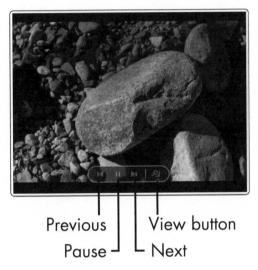

Previous   View button

Pause   Next

Figure 10-4

Figure 10-5

4. Click OK to close the dialog box.

 When you click the View button to display the current slide in Windows Photo Viewer, you can use tools to modify the image, print it, e-mail it, or even create a movie. See Chapter 13 for more about using Windows Photo Viewer.

Use the Windows Calendar

1. The Calendar gadget isn't an organizer, it just helps you remember dates with a Calendar display you can place on your desktop. Add the Calendar gadget (see **Figure 10-6**) to the desktop. (See the earlier task "Open the Gadget Gallery and Add Gadgets to the Desktop.")

Figure 10-6

2. Move your mouse over the calendar and click the Size tool to move between the larger size, which displays both the monthly and daily sections (as shown in **Figure 10-7**), and the smaller size, which displays only the daily display by default.

The Size tool

Figure 10-7

3. With the larger calendar displayed, click the Next or Previous arrow to move to another month; double-click a date to display it in the lower part of the calendar; and click the red tab in the lower-left corner to return to today's date.

> If you prefer to use the smaller size calendar but want to have it display the monthly calendar rather than the daily calendar, just double-click the small display and it toggles between month and day.

> With the monthly display shown in the smaller size, you can jump to the daily display for a specific date by double-clicking that date in the monthly view.

Play with a Puzzle

1. Add the Picture Puzzle gadget to the desktop. (See the earlier task "Open the Gadget Gallery and Add Gadgets to the Desktop.")

2. Click either of the tools along the top of the puzzle (see **Figure 10-8**) to do the following:

- **Pause timer** stops the automatic count of seconds of play.

- **Show Picture** displays the completed picture; release it and you go back to where you were in the game.

- **Solve** ends the game and displays the completed picture.

Pause   Show
timer   Picture

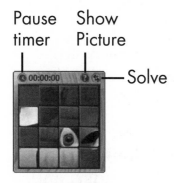

Solve

Figure 10-8

3. To play the game, click any piece adjacent to a blank square. It moves into the blank space. Keep clicking and moving pieces until you get the picture pieces arranged to form a picture.

4. Click the Settings button to the right of the puzzle to display its settings dialog box (see **Figure 10-9**).

Picture Puzzle

1 of 11

OK   Cancel

Figure 10-9

5. Click the Previous or Next button to scroll through available pictures for the puzzle.

6. When you find the picture you want, click OK to close the dialog box.

Convert Currency

1. Need to change dollars to euros? If you have an Internet connection, you can get up-to-the-minute currency values. Start by adding the Currency Conversion gadget to the desktop. (See the earlier task "Open the Gadget Gallery and Add Gadgets to the Desktop.")

2. Connect to the Internet to access the latest currency rates (as shown in **Figure 10-10**), and do any of the following.

   • Enter the number of dollars; the number of equivalent euros is displayed.

Figure 10-10

   • Click one of the currency names and a list of available currencies appears (see **Figure 10-11**). Click another currency to change which currencies to convert from and to.

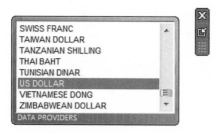

Figure 10-11

 To view the online source for the latest currency conversion rates, with the larger size Currency gadget displayed, click the Data Providers link. The Money-Central MSN page opens. Click the Banking tab and then click the Currency Exchange Rates link to view current rates.

 If you want to, you can display several Currency Conversion gadgets to compare multiple currencies at the same time.

Use the Feed Headlines Gadget

1. If you like to read the latest headlines (this requires an Internet connection), add a news feed to your desktop. First, add the Feed Headlines gadget to the desktop. (See the earlier task "Open the Gadget Gallery and Add Gadgets to the Desktop.")

2. Click the Feed Viewer window to connect to the default RSS feed (see **Figure 10-12**).

3. At the Web site that appears, you can view blog entries, submit an entry, or subscribe to additional feeds.

Figure 10-12

4. Click the Settings button. In the resulting Feed Headlines dialog box (see **Figure 10-13**), select the default feed.

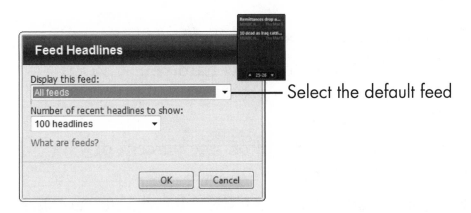

Select the default feed

Figure 10-13

5. Click OK to close the dialog box.

 Use the Show Next Set of Feeds and Show Previous Set of Feeds arrows that appear at the bottom of the View Feeder gadget when you move your mouse over it to scroll through available feeds.

Monitor Your CPU

1. Is your computer acting sluggish? Check its performance using the CPU Meter. Add the CPU Meter gadget (see **Figure 10-14**) to the desktop. (See the earlier task "Open the Gadget Gallery and Add Gadgets to the Desktop.")

Figure 10-14

2. Use the readouts to monitor the following:

- CPU (on the left) monitors how hard your CPU is working to process various programs and processes running on your computer.

- Memory (on the right) monitors the percent of your computer memory that is being used.

 That's about all there is to CPU Meter! You can click the Size button to toggle between a larger and smaller version, but you can't make any settings for it. It's just a little reminder that helps you keep track of your computer's performance. If memory is almost at 100 percent, consider freeing some space. If the CPU is at a higher percentage, odds are you've got lots of programs running which could be slowing down your computer's performance; consider shutting some down!

If you want more details about your computer memory, use the Start menu to display the Control Panel and choose System and Security. The System links allow you to view the processor speed and the amount of RAM available.

Chapter 11

Creating Documents with Works Word Processor

Get ready to . . .

The two kinds of software programs that people use most often are word processors (for working with words) and spreadsheets (for working with numbers). In this chapter, you get to see the basic tools of the word processor built into Microsoft Works.

Works or a trial version of the product comes preinstalled on many Windows computers. If not, the program is relatively inexpensive (anywhere from $30 to $40 depending on where you shop), so it's a good entry-level program you may want to have on your computer.

With a word processor, you can create anything from simple letters to posters or brochures. You can use both text and graphics to add style to your documents. You can even use a word processor to print envelopes or labels so you can send those holiday newsletters or brochures for the local food co-op on their way.

In this chapter, you explore the following:

➤ Enter text and format it by applying different fonts, colors, and effects.

➤ Insert tables for organizing information.

➤ Insert graphics and arrange them on the page.

➤ Prepare your document for printing by using spelling- and grammar-checking tools, modifying the page setup, and finally, printing it!

Open a New Document and Enter and Edit Text

1. Your first step in creating any document is to open your word processor and enter and edit some text. Choose Start⇨All Programs⇨Microsoft Works and then select the Microsoft Works Word Processor. The program opens, and a blank document is displayed (see **Figure 11-1**).

2. Begin typing your text. Works (like all word-processing programs) *wraps* the text, which means it automatically moves to the next line within a paragraph as you type. Press Enter twice on your keyboard only when you want to start a new paragraph.

3. To edit text you have entered, perform any of the following actions:

   • Click anywhere within the text and press Backspace on the keyboard to delete text to the *left* of the mouse cursor.

   • Click anywhere within the text and press the Delete key to delete text to the *right* of the mouse cursor.

   • Click and drag your cursor over text to select it and press Delete or Backspace to delete the selected text.

   • Click anywhere within the text and type additional text.

Begin typing in a blank document

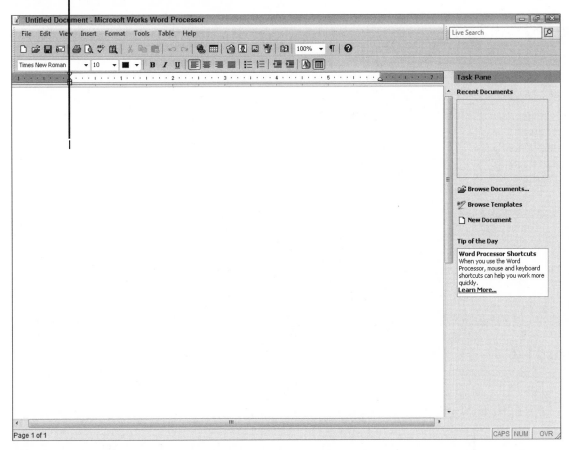

Figure 11-1

Save a Document

1. To save a document for the first time, choose File⇨Save.

2. In the resulting Save dialog box (see **Figure 11-2**), click the arrow on the right of the Save In field and click a different folder.

3. Type a name for the document in the File Name text box.

Type a name for your document

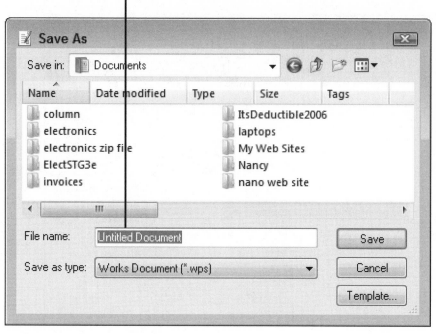

Figure 11-2

4. Click Save.

If you want to save the document in another format (for example, you can save a Works document as plain text so any word processor can open it), click the arrow in the Save As Type field in the Save As dialog box and choose a different format before you click the Save button.

Open an Existing Document

1. After you create a file and save it, you can open it to add to or edit the contents, or you can print it. To open a file after you save it, with the Works word processor open, choose File⇨Open.

214

2. In the Open dialog box that appears (see **Figure 11-3**), locate the file on your computer or storage disc by clicking the arrow in the Look In field and clicking the disc or folder where your file is located.

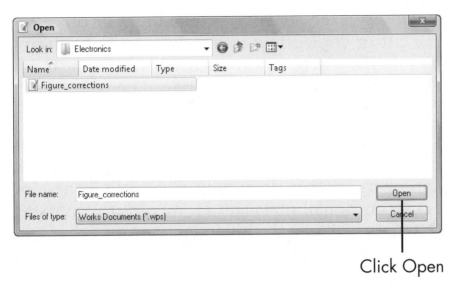

Click Open

Figure 11-3

3. When you locate the file, click it and then click the Open button. The file opens, ready for you to edit or print it.

Cut, Copy, and Paste Text

1. You can cut and paste or copy and paste selected text to move it to or duplicate it in another location in your document. With a document open in Works word processor, click and drag over text to select it; the text is highlighted (see **Figure 11-4**).

2. Perform either of the following two steps, depending on whether you want to *cut* the text (remove it) or *copy* it (leave the existing text and make a copy of it):

- Click the Cut button on the toolbar to cut the text.

- Click the Copy button on the toolbar to make a copy of the text.

3. Windows places the cut or copied text on its *Clipboard*, a temporary holding place for cut or copied text or objects. To paste the cut or copied text to another location within the document, click where you want the text to appear and click the Paste button on the toolbar. The text appears in the new location.

 After you place text or an object on the Windows Clipboard, you can paste it anywhere. For example, you can open another document and paste it there or paste it in an e-mail message. However, it won't stay on the Clipboard forever. If you cut or copy other text or objects, your earlier item will soon be removed from the Clipboard, which holds only a few items at a time.

Click Cut

Click Copy

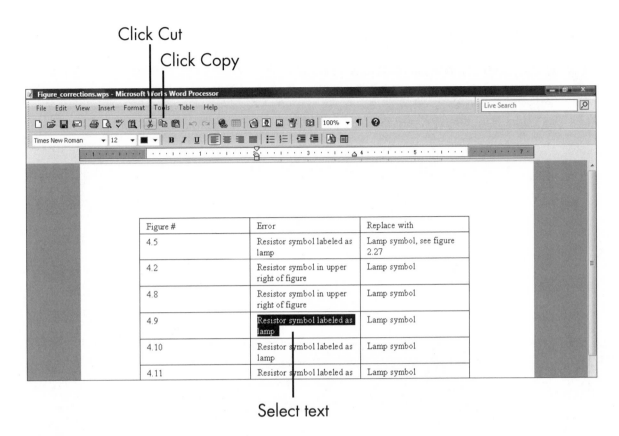

Select text

Figure 11-4

Format Text

1. To format text means to change its size, apply effects such as bold or italic to it, or change the font (that is, a family of typeface with a certain look and feel to it). You start by selecting the text you want to format. Click and drag your mouse over the text you want to format to select it. (**Figure 11-5** shows how the selected text is highlighted in black.)

Click and drag to select text

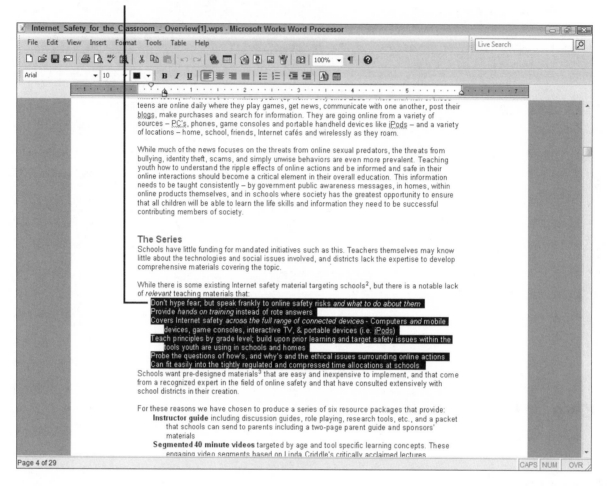

Figure 11-5

2. Choose Format⇨Font. In the resulting Font dialog box (see **Figure 11-6**), make any of the following formatting choices:

• Select a font from the list of available fonts. Use the scroll bar in this list to see more choices and click the one you want to select it. The font is previewed in the large box near the bottom of the dialog box.

• Select a font style such as Bold or Italic from the Font Style list. Font styles are useful for emphasis.

- Choose a different text size by selecting a point size setting from the Size list. The greater the point size, the larger the text.

- If you want to underline the selected text, choose a style from the Underline drop-down list.

- Click the arrow on the Color drop-down list and select a different color for the text.

- Click any of the Effects check boxes to apply effects to the text.

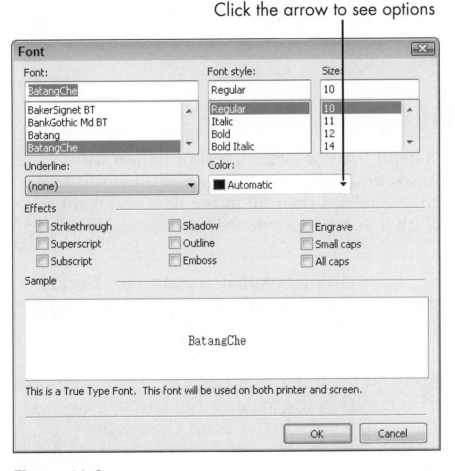

Figure 11-6

3. Click OK to apply the formatting options you have selected.

 You can also use the Formatting toolbar to apply individual formatting settings to selected text. For example, you can click the Bold button or choose a different font from the Font drop-down list. If you don't see the Formatting toolbar, choose View⇨Toolbars⇨Formatting.

 Try not to use too many formatting bells and whistles in a single document, as the formatting might become distracting or make the document difficult to read. A good guideline is to use only two fonts on a single page and use effects such as bold or shadowed text for emphasis only.

Insert a Table

1. A table is a handy way to organize information with headings, rows, and columns. You can easily insert tables in word processors and then fill in the data you want to organize. With a document opened, choose Table⇨Insert Table.

2. In the Insert Table dialog box that appears (see **Figure 11-7**), click a predesigned format for the table in the Select a Format list box. A sample of the format is displayed.

3. Use the arrows on the other four fields to set the number of rows and columns in the table and to specify row height and column width. If you don't change the height and width settings, rows and columns will adjust automatically to the text you enter in each table cell.

4. Click OK to insert the table. In the blank table that appears (see **Figure 11-8**), the cursor is ready and waiting for you in the top-left cell, and if that's where you want your first entry, you can simply begin typing your table contents.

Select a table style

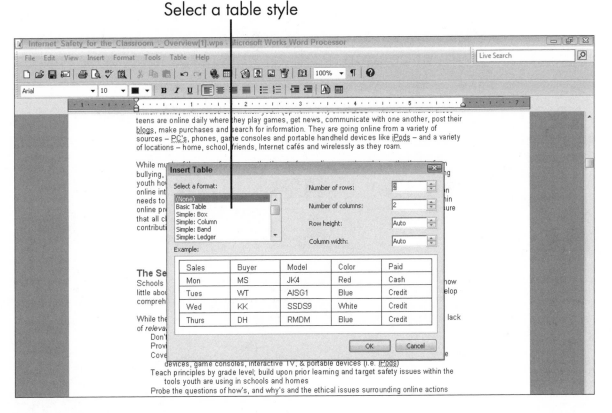

Figure 11-7

5. Press Tab to move to the next cell in the table. If you reach the last cell in the last row and press Tab, a new row is inserted. Alternatively, you can click in any cell where you want to add text.

 You can format text you enter in a table just as you do any other text in your document. Just click and drag to select the cells you want to format and then follow the steps in the preceding task, "Format Text."

 To insert additional columns after you've created your table, click in the column next to which you want to insert a column and choose Table⇨Insert Column. Then choose either the Before or After Current Column option, depending on whether you want the new column to appear to the left or right of the current column.

Type text in the table cells

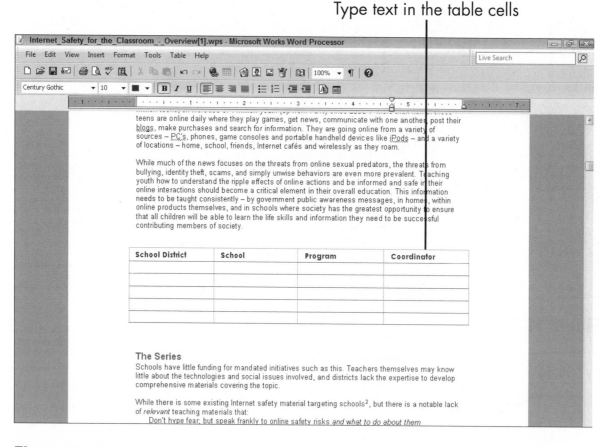

Figure 11-8

Add Graphics

1. If you have files that contain a drawing or photo, you can insert them in your document to spruce it up or help you make a point. With a document open, choose Insert⇨Pictures⇨From File.

2. In the resulting Insert Picture dialog box (see **Figure 11-9**), click the file in your Pictures folder to select it. If the picture file is in a subfolder within the Pictures folder, double-click the folder to display those files. If you want to use a picture file located elsewhere, click the arrow in the Look In field and choose another location.

3. Click the Insert button. The picture is inserted in your document.

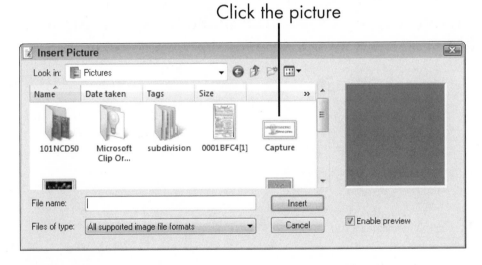

Figure 11-9

 You can also insert built-in drawings and photos called *Clip Art* by choosing Insert⇨Picture⇨Clip Art. In the dialog box that appears, select a category and subcategory to display picture previews. Then click a picture and click the Insert button to place it in your document.

Resize Objects

1. After you insert a picture or piece of art, you may want to resize it. Click the object (such as a photo or Clip Art) to select it. Small boxes called *handles* appear around its edges. See **Figure 11-10**.

2. Do any of the following to resize the object:

- Click the center handles on the left or right side of the object and drag outward to make the object wider, or drag inward to make the object narrower. This distorts the original proportions.

- Click the center handles on the top or bottom of the object and drag up or down to make the object higher or shorter. This action also distorts the proportions.

File   Edit   View   Insert   Format   Tools   Table   Help

Live Search

Arial   10   B   I   U

education is to ensure students have both the understanding and skills needed to make, and successfully implement, informed Internet Safety choices.

Objective:
The objective of Internet Safety Education is to teach safety *principles*; help students identify their own, their family's and their friend's safety needs and personal values; and learn the skills needed to apply safety principles plus their personal values to online encounters. These principles, values and skills are first applied and practiced against known examples, then solidified so students are able to apply their knowledge against future risks.

Click a handle and drag

Figure 11-10

- Click a handle in any corner and drag outward to enlarge the object and keep it in proportion, or drag inward to shrink the object, again keeping it in proportion to its original size.

 You can use another method to resize objects. Select the object and choose Format⇨Object to display the Format Object dialog box. Click the Size tab and enter new Height and Width settings. Click OK to accept the new settings. Depending on the dimensions you enter, the resulting object might be out of proportion.

Check Spelling

1. If you never won spelling bees in school, you'll be glad to hear that Works has a tool that helps you check and correct your spelling. Although the tool won't catch every error (if you typed *sore* instead of *soar*, the tool won't catch it), it can catch many spelling mistakes. With the document you want to check open, choose Tools⇨Spelling and Grammar. If you didn't make any discernable errors, a message appears that the spelling check is complete, but if you did, a dialog box appears.

2. In the resulting Spelling and Grammar dialog box (see **Figure 11-11**), take any of the following actions:

   • Click Ignore Once to ignore the current instance of the word not found in the dictionary.

   • Click Ignore All to ignore all instances of this word.

   • Click Add to add the word to the dictionary so it is no longer questioned in a Spelling and Grammar check.

   • Click a suggested spelling and then click Change to change just this instance of the word.

   • Click a suggested spelling and click Change All to change all instances of the word.

3. The Spell Checker moves to the next suspect word, if any, and you can use any of the options in the preceding list to fix mistakes. This continues until the Spell Checker tells you the Spell Check is complete.

4. Click Close to close the dialog box.

If you would also like to have Works check your grammar, you can select the Check Grammar checkbox in the Spelling and Grammar dialog box. When you next run the Spelling and Grammar check, Works displays sentences with possible grammatical problems and suggestions for how to fix them.

Click to select an alternate spelling

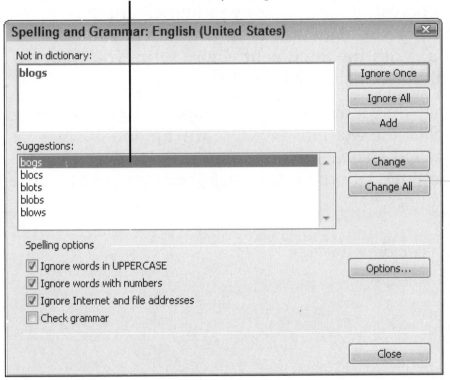

Figure 11-11

 It's a good idea to use the Add feature to put unusual words or acronyms you use often in the dictionary. For example, you might add unrecognized names of people or companies, scientific terms, or acronyms such as IBM or MTV. By adding such words to the dictionary, you save yourself the time it takes to tell

227

Works over and over again that those words are correct.

Change Page Setup

1. Word processors use default page setup that includes
settings such as margins and orientation of your contents
on the document page. If you want to change those
settings, you can do that when you first create the
document, or you may wait until you're ready to print the
document. With the document whose setup you want to
change displayed, choose File⇨Page Setup.

2. In the Page Setup dialog box that appears (see **Figure
11-12**), click the Margins tab. Use the up and down
arrows (called *spinner arrows*) to increase or decrease
margin settings, or type a new measurement in any of the
Margins boxes.

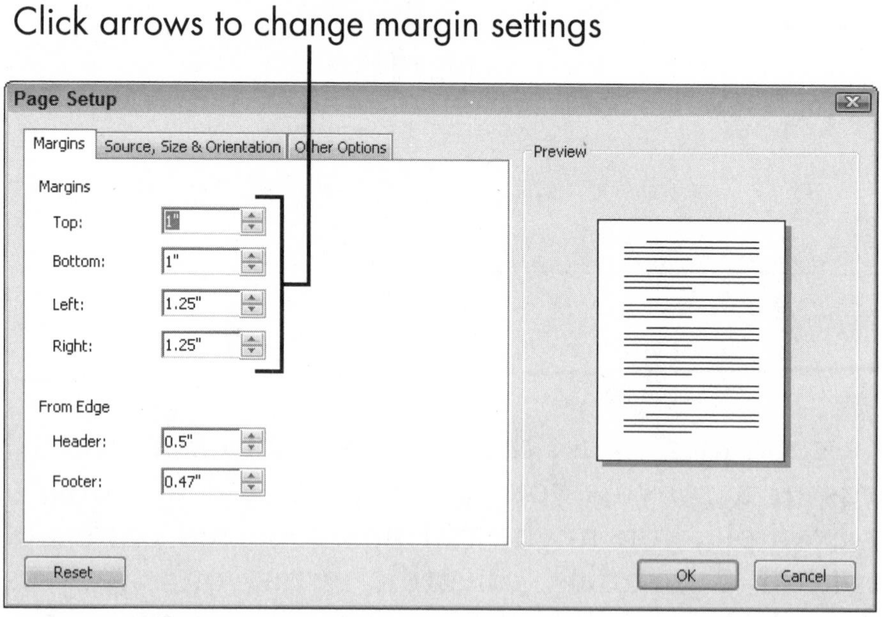

Click arrows to change margin settings

Figure 11-12

3. Click the Source, Size & Orientation tab (see **Figure 11-13**). Select a radio button for either Portrait orientation (with the longer edges of the paper on the sides) or Landscape (with the shorter edges of the paper on the sides).

4. Also on the Source, Size & Orientation tab, you can use the Paper settings to specify the size of paper you will print to, and, if you have multiple paper trays, to select the source for the paper.

5. Click OK to save the new settings.

Choose an orientation

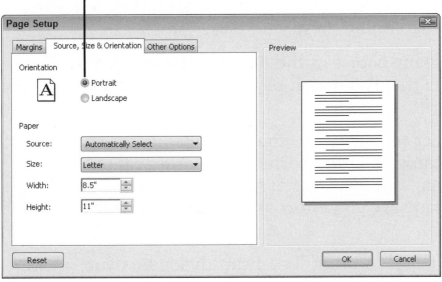

Figure 11-13

 If you're inserting a header or footer (for example, a page number or the name of the document that you want to appear on every page on either the top or bottom), you should check some settings in this dialog box. On the Margins tab, you can specify how far

229

from the edge of the paper the header or footer should appear. On the Other Options tab, you can control what page number you start with and whether the header or footer should appear on the first page of the document. (To insert headers or footers in your document, use the Header and Footer command on the View menu.)

Print a Document

All Windows software uses a similar procedure to print files, and Works is no different. You simply choose File⇨Print (or in Office 2007 and later programs, click the Office button and choose Print) and use the settings shown in **Figure 11-14** to determine these variables:

- How many copies of the document you want to print: Be sure there's enough paper in your printer to handle them all!

- Whether to collate the copies: Collating assembles sets of documents in the correct page order rather than printing, say, five page 1s, then five page 2s, and so on. This can save you effort assembling your documents yourself.

- What pages to print: The Print dialog box you see in Windows software allows you to print the current page, text you select before giving the Print command, the entire document, or a specified page or range of pages.

- Which printer to print to and preferences for that printer: You can determine preferences such as the print quality and whether to print in color or grayscale.

Always remember before you print to proofread your document and run a Spell Check to make sure it's letter perfect.

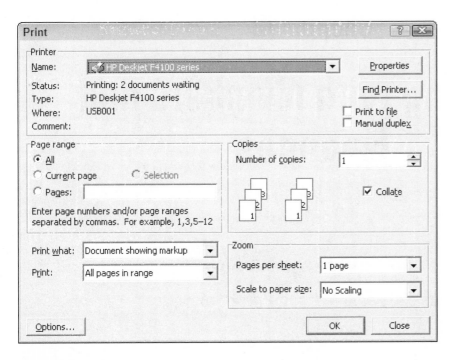

Figure 11-14

Chapter 12

Working with Numbers and Finances

A spreadsheet program allows you to automate both simple and complex calculations. You enter numbers and then perform actions on them such as calculating an average or generating a sum for a range of numbers. You can format the data in a spreadsheet and also generate charts based on the numbers you enter.

Microsoft Works 9 includes a spreadsheet program that provides some pretty sophisticated tools for working with numbers and charts. You can also use this and other spreadsheet programs to create tables of data, such as your home inventory or investments.

In addition to working with a spreadsheet program, there are several ways you can get information about your investments and perform financial transactions online. Together, a spreadsheet program and the financial tools you can use on the Internet can make managing your financial life much easier.

Explore the Structure of a Spreadsheet

Spreadsheet software, such as Microsoft Works Spreadsheet and Microsoft Excel, uses a grid-like structure for entering data. The individual cells of the grid are formed by the intersection of a row with a column, so a cell is identified by a column letter followed by a row number. For example, B3 identifies the cell located at the intersection of the second column over and third row down.

Here are some additional facts you should know about spreadsheets:

- You can enter text or numbers in spreadsheets.

- When you click in a cell, the Formula bar becomes active. You can enter contents and edit those contents in the Formula bar (see **Figure 12-1**).

- Use the two scroll bars, the one to the right and the one at the bottom, to move vertically or horizontally through a large spreadsheet.

- You can perform calculations on numbers that you've entered in a spreadsheet, such as adding numbers or calculating an average of several numbers.

- You can format the contents of cells or use an AutoFormat feature to apply predesigned styles to selected cells. Note that in some predesigned formats, the grid lines are neither displayed nor printed.

- After you've entered some data into your spreadsheet, you can easily generate a chart representing that data graphically.

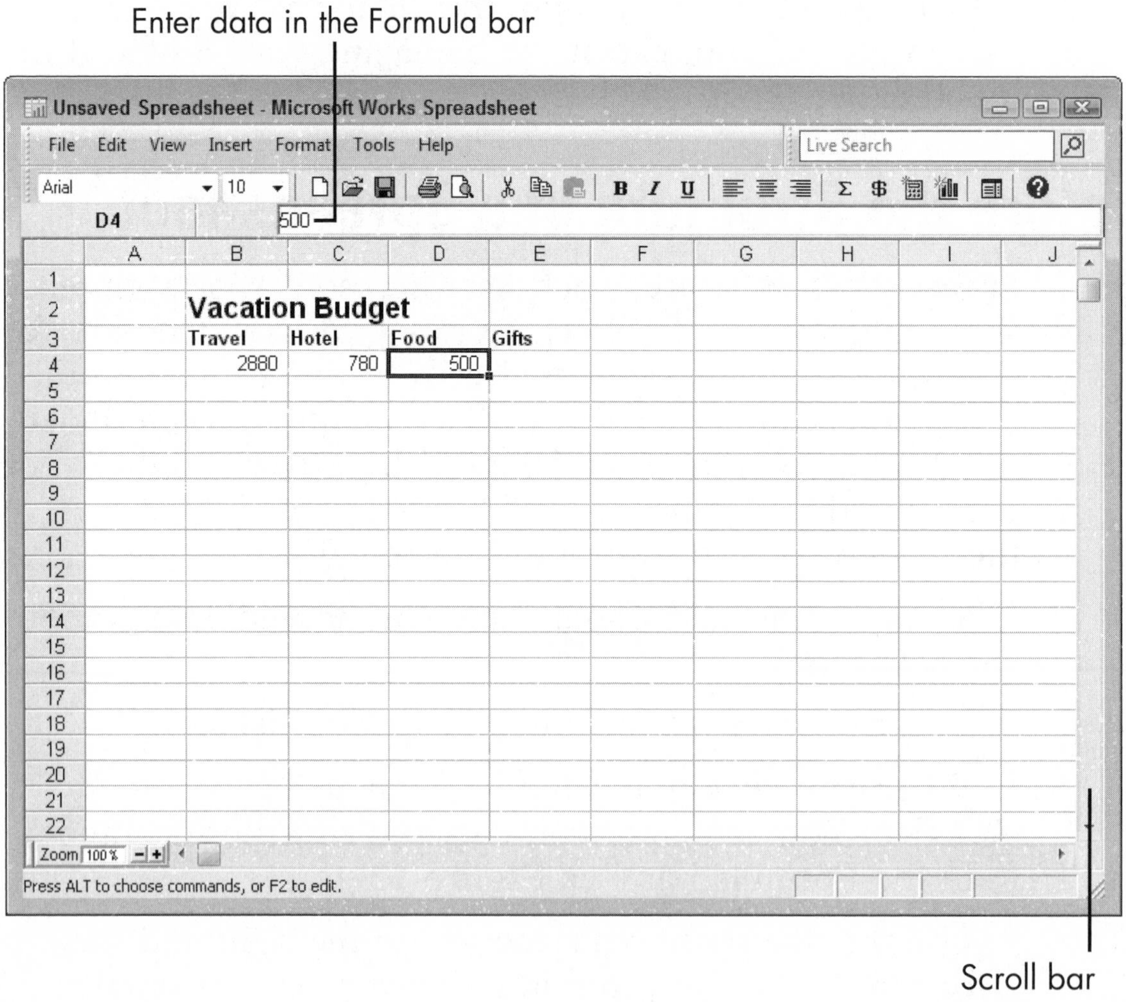

Figure 12-1

Open Works Spreadsheet and Enter Text

1. To start a new spreadsheet and begin filling it with information, first choose Start⇨All Programs⇨Microsoft Works⇨Microsoft Works Spreadsheet.

2. In the blank spreadsheet that appears, click in a cell to make it active (see **Figure 12-2**).

3. Begin typing; notice that what you type appears in both the cell and the Formula bar.

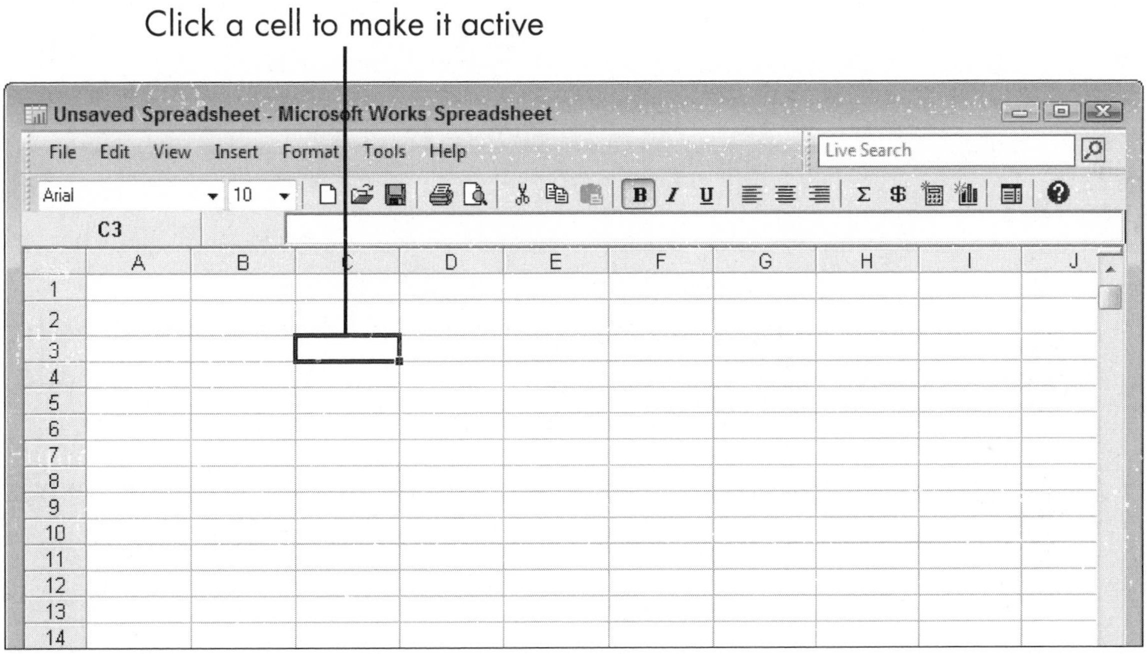

Click a cell to make it active

Figure 12-2

4. Press Tab to complete the entry and move to the next cell. Note that you can also click the Enter button (see **Figure 12-3**), which looks like a check mark, to complete your entry and keep the current cell active.

The Enter button

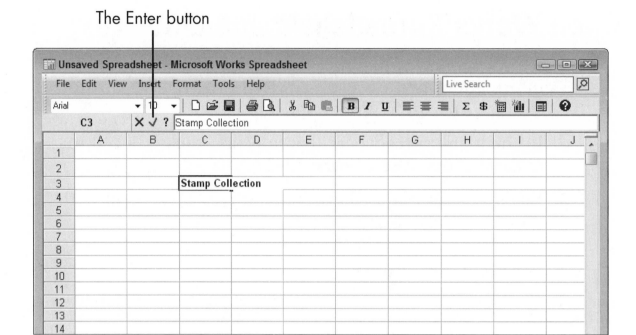

Figure 12-3

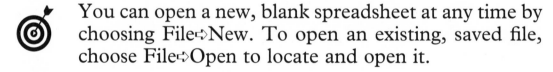 You can open a new, blank spreadsheet at any time by choosing File⇨New. To open an existing, saved file, choose File⇨Open to locate and open it.

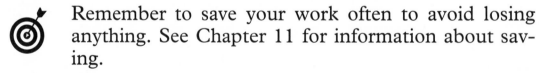 Remember to save your work often to avoid losing anything. See Chapter 11 for information about saving.

Format Numbers

1. You can format text in the cells of a spreadsheet by applying effects or changing the text font or color, just as you do for text in a word processor (see Chapter 11). However, formatting numbers in a spreadsheet is a bit different. In this procedure, you format the number to fit a category such as currency or to include a certain number of decimal points. To begin formatting numbers, first click the cell containing the numbers you want to format. To select multiple cells, click a cell and drag up, down, right, or left to select a range of cells.

2. Choose Format⇨Number.

3. In the Format Cells dialog box that appears with the Number tab displayed (see **Figure 12-4**), click an option in the Select Format Type list, such as Currency or Percent.

4. Click the up or down arrow in the Set Decimal Places field to specify how many decimal places the number should have; for example, 22.10 (two decimals), 22.1 (one decimal), or 22 (no decimals). Your settings appear in the Preview box.

5. Click OK to apply your formatting selections and close the dialog box.

 Currency and General are common options for formatting numbers in lists or budgets, but they aren't the only ones. You can even format numbers to display as dates, times, or fractions. If you want zero to appear as False (in other words no value) and any number (that is any value at all) to appear as True, choose the True/False number type.

Click a number format

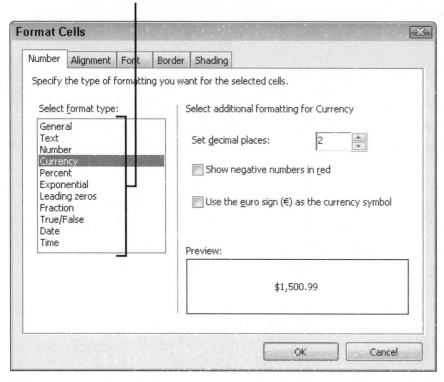

Figure 12-4

Apply AutoFormats to Cells

1. You can also format sets of cells by using AutoFormats, which are predesigned sets of formatting choices such as cell shading or borders. Click and drag to select a range of cells.

2. Choose Format↷AutoFormat.

3. In the AutoFormat dialog box that appears (see **Figure 12-5**), select a format from the list provided. You see a preview of the design.

Click a format

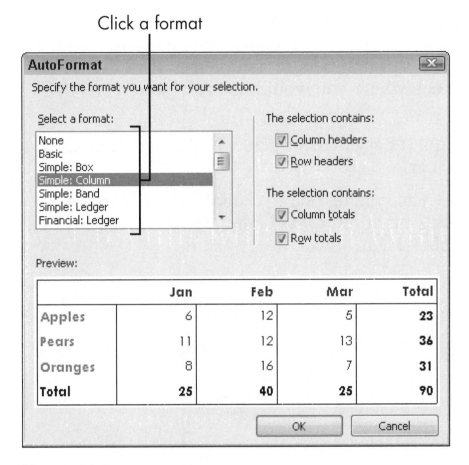

AutoFormat ⊠

Specify the format you want for your selection.

Select a format:

| None |
| Basic |
| Simple: Box |
| Simple: Column |
| Simple: Band |
| Simple: Ledger |
| Financial: Ledger |

The selection contains:

☑ Column headers

☑ Row headers

The selection contains:

☑ Column totals

☑ Row totals

Preview:

	Jan	Feb	Mar	Total
Apples	6	12	5	23
Pears	11	12	13	36
Oranges	8	16	7	31
Total	25	40	25	90

OK   Cancel

Figure 12-5

4. If you like, you can modify the settings for including column and row headings and totals by selecting or deselecting any of the four check boxes on the right of the dialog box.

5. Click OK to apply the selected formatting to the cell range.

Perform Simple Calculations

1. A spreadsheet program is way more than just a place to list numbers and text. After you've entered some numbers in your spreadsheet, you can use powerful spreadsheet tools to perform simple or complex calculations, from averaging a set of numbers to complex statistical analysis. Click in a cell where you would like calculation results to appear.

2. Choose Tools⇨Easy Calc or press the Easy Calc button on the toolbar.

3. In the Easy Calc dialog box that appears (see **Figure 12-6**), click a function in the Common Functions list box and then click Next.

Click a function

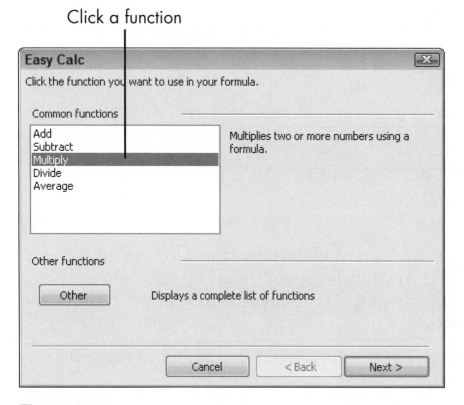

Figure 12-6

4. In the following dialog box (see **Figure 12-7**), enter a range of cells, such as A1:C4, in the Range field. Or click

the button on the right of the Range field; the dialog box is then hidden, allowing you to click and drag on your spreadsheet to select the cells you want to calculate. After you make the selection, the dialog box appears again.

5. Click Next. In the Final Result dialog box, you can enter a different cell location, such as G5, in the Result At text box, and the result will be saved in the cell you indicate. Click Finish to complete the calculation. The result of the calculation now appears in the designated cell.

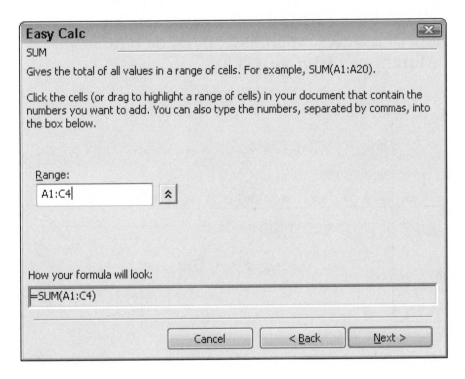

Figure 12-7

 To quickly add numbers, you can simply click in the cell where you want to place the results and then click the AutoSum button on the toolbar (which looks kind of like a capital *M* turned sideways). Spreadsheet suggests cells you might want to include in the calcula-

241

tion, but you can click and drag to select more or different cells. Click or press Enter to complete the sum.

Complete a Series with Fill

1. Life consists of patterns, and spreadsheets make entering items with patterns quick and easy. For example, if you are entering a series of odd numbers (1, 3, 5, and so on), you can use tools to complete the series automatically. Enter some data in sequential cells that constitutes the beginning of a series, such as 1, 2, 3, or January, February, March (see **Figure 12-8**).

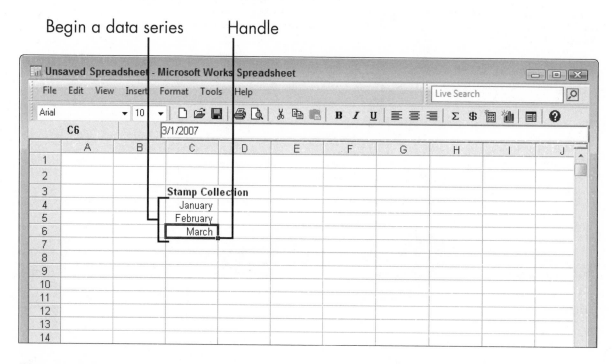

Figure 12-8

2. Click and drag over the data; a small handle appears at the end of the series (in the bottom-right corner for items

242

in a column or at the far right for items in a row).

3. Click and drag the handle to add items to your series (see **Figure 12-9**). For a series in a column, drag down, but for a series in a row, drag to the right. For example, if you entered January, February, and March, you might drag over nine blank cells to add the rest of the months of the year. Works Spreadsheet completes the series.

 Items in a series don't have to be sequential. Works Spreadsheet can detect patterns as well. For example, if you enter 11, 22, and 33 and fill out the series, you get 44, 55, 66, and so on. However, if selected data has no discernable pattern, when you drag to fill, the data will simply be repeated again and again.

Drag the handle to fill out the series

	A	B	C	D	E	F	G	H	I	J
1										
2										
3			Stamp Collection							
4			January							
5			February							
6			March							
7										
8										
9										
10										
11										
12										
13										
14										

Unsaved Spreadsheet - Microsoft Works Spreadsheet

File   Edit   View   Insert   Format   Tools   Help

Arial   10   C4:C6   1/1/2007

Figure 12-9

Insert a Chart

1. If you want to see your data represented visually, the Works spreadsheet can create attractive charts from your data. To start, you have to first enter the data you want your chart to be based on.

2. Click and drag over the data to select it and then click the New Chart button on the toolbar.

3. In the resulting New Chart dialog box (see **Figure 12-10**), click a Chart Type image to select it.

4. Enter a title for the chart in the Chart Title text box. Click the Show Border or Show Gridlines checkbox to apply those effects.

5. Click OK to display the chart (see **Figure 12-11**). To go back to the spreadsheet, you can choose View⇨Spreadsheet.

Click a chart type

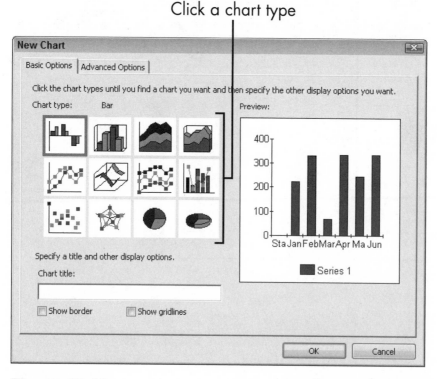

Figure 12-10

244

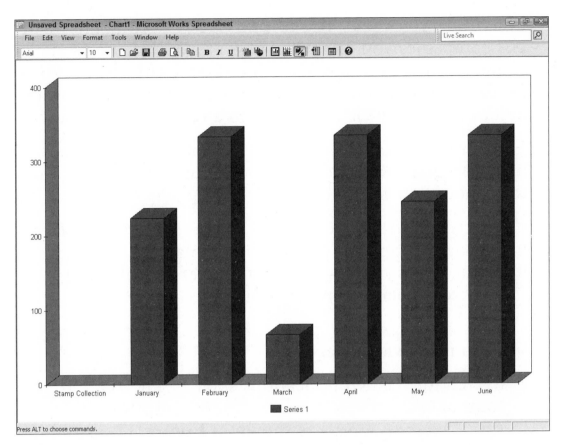

Figure 12-11

 After you insert a chart, you can use tools on the Format menu or on the Chart toolbar, such as the Chart Type button or the Borders button, to make changes to chart type, borders used around the chart, or font style or size.

Get Advice about Finances Online

You can use the Internet to access a wealth of financial information online. You can read current news stories, get advice about how to invest, and connect with others to share information. Keep in mind that the quality of information online can vary drastically, and you can't always believe

245

everything you read. Try to find sites of reputable financial companies you might know from your offline financial dealings, such as Merrill Lynch or Forbes Magazine. Also, never give out financial account numbers to anybody via e-mail, even if they claim to be with a reputable company.

Here are some of the resources available to you for planning and monitoring your finances (see Chapter 16 for details about how to go to any Web site):

- Visit sites such as `www.money.cnn.com/magazines/moneymag/money101` for simple financial lessons about topics such as setting a budget and planning your retirement from CNNMoney.

- Visit `www.financialplan.about.com` for financial planning advice by age.

- Search for online publications such as The Wall Street Journal (`www.wallstreetjournal.com`), Forbes (`www.forbes.com`), as shown in **Figure 12-12,** or Kiplinger's (`www.kiplinger.com`) for articles about the latest financial and investing trends.

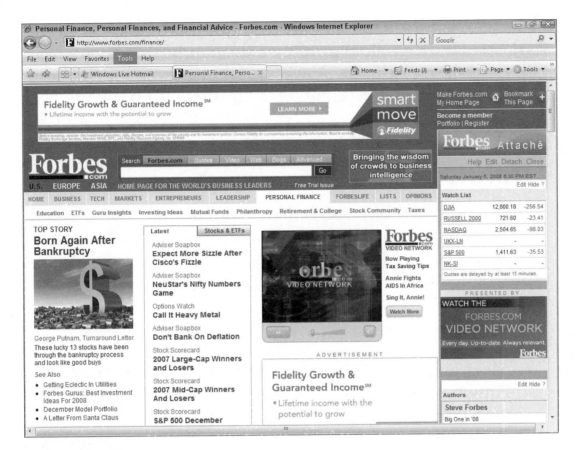

Figure 12-12

- Check out online discussion forums such as `www.money.MSN.com` to connect with others who are interested in learning more about finances. However, be very careful not to reveal too much personal information to anybody you meet online, especially about your specific finances and accounts.

 In the United States, you're entitled to order a free credit report from major credit report organizations every year, and you can order those reports online. Visit `www.annualcreditreport.com` to get started.

Windows 7 lets you display *gadgets* (little programs, such as a calculator, that do handy things) on your desktop. Add the Stocks gadget to check stock quotes at a glance. See Chapter 10 for details on adding gadgets.

Bank Online

Many people today are banking online because it's convenient. You can typically make account transfers, check your balance, and even download your account activity to a program such as Quicken to manage your financial records or work with your taxes.

Consider this information when banking online:

- Most online banks, such as Barclays in the United Kingdom (see **Figure 12-13**), have very strong security measures in place; however, you should be sure that you're using a secure Internet connection to go online. If you use a wireless home network that isn't protected, for example, it's possible for someone to tap into your online transactions, so you should have whoever sets up your network enable security and a firewall. (See Chapter 21 for an introduction to basic security.) Also, if you use a public wireless network such as those in airports or hotels, don't log on to any financial accounts.

- You may need to set things up with your bank so that you can access your account online and make transfers among your different accounts. Talk to your bank about what they require.

- Be careful to choose strong passwords (random combinations of letters, numbers, and punctuation are best) for accessing your bank accounts. If you write the passwords down, put them someplace safe. See Chapter 18 for advice about strong passwords.

- Be aware of your financial rights, such as how credit cards and bank accounts are protected by law. The FDIC Web site offers lots of information about your banking and financial life at `www.fdic.gov`. It's specific to the United States, but some of the advice about online financial dangers is pertinent no matter where you live.

Figure 12-13

Invest Online

Every major broker has an online presence. Investing online is convenient, and online brokers enable you to place buy or sell orders very quickly and inexpensively. In addition, you can manage investment accounts online.

Here are some tips for online investing:

- **Understand the fees.** Online brokerage fees are typically lower than working with a full-service broker. However, online broker fees can vary widely. Shop around for a broker you trust and who has reasonable fees.

- **Buyer beware.** Though online banking is protected by most federal governments, including the United States, online investment accounts don't always share similar protections, depending on what country you live in. Consider asking your investment counselor for advice about how protections work in your country.

- **Handle various types of investments.** Beyond buying and selling stocks, you can invest in bonds, deposit to your IRA or other retirement accounts, and more. Companies such as Fidelity (www.fidelity. com) give you lots of investment choices.

- **Retain offline access to your account.** Remember that one downside to online investing is that if your computer connection is down or your broker's server is down, you can't get to your online brokerage to invest. Keep a phone number handy so you can reach your broker by an alternative method in the case of technical glitches.

- **Check what others have to say.** Visit sites such as

The Motley Fool (see **Figure 12-14**) for articles and advice on investing.

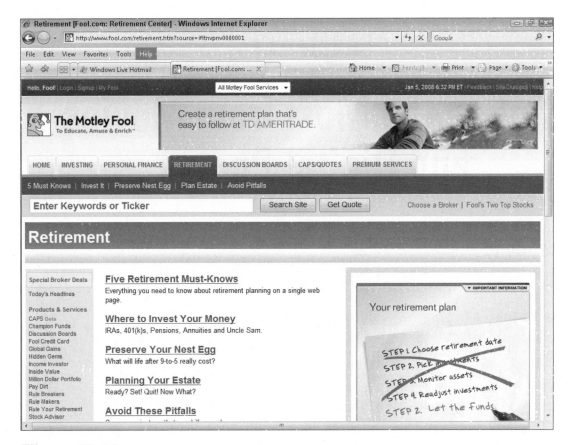

Figure 12-14

Chapter 13

Getting the Most from Movies and Digital Photos

Apicture is worth a thousand words, and that's probably why everybody is in on the digital image craze. Most people today have access to a digital camera (even if only on their cell phones) and have started manipulating and swapping photos like crazy, both online and off.

In this chapter you discover how to

➤ Play movies with Windows Media Player.

➤ Upload photos from your digital camera.

➤ View your photos and add tags and ratings to help you organize and search through photos.

➤ E-mail a photo to others.

➤ Burn photos to a DVD to pass around to your friends.

Work with Media Software

Your computer is a doorway into a media-rich world full of music, digital photos, and movies. Your computer provides you with all kinds of possibilities for working with media. Windows 7 has two useful media programs built right into it: Windows Media Player and Windows Photo Viewer. In combination, they give you the ability to play music and set up libraries of music tracks; view, organize, and edit photos; and edit and play your own home movies.

Here's what you can do with each of these programs:

➤ **Windows Media Player** (see **Figure 13-1**) is just what its name suggests: a program you can use to play music, watch movies, or view photos. It also offers handy tools to create *playlists* (customized lists of music you can build and play) and set up libraries of media to keep things organized. You can even burn media to a DVD so you can play it on your DVD player or another computer.

→ **Windows Photo Viewer** (see **Figure 13-2**) enables you to work with digital photos; it opens automatically when you double-click a photo file. You can also burn media to a disc or order prints from within Photo Viewer.

→ Using photo properties in the **Pictures library** (see **Figure 13-3**) you can organize your photos by adding tags that help you search for just the photo you need. You can also run slide shows using the Picture library.

Figure 13-1

Figure 13-2

Figure 13-3

Play Movies with Windows Media Player

1. To open Windows Media Player and begin working with music and movie files, click the icon with an orange circle containing a right-facing arrow on the taskbar, or choose Start➪All Programs➪Windows Media Player. If this is your first time using the player, you may be prompted to make some basic settings.

2. Click the Maximize button in the resulting Media Player window. (Maximize is in the upper-right corner of the window, next to the X-shaped Close button, and has a square icon.)

3. Click Videos in the navigation pane to the left.

4. In the window listing video files that appears, click the Library folder that contains the movie you want to play (as shown in **Figure 13-4**).

Click the folder that contains the movie you want to play

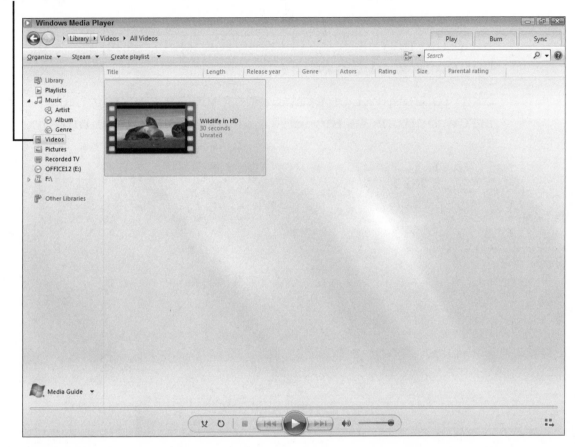

Figure 13-4

5. Double-click a file to begin the playback (see **Figure 13-5**). Use tools at the bottom of the screen to do the following (if they disappear during playback, just hover your mouse over that area to display them again):

• Adjust the volume of any soundtrack by clicking and dragging the slider left (to make it softer) or right (to make it louder). Click the megaphone-shaped volume icon to mute the sound (and click it again to turn the sound back on).

- Pause the playback by clicking the round Pause button in the center of the toolbar.

- Stop the playback by clicking the square-shaped Stop button toward the left.

- Skip to the next or previous movie by clicking the arrow buttons to the left or right of the Pause button.

Figure 13-5

6. Click the Close button to close Media Player.

 To stop the movie before it finishes, click the Stop button. Note that the Rewind and Fast Forward tools aren't available for single movie clips — they jump

258

you from one track to another when playing sound files.

Upload Photos from Your Digital Camera

Uploading photos from a camera to your computer is a very simple process, but it helps to understand what's involved. (This is similar to the process you can use to upload movies from a camcorder — in both cases, check your manual for details.) Here are some highlights:

➤ **Making the connection:** To upload photos from a digital camera to a computer requires that you connect the camera to a USB port on your computer using a USB cable that typically comes with the camera. Power on the camera or change its setting to a playback mode as instructed by your user's manual.

➤ **Installing software:** Digital cameras also typically come with software that makes uploading photos to your computer easy. Install the software and then follow the easy-to-use interface to upload photos. If you're missing such software, you can simply connect your camera to your computer and use Windows Explorer to locate the camera device on your computer and copy and paste photo files into a folder on your hard drive. (Chapter 3 tells you how to use Windows Explorer.)

➤ **Printing straight from the camera:** Some cameras save photos onto a memory card, and many printers include a slot where you can insert the memory card from the camera and print directly from it without having to first upload pictures. Some cameras also connect directly to printers. However, if you want to keep a copy of the photo and clear up space in your camera's memory, you should upload even if you can print without uploading.

View a Digital Image in the Windows Photo Viewer

1. To peruse your photos and open them in Windows Photo Viewer, click Start⇨Pictures.

2. In the resulting window, if there are folders in this library, double-click on one to display files within it. Double-click on any photo in any Pictures Library folder. In the Windows Photo Viewer window, shown in **Figure 13-6,** you can use the tools at the bottom (see **Figure 13-7**) to do any of the following:

Figure 13-6

- The **Previous** and **Next** icons move to a previous or following image in the same folder.

- The **Display Size** icon, in the shape of a magnifying glass, displays a slider you can click and drag to change the size of the image thumbnails.

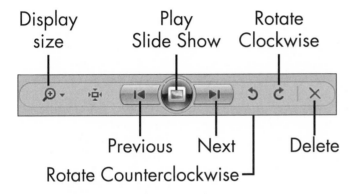

Figure 13-7

- The **Delete** button deletes the selected image.

- The **Rotate Clockwise** and **Rotate Counterclockwise** icons spin the image 90 degrees at a time.

- The center **Play Slide Show** button, with a slide image on it, displays the images in your Picture folder in a continuous slide show.

 If you want to quickly open a photo in another application, click the Open button at the top of the Windows Photo Viewer window and choose a program such as Paint or Microsoft Office Picture Manager.

Add a Tag to a Photo

1. Tags help to categorize photos so you can search for them easily. To create a new tag, choose Start⇨Pictures. Locate the photo you want, right-click it, and choose Properties.

2. In the Properties dialog box that appears, click the Details tab (see **Figure 13-8**).

Click the Details tab

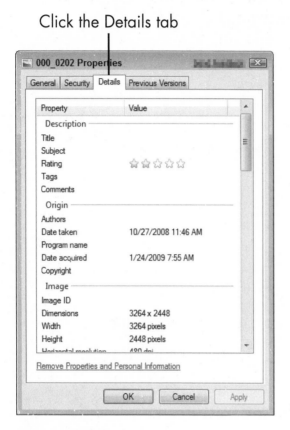

Figure 13-8

3. Click the Tags item and a field appears. Enter a tag(s) in the field (see **Figure 13-9**) and click OK to save the tag.

4. Now if you display your Pictures library in Windows Explorer in a Details view, the tag will be listed next to the photo. Tags are also used when you view photos in Windows Media Center.

 To delete a tag, just display the photo Properties dialog box again, click to the right of the tag, and press

262

Backspace.

 To see a list of all photos in the Photo Gallery organized by tags, click the arrow on the Arrange By item and choose Tag.

Enter a tag here

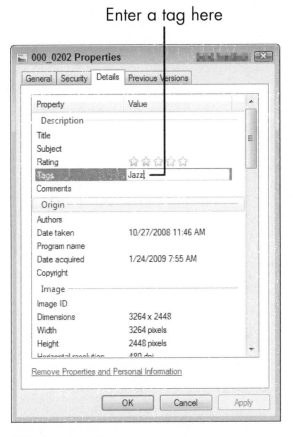

Figure 13-9

E-Mail a Photo

1. Choose Start⇨Pictures. In Pictures Library, shown in **Figure 13-10** in Details view, click to the left of the thumbnail to select the photo; a checkmark appears in a checkbox to indicate it is selected. To choose multiple

263

photos, click additional thumbnails.

2. Choose File⇨Send To⇨Mail Recipient. In the Attach Files dialog box that appears (see **Figure 13-11**), change the photo size by clicking the Picture Size drop-down arrow and choosing another size from the list if you wish.

3. Click Attach. An e-mail form from your default e-mail appears with your photo attached.

Selected photos

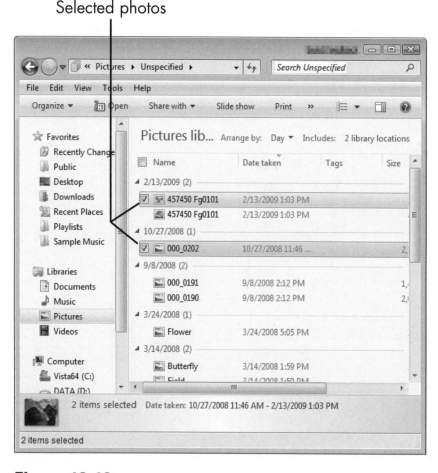

Figure 13-10

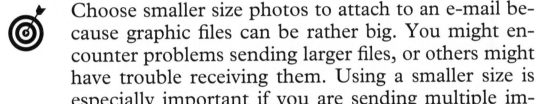

Click to change
the photo size

Figure 13-11

4. Fill out the e-mail form with an addressee, subject, and message (if you wish), and then click Send.

 Choose smaller size photos to attach to an e-mail because graphic files can be rather big. You might encounter problems sending larger files, or others might have trouble receiving them. Using a smaller size is especially important if you are sending multiple images. Note that although you can send a video file as an e-mail attachment, you can't resize it; video files make photo files look tiny by comparison, so it's probably better to send one at a time, if at all.

 You can also open an e-mail form first. Then, with the Photo Viewer open, click and drag a photo to your e-mail. This method attaches the original file size to the message.

Burn a Photo to a DVD

1. You can burn a copy of your photos to a DVD to share them or to have a backup. Insert a writable DVD into your disc drive.

2. With the Pictures Library open in Windows Explorer, display a photo by locating it with the navigation pane and double-clicking the thumbnail to display it in Windows Photo Viewer.

3. Click the Burn button and then choose Data Disc.

4. A balloon message appears on the taskbar indicating that you have files waiting to be burned to DVD. Click the balloon and a list of files waiting to be burned appears, as shown in **Figure 13-12.**

5. Click the Burn to Disc button. In the Burn to Disc dialog box that appears, enter a name in the Disc Title (the default name is today's date), and if you wish, change the recording speed; click Next.

6. A progress window appears (see **Figure 13-13**).

7. When the files have been burned to the disc, a confirming dialog box appears, and your disc drawer opens. Click Finish to complete the process and close the dialog box.

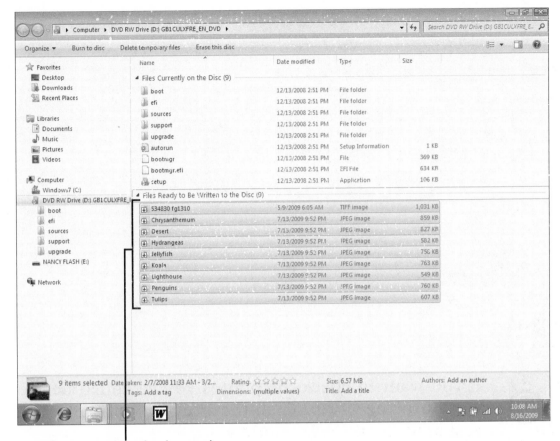

Files waiting to be burned

Figure 13-12

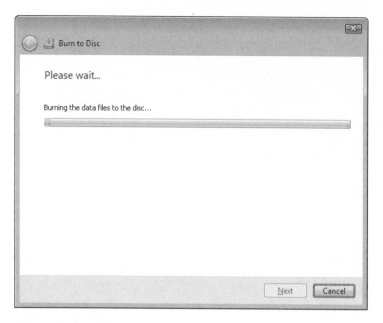

Figure 13-13

 If you want to check the photos you've added before you burn the DVD, click the Preview button in the Ready to Burn DVD window.

Create and Play a Slide Show

1. You can use the photos in your Pictures Library to run your own slide show. Choose Start⇨Pictures. Double-click the Picture Library to display all pictures within it.

2. Click an image to select it. Holding down the Ctrl key, repeat this to select all the photos you want to appear in the slide show (see **Figure 13-14**).

Photos selected for slide show

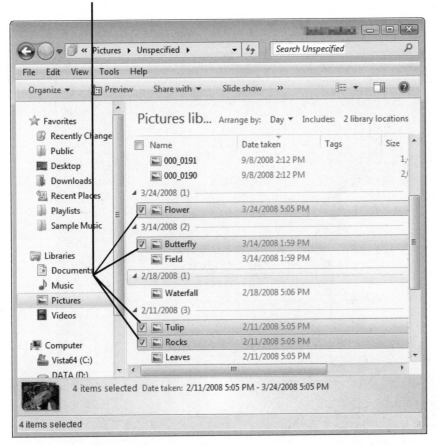

Figure 13-14

3. Click the Slide Show button. The first image appears in a separate full-screen display. The slides move forward automatically, cycling among the photos repeatedly (see **Figure 13-15**).

4. Press Escape to stop the slide show.

 If you want a more sophisticated slide show feature, check out Windows Media Center. Here you can create and save any number of custom slide shows, reorganize slides, and edit slide shows to add or delete photos. You might also consider a commercial slide

show program such as PowerPoint if you want to create more complex slide shows.

Figure 13-15

Chapter 14

Playing Music in Windows 7

Music is the universal language, and your computer opens up many opportunities for appreciating it. Your computer makes it possible for you to listen to your favorite music, download music from the Internet, play audio CDs and DVDs, and organize your music by creating playlists. You can also save (or *burn* in computer lingo) music tracks to a CD/DVD or portable music device such as the hugely popular iPod.

With a sound card installed and speakers attached, you can use Windows media programs to do the following:

➡ Getting your computer ready for listening by setting up your speakers and adjusting the volume

➡ Playing music using Windows Media Player

➡ Managing your music by creating playlists of tracks you download

➡ Burning tracks to CD/DVD or syncing with portable music devices

➡ Making settings to copy music from CD/DVDs to your computer (called *ripping*)

Set Up Speakers

1. Attach speakers to your computer by plugging them into the appropriate connection (often labeled with a little megaphone or speaker symbol) on your CPU, laptop, or monitor.

2. Choose Start⇨Control Panel⇨Hardware and Sound; then click the Manage Audio Devices link (under the Sound category).

3. In the resulting Sound dialog box (see **Figure 14-1**), click the Speakers item and then click the Properties button.

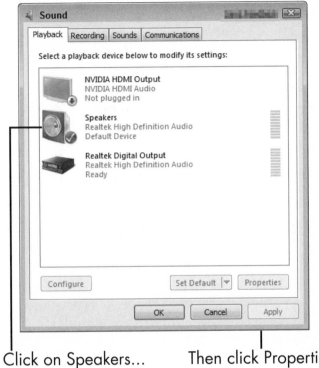

Click on Speakers...   Then click Properties

Figure 14-1

4. In the resulting Speakers Property dialog box, click the
Levels tab, shown in **Figure 14-2,** and then use the
Speakers slider to adjust the speaker volume. ***Note:*** If
there is a small red x on the speaker button, click it to
activate the speakers.

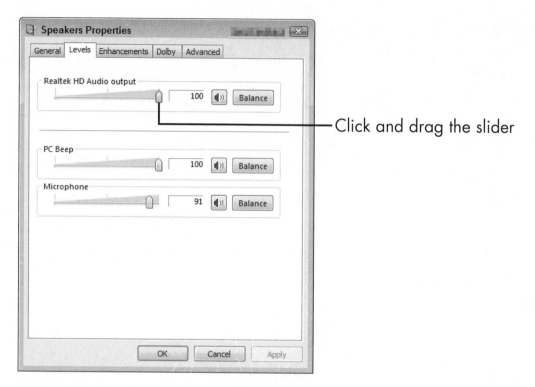

Click and drag the slider

Figure 14-2

5. Click the Balance button. In the resulting Balance dialog box, use the L(eft) and R(ight) sliders to adjust the balance of sounds between the two speakers.

6. Click OK three times to close all the open dialog boxes and save the new settings.

 If you use your computer to make or receive phone calls, check out the Communications tab of the Sound dialog box. Here you can make a setting to have Windows automatically make adjustments to sounds to minimize background noise.

Adjust System Volume

1. You can set the master system volume for your computer

274

to be louder or softer. Choose Start⇨Control Panel⇨ Hardware and Sound.

2. Click the Adjust System Volume link under Sound to display the Volume Mixer dialog box (shown in **Figure 14-3**).

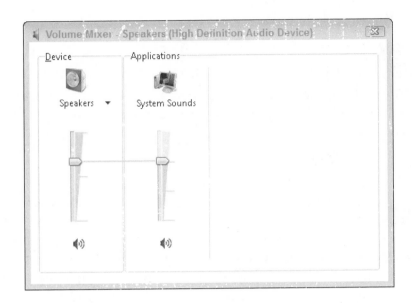

Figure 14-3

3. Make any of the following settings:

   • Move the Device slider to adjust the system's speaker volume up and down.

   • For sounds played by Windows (called *system sounds*), adjust the volume by moving the Applications slider.

   • To mute either the main or application volume, click the speaker icon beneath either slider so that a red circle appears.

4. Click the Close button twice.

Here's a handy shortcut for quickly adjusting the volume of your default sound device. Click the Volume button (which looks like a little gray speaker) in the notifications area of the taskbar. To adjust the volume, use the slider on the Volume pop-up that appears, or select the Mute Speakers button to turn off sounds temporarily.

 Today many keyboards include volume controls and a mute button to control sounds from your computer. Some even include buttons to play, pause, and stop audio playback. Having these buttons and other controls at your fingertips can be worth a little extra in the price of your keyboard.

Create a Playlist

1. A *playlist* is a saved set of music tracks you can create yourself — like building a personal music album. Choose Start⇨All Programs⇨Windows Media Player.

2. Click the Library button and then click the Create Playlist button. A playlist appears in the navigation pane on the left. Type a name for the playlist and then click anywhere outside the playlist to save the name.

3. Double-click a category (for example, Music) to display libraries, and then double-click a library in the left pane; the library contents appear (see **Figure 14-4**). Click an item and then drag it to the new playlist in the navigation pane. Repeat this step to locate additional titles to add to the playlist.

4. To play a playlist, click it in the Library pane and then click the Play button.

5. You can organize playlists by clicking the Organize button (see **Figure 14-5**) and then choosing Sort By. In the submenu that appears, sort by features such as title, artist, or release date.

Click a library   Drag items to the new playlist

Figure 14-4

Click the Organize button

Figure 14-5

You can also right-click a playlist in the Library pane and choose Play to play it or choose Delete to delete the list, though the original tracks that make up the list still exist.

Burn Music to a CD/DVD

1. Saving music files to a storage medium such as a CD or DVD is referred to as *burning.* You might burn music to a disc so you can take it to a party or another computer location. Insert a blank CD or DVD suitable for storing audio files in your computer CD/DVD-RW drive.

2. Open the Windows Media Player, click the Burn tab, and then click one or more songs, albums, or playlists and

278

drag them to the Burn pane (see **Figure 14-6**).

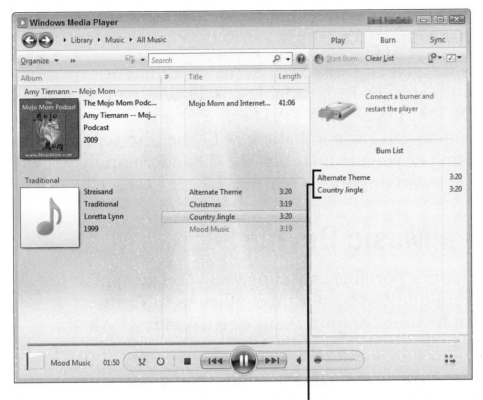

Songs placed in the Burn pane

Figure 14-6

3. Click Start Burn. Windows Media Player begins to burn the items to the disc. The Status column for the first song title reads `Writing to Disc` and changes to `Complete` when the track is copied.

4. When the burn is complete, your disc is ejected (although you can change this option by clicking the Burn Options button and choosing Eject Disc After Burning to deselect it).

If you swap music online through various music-sharing services and then copy them to CD/DVD and pass them around to your friends, always do a virus check on the files before handing them off. Also, be sure you have the legal right to download and swap that music with others.

 Note that optical discs come in different types, including CD-R (readable), CD-RW (read/writable), DVD+, DVD– and DVD+/–. You must be sure your optical drive is compatible with the disc type you are using or you cannot burn the disc successfully. Check the packaging for the format before you buy!

Sync with a Music Device

1. If you have a portable music player, you can sync it to your computer to transfer music files to it. Connect a device to your computer and open Windows Media Player.

2. Click the Sync tab; a Device Setup dialog box appears (see **Figure 14-7**).

3. Name the device, and click Finish. The device is now synced with Windows Media Player and will be automatically updated whenever you connect it to your computer.

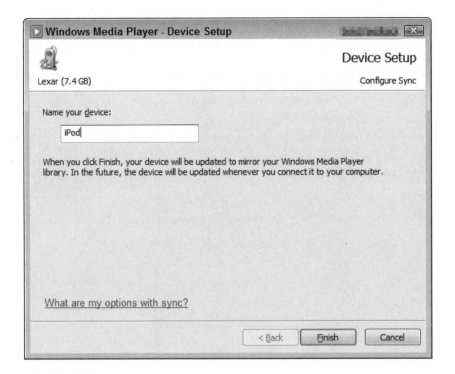

Figure 14-7

🎯 To add items to be synced to a device, with the Sync tab displayed, simply drag items to the right pane. If you are connected, or the next time you connect, the items are copied onto the device automatically.

🎯 If you want to be sure that the sync is progressing, click the Sync Options button (it's on the far right of the top of the Sync tab and looks like a little box with a checkmark in it) and choose View Sync Status.

Play Music

1. Choose Start⇨All Programs⇨Windows Media Player.

2. Click the Library button and then double-click Music or Playlists to display a library like the one shown in **Figure 14-8.** Double-click an album or playlist to open it; the

281

titles of the songs are displayed in the right pane.

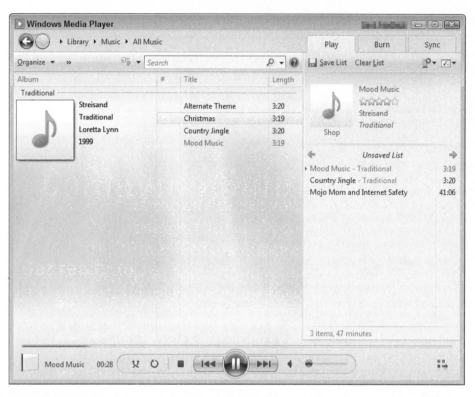

Figure 14-8

3. Use the buttons on the bottom of the Player window (as shown in **Figure 14-9**) to do the following:

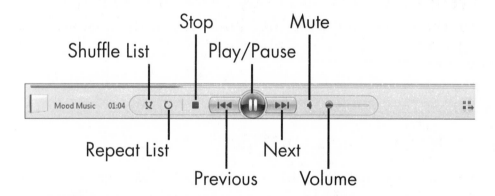

Figure 14-9

- Click a track, and then click the **Play** button to play it. When a song is playing, this button changes to the **Pause** button.

- Click the **Stop** button to stop playback.

- Click the **Next** or **Previous** button to move to the next or previous track in an album or playlist.

- Use the **Mute** and **Volume** controls to pump the sound up or down without having to modify the Windows volume settings.

Tired of the order in which your tracks play? You can use the List Options button on the Play pane and choose Shuffle List to have Windows Media Player move around the tracks on your album randomly. Click this button again to turn the shuffle feature off.

To jump to another track, rather than using the Next and Previous buttons you can double-click a track in the track list in the Media Player window. This can be much quicker if you want to jump several tracks ahead or behind of the currently playing track.

Make Settings for Ripping Music

1. If you place a CD/DVD in your disc drive, Windows Media Player will ask if you want to *rip* the music from the disc to your computer. Doing so stores all the tracks on your computer. To control how ripping works, with Windows Media Player open, click the Organize button and choose Options.

2. Click on the Rip Music tab to display it.

3. In the resulting window (see **Figure 14-10**) you can make the following settings:

- Click the **Change** button to change the location where ripped music is stored; the default location is your Music folder.

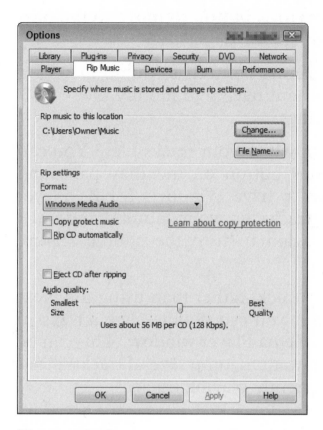

Figure 14-10

- Click the **File Name** button to choose the information to include in the filenames for music that is ripped to your computer (see **Figure 14-11**).

- Choose the audio format to use by clicking the **Format** drop-down list.

- Many audio files are copyright protected. If you have permission to copy and distribute the music, you may not want to choose the **Copy Protect Music** checkbox; however, if you are downloading music you paid for and therefore should not give away copies of, you should ethically choose to Copy Protect music so that Windows prompts you to download media rights or purchase another copy of the music when you copy it to another location.

Figure 14-11

- If you don't want to be prompted to rip music from CD/DVDs you insert in your drive, but instead want all music ripped automatically, click the **Rip CD Automatically** checkbox.

- If you want the CD/DVD to eject automatically after ripping is complete, select the **Eject CD after Ripping** checkbox.

4. When you finish making settings, click the OK button to save them and close the Options dialog box.

 Use the Audio Quality slider to adjust the quality of the ripped music. The smallest size file will save space on your computer by compressing the file, but this causes a loss of audio quality. The Best Quality will provide optimum sound, but these files can be rather large. The choice is yours based on your tastes and your computer's capacity!

Chapter 15

Playing Games in Windows 7

Get ready to . . .

All work and no play is just wrong no matter how you look at it. So, Microsoft has built plenty of games into Windows to keep you amused.

Many computer games are essentially virtual versions of games that you already know, such as Solitaire and Chess. But Windows has added some interesting treats to the mix — several that depend to a great extent on some neat on-

287

screen animation.

Altogether, you can access eleven games through Windows, and this chapter gives you a sampling of the best of them. Here's what you can expect:

➼ Traditional card games, such as Solitaire and Hearts

➼ Games of dexterity, such as Minesweeper, where the goal is to be the fastest, smartest clicker in the West

➼ An online version of chess called Chess Titans that helps you hone your chess strategy against another player or your computer

➼ A world of online gaming

No matter what your comfort level with computers, these games are pretty darn easy to play and they're fun, so why not give them a try?

Play Solitaire

1. Choose Start⇨Games. If this is the first time you're playing games, Windows displays a Set Up Game dialog box. If it does, make choices (like whether to automatically check for game updates) and click OK. In the resulting Games window (see **Figure 15-1**), double-click Solitaire.

Double-click Solitaire

Figure 15-1

2. In the resulting Solitaire window, if you need help with game rules, read the How to Play message that appears. When you're ready to play, click a card (see **Figure 15-2**) and then click a card in another deck that you want to move it on top of. The first card you click moves.

Click a card

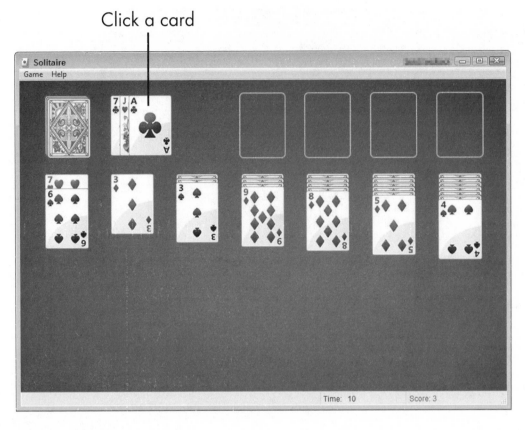

Figure 15-2

3. When playing the game, you have the following options:

- If no moves are available, click the stack of cards in the upper-left corner to deal another round of cards.

- If you move the last card from one of the six laid-out stacks, leaving only face-down cards, click the face-down cards to flip one up. You can also move a King onto any empty stack.

- When you reach the end of the stack of cards in the upper-left corner, click them again to redeal the cards that you didn't use the first time.

- You can play a card in one of two places: either

building a stack from King to Ace on the bottom row, alternating suits; or starting from Ace in any of the top four slots, placing cards from Ace to King in a single suit.

- When you complete a set of cards (Ace to King), click the top card and then click one of the four blank deck spots at the top-right of the window. If you complete all four sets, you win.

4. To deal a new game, choose Game⇨New Game (or press F2). Unlike life, it's easy to start over with Solitaire! When prompted, choose Quit and Start a New Game.

5. To close Solitaire, click the Close button.

 To change settings for the game, choose Game⇨Options. The two main settings you'll probably deal with here are Draw (which gives you an option of turning over one card or a stack of three cards on each deal) and Scoring (which offers the option of not using scoring at all, or using Standard or Vegas-style scoring). Standard scoring starts you off with nothing in the bank and pays you $5 or $10 for every card you place depending on whether you place it on the lower stacks or the area where you place Aces. Vegas-style is a bit more complex, starting you off with a $52 debit ($1 per card in the deck), and crediting you $5 per card you place in the Aces area, with the object being to come out in the black (money-wise, that is) at the end. You can also choose to time your game.

 Don't like a move you just made? Undo it by choosing Game⇨Undo. This only works for the last move, however. You can also get unstuck if you're on a losing streak by choosing Game⇨Hint.

Play FreeCell

1. FreeCell is a variation on solitaire. Choose Start⇨Games; in the Games Windows, double-click FreeCell.

2. In the resulting FreeCell window, shown in **Figure 15-3,** a game is ready to play. If you want a fresh game, you can always choose Game⇨New Game; a new game is dealt and ready to play.

 The goal is to move all the cards, grouped by the four suits, to the home cells (the four cells in the upper-right corner) stacked in order from Ace at the bottom to King at the top. The trick here is that you get four free cells (the four cells in the upper-left corner) where you can manually move a card out of the way to free up a move. You can also use those four slots to allow you to move up to four cards in a stack at once. (For example, you can move a Jack, 10, 9, and 8 all together onto a Queen.) You can move only as many cards as there are free cells available plus one. Free spaces in the rows of card stacks also act as free cells. You win when you have four stacks of cards for each of the four suits placed on the home cells.

3. Click a card; to move it, click a free cell or another card at the bottom of a column. **Figure 15-4** shows a game where two free cells are already occupied.

 If you move a card to a free cell, you can move it back to the bottom of a column, but only on a card one higher in an alternate color. You could move a 3 of hearts to a 4 of spades, for example. You stack the cards in the columns in alternating colors, but the cards in the home cells end up in order and all in one suit.

292

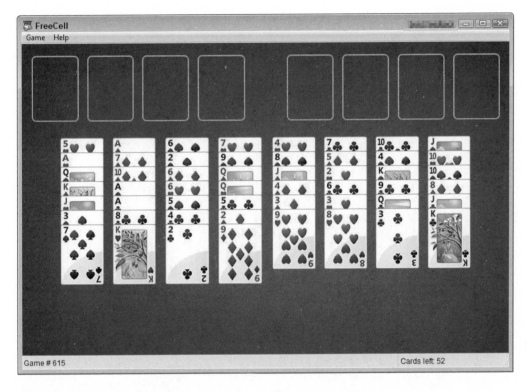

Figure 15-3

Two occupied free cells

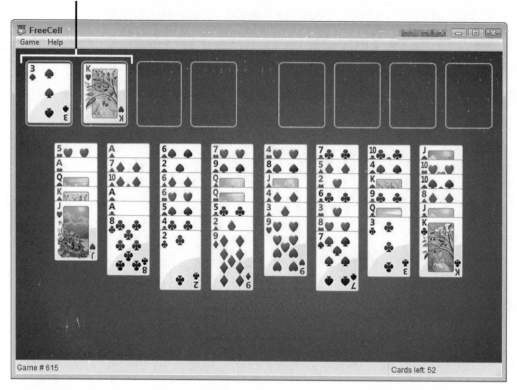

Figure 15-4

 If you get hooked on this game, try going to www. freecell.org, a Web site devoted to FreeCell. Here you can engage in live games with other players, read more about the rules and strategies, and even buy FreeCell merchandise. Don't say I didn't warn you about the possibility of addiction.

Play Spider Solitaire

1. Choose Start⇨Games; in the Games windows, double-click Spider Solitaire. If you've never played the game before, the Select Difficulty window appears. Click your comfort level: Beginner, Intermediate, or Advanced.

2. In the resulting game window, click a card and then click another card or drag it to the bottom of another stack or to an empty stack so that you match the same suit in each stack, moving in descending order from King to Ace (see **Figure 15-5**).

Stack same-suited cards in descending order

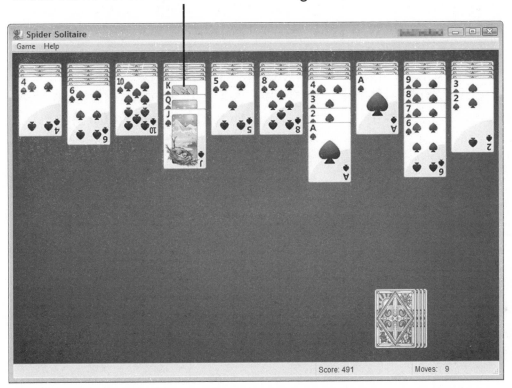

Figure 15-5

3. Move a card to automatically turn over a new card in the stack.

4. After you complete a set of cards in a suit, those cards are moved off the game area. The goal is to remove all the cards in the fewest moves. You can

- **Deal a new set of cards.** Choose Game⇨New Game

295

or click the stack of cards in the bottom-right corner to deal a new set of cards. (**Note:** You are prompted to quit, restart, or keep playing; choose Keep Playing.)

- **Save your game.** Choose Game⇨Exit and then click Save in the Exit Game dialog box to save your game.

- **Change the options.** Choose Game⇨Options (see **Figure 15-6**) and select a new difficulty level. Other options mainly affect how or whether you save games and open them to continue, and whether the variously annoying or angelic sounds play when you click a card, deal a card, or fold a stack (assuming your computer system is set up with a sound card and speakers).

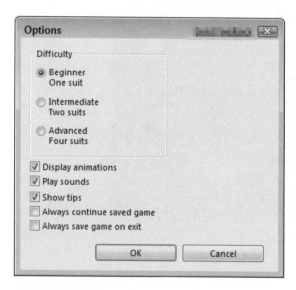

Figure 15-6

5. When you finish playing, click the Close button and either click Save or Don't Save in the Exit Game dialog box.

 Stuck for a move? Try choosing Game⇨Hint. Various combinations of cards are highlighted in sequence to suggest a likely next step in the game. If you're not stuck but just bored with the appearance of the game, choose Game⇨Change Appearance and select other desk and background styles.

Play Minesweeper

1. Choose Start⇨Games; in the Games window, double-click Minesweeper. If you've never played the game, a Select Difficulty dialog box appears. Click on your selection.

2. The Minesweeper game board opens (see **Figure 15-7**). Click a square on the board, and a timer starts counting the seconds of your game.

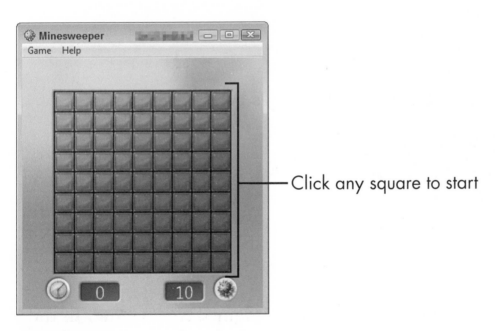
Click any square to start

Figure 15-7

- If you click a square and numbers appear in various squares, the number tells you how many mines are within the up to eight squares surrounding that square;

if it remains blank, there are no mines within the eight squares surrounding it.

- If you click a square and a bomb appears, all the hidden bombs are exposed (see **Figure 15-8**), and the game is over.

- Right-click a square once to place a flag on it marking it as a mine. Right-click a square twice to place a question mark on it if you think it might contain a bomb to warn yourself to stay away for now.

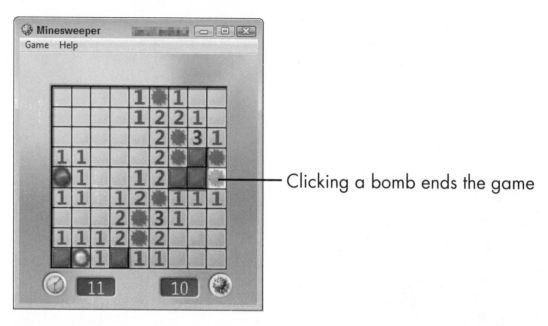
Clicking a bomb ends the game

Figure 15-8

3. To begin a new game, choose Game⇨New Game. In the New Game dialog box, click Quit and Start a New Game. If you want to play a game with the same settings as the previous one, click Restart This Game.

4. You can set several game options through the Game menu:

- To change the expertise required, choose Game⇨Options and then choose Beginner, Intermediate, or Advanced.

- To change the color of the playing board, choose Game⇨Change Appearance.

- If you want to see how many games you've won, your longest winning or losing streak, and more, choose Game⇨Statistics.

5. To end the game, click the Close button, and when prompted to save the game, click Save or Don't Save.

 If you want a bigger game board (more squares, more bombs, more fun), choose Game⇨Options and then click Custom and specify the number of squares across and down and the number of bombs hidden within them.

Play Hearts

1. Choose Start⇨Games and double-click Hearts.

2. In the resulting Hearts window, shown in **Figure 15-9,** your hand is displayed while others are hidden. Begin play by clicking three cards to pass to your opponent, and then click the Pass Left button.

3. Each player moving clockwise around the window plays a card of the same suit by clicking it. The one who plays the highest card of the suit in play wins the trick. (A *trick* is the cards you collect when you play the highest card of the suit.)

4. Choose Game⇨Options to change the settings shown in **Figure 15-10.** You can rename the other three players, play sounds, show tips, or specify how to save a game.

5. To end the game, choose Game⇨Exit or click the Close button. When prompted, either Save or Don't Save the game.

Click to pass three selected cards

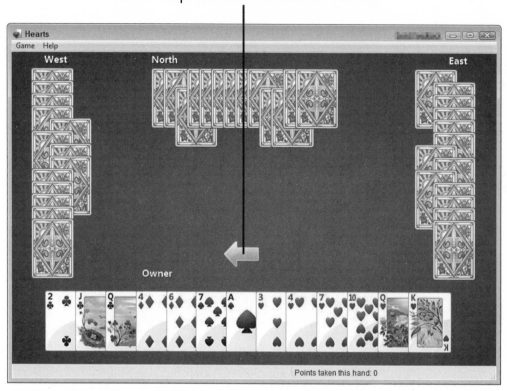

Figure 15-9

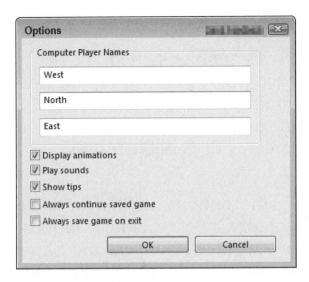

Computer Player Names

West

North

East

☑ Display animations
☑ Play sounds
☑ Show tips
☐ Always continue saved game
☐ Always save game on exit

OK   Cancel

Figure 15-10

 Check out the menus in the Games window for organizing and customizing the various games that Windows 7 makes available and to set Parental Controls.

Play Chess Titans

1. Chess is an ancient game of strategy. If you're a chess buff, you'll enjoy playing a computer opponent in the Windows version, Chess Titans. To begin playing chess, choose Start⇨Games; in the Games window, double-click Chess Titans. The first time you play the game, the Select Difficulty window appears. Click a skill level to start a game.

2. In the resulting Chess Titans window, a new game is ready to play. By default, a new game will be played against the computer, but you can choose to play another person when you start a new game. If you want to start a new game at any time, you can always choose Game⇨New Game Against Computer or New Game

Against Human; a new game is ready to play.

3. Click a piece; all possible moves are highlighted. To move the piece, click the space where you want to move it. Once you make a play, your opponent (either the computer or another human) moves a piece. **Figure 15-11** shows a game in progress with possible moves highlighted.

 You can change the game options so that possible moves are not highlighted. Choose Game⇨Options. In the resulting Options window, deselect the Show Valid Moves checkbox and then click OK. The Options dialog box also lets you control a variety of other settings, including whether you're playing as black or white, whether to show tips or play sounds, and the quality of graphics. If you're new to the game, which is rather complex, try visiting www.chess.com for beginner instructions and strategies.

Possible moves are highlighted

Figure 15-11

 Don't like the look of your chess board? You can modify it to look like a different material, such as wood. Choose Game⇨Change Appearance. In the Change Appearance window, click a style of chess piece and a style of chess board. Click OK to save your settings.

Play Online Games

There are thousands of gaming sites online that let you interact with other players from around the world. Search in your browser using keywords such as "card games" or "Chess" to find them. Some are simple games like Poker or Chess. Others are part of sophisticated virtual worlds where you take on a personality, called an avatar, and can even acquire virtual money and goods.

Here are some tips for getting involved in online gaming and some advice for staying safe:

➤ Safety first! You're playing games with strangers, so avoid giving out personal information or choosing a revealing user name. If somebody gets inappropriately emotional or abusive while playing the game, leave the game immediately and report the player to the site owner.

➤ In some cases, you can play a computer; in others, you play against other people the game site matches you up with. You can usually request a level of play, so if you're a beginner, you can feel comfortable that you'll be matched with other beginners.

➤ To play some games, you may need additional software, such as Adobe Shockwave Player or software to enable your computer to play animations. If you see such a message on a game site, be sure you're downloading software from a reputable source that has a good privacy policy for users and credentials like a Better Business Bureau seal so you don't download a virus or spyware.

➤ Many games are free, though some require that you enter information about yourself to become a member. Read the fine print carefully when signing up.

➤ Many game sites offer tutorials or practice games to help you learn and improve. **Figure 15-12** shows the Tutorial page for Legends of Norrath, a multiplayer, online, role-playing game.

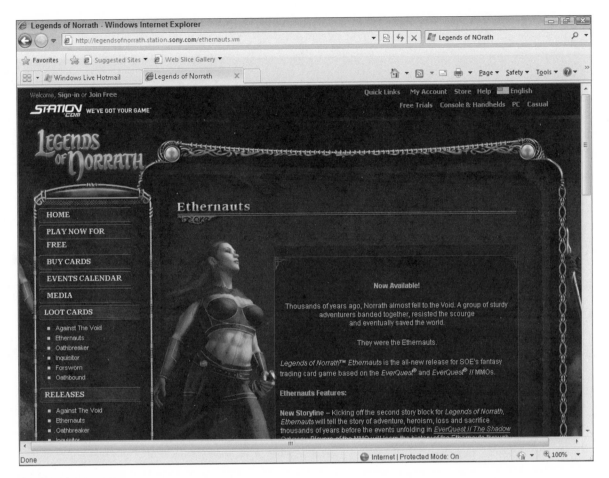

Figure 15-12

➤ Some games allow several players to participate at once, so you might have to be on your toes! In addition to manipulating pieces or characters, you might also be able to communicate with other players using instant messaging or even voice messages. Chapter 20 explains how instant messaging works.

➤ Online gaming can be addictive, so be as moderate in your playing online as you are offline. Remember that these games are just for fun.

Part III
Exploring the Internet

The 5th Wave   By Rich Tennant

"Since we got it, he hasn't moved from that spot for eleven straight days. Oddly enough they call this 'getting up and running' on the Internet."

Chapter 16

Understanding Internet Basics

For many people, going online might be the major reason to buy a computer. You can use the Internet to check stock quotes, play interactive games with others, and file your taxes, for example. For seniors especially, the Internet can provide wonderful ways to keep in touch with family and friends located around the country or on the other side of the world via e-mail or instant messaging. You can share photos of your grandchildren or connect with others who share your hobbies or interests.

But before you begin all those wonderful activities, it helps to understand some basics about the Internet and how it works.

This chapter helps you to understand what the Internet and World Wide Web are, as well as some basics about connecting to the Internet and navigating around.

Understand What the Internet Is

The Internet, links, the Web . . . people and the media bounce around many online-related terms these days, and folks sometimes use them incorrectly. Your first step in getting familiar with the Internet is to understand what some of these terms mean.

Here's a list of common Internet-related terms:

➼ The *Internet* is a large network of computers that contain information and technology tools that can be accessed by anybody with an Internet connection. (See the next section for information about Internet connections.)

➼ Residing on that network of computers is a huge set of documents, which form the *World Wide Web,* usually referred to as just the *Web.*

➼ The Web includes *Web sites,* which are made up of collections of *Web pages* just as a book is made up of individual pages. Web sites can be informational, host communication tools such as *chats* or *discussion boards* that allow people to "talk" via text messages.

➼ You can buy, sell, or bid for a wide variety of items in an entire online marketplace referred to as the world of **e**-*commerce.*

➡ To get around online, you use a software program called a *browser.* There are many browsers available, and they're free. Internet Explorer is Microsoft's browser; others include Mozilla Firefox, Google Chrome, and Opera. Browsers offer tools to help you navigate from Web site to Web site and from one Web page to another.

➡ When you open a Web site, you might see colored text or graphics that represent *hyperlinks,* also referred to as *links.* You can click links to move from place to place within a Web page, on a Web site, or between Web sites. **Figure 16-1** shows some hyperlinks indicated by highlighted text or graphics.

A link can be a graphic (such as a company logo) or text. A text link is identifiable by colored text, and it's usually underlined. After you click a link, it usually changes color to show that you've followed the link.

Click a graphical hyperlink

Click a text hyperlink

Figure 16-1

Explore Different Types of Internet Connections

Before you can connect to the Internet for the first time, you have to have certain hardware in place and choose your *Internet service provider* (also referred to as an *ISP* or simply a *provider*). An ISP is a company that owns dedicated computers (called *servers*) that you use to access the Internet. ISPs charge a monthly fee for this service.

In the past, you could sign up with an ISP such as Microsoft's MSN to get dial-up access (that is, access via your regular phone line) to the Internet. Today many people pay to access the Internet through their telephone or cable television provider, whose connections are much faster than a dial-up connection. Companies such as AOL now focus on content they provide such as news, human interest stories, horoscopes, and games.

You can choose a type of connection to go online. Depending on the type of connection you want, you will go to a different company for the service. For example, a DSL connection might come through your phone company, whereas a cable connection is available through your cable-TV company. Not every type of connection is necessarily available in every area, so check with phone, cable, and small Internet providers in your town to find out your options and costs (some offer discounts to AARP members, for example).

Here are the most common types of connections:

- **Dial-up connections:** With a dial-up connection, you use a phone line to connect to the Internet, entering a phone number that's provided by your ISP. This is the slowest connection method, but it's relatively inexpensive. Your dial-up Internet provider will give you *local access numbers,* which you use to go online. Using these local access numbers, you won't incur long distance charges for your connection. However, with this type of connection, you can't use a phone line for phone calls while you're connected to the Internet, so it's no longer a very popular way to connect.

➤ **Digital Subscriber Line:** DSL also uses a phone line, but your phone is available to you to make calls even when you're connected to the Internet. DSL is a form of broadband communication, which may use phone lines and fiber-optic cables for transmission. You have to subscribe to a broadband service (check with your phone company) and pay a monthly fee for access.

➤ **Cable:** You may also go through your local cable company to get your Internet service via the cable that brings your TV programming rather than your phone line. This is another type of broadband service and is also faster than a dial-up connection. Check with your cable company for monthly fees.

➤ **Satellite:** Especially in rural areas, satellite Internet providers may be your only option. This requires that you install a satellite dish. BlueDish and Comcast are two providers of satellite connections to check into.

➤ **Wireless hotspots:** If you take a wireless-enabled laptop computer with you on a trip, you can piggyback on a connection somebody else has made. You will find wireless hotspots in many public places, such as airports, cafes, and hotels. If you're in range of such a hotspot, your computer usually finds the connection automatically, making Internet service available to you for free or for a fee.

Internet connections have different speeds that depend partially on your computer's capabilities and partially on the connection you get from your provider. Before you choose a provider, it's important to understand how faster connection speeds can benefit you:

➤ Faster speeds allow you to send data faster. In addition, Web pages and images display faster.

➤ Dial-up connection speeds run at the low end about 56 kilobits per second, or Kbps. Most broadband connections today are around 500 to 600 Kbps. If you have a slower connection, a file might take minutes to upload (for example a file you're attaching to an e-mail). This same operation might take only seconds at a higher speed.

Depending on your type of connection, you'll need different hardware:

➤ A broadband connection uses an Ethernet cable and a modem, which your provider should make available, as well as a connection to your phone or cable line.

➤ Many desktop and laptop computers come with a built-in modem for dial-up connections (though these are being left out more and more as people move to wireless connections) and are enabled for wireless. If you choose a broadband connection, your phone or cable company will provide you with an external modem and wireless router (usually for a price).

➤ If you have a laptop that doesn't have a built-in wireless modem, you can add this hardware by buying a wireless CardBus adapter PC card at any office supply or computer store. This card enables a laptop to pick up wireless signals.

Many providers offer free or low-cost setup when you open a new account. If you're not technical by nature, consider taking advantage of this when you sign up.

USE CD
FROM ISP
SEE PAGE 318

Set Up an Internet Connection

1. The first step is to set up a connection in Windows so you can access the Internet. Choose Start⇨Control Panel⇨Network and Internet.

2. In the resulting window, click Network and Sharing Center.

3. In the resulting Network and Sharing Center window (see **Figure 16-2**), click the Set Up a New Connection or Network link.

Click this link

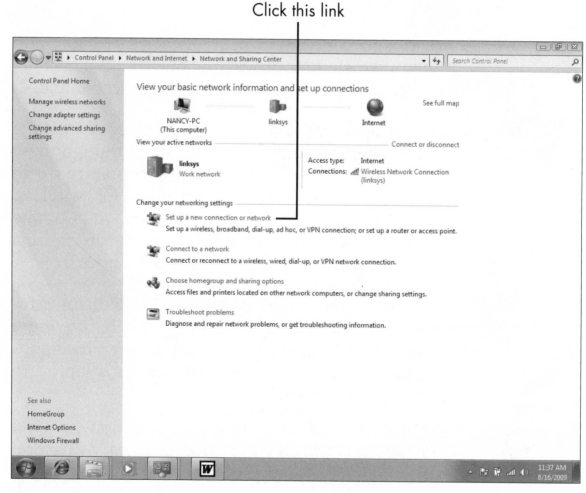

Figure 16-2

4. In the Choose a Connection Option window, click Next to accept the default option of creating a new Internet connection. If you are already connected to the Internet, a window appears; click Set Up a New Connection Anyway.

5. In the resulting dialog box, click your connection. (These steps follow the selection of Broadband.)

6. In the resulting dialog box, shown in **Figure 16-3,** enter your user name, password, and connection name (if you want to assign one) and then click Connect. Windows automatically detects the connection, and the Network and Sharing Center appears with your connection listed.

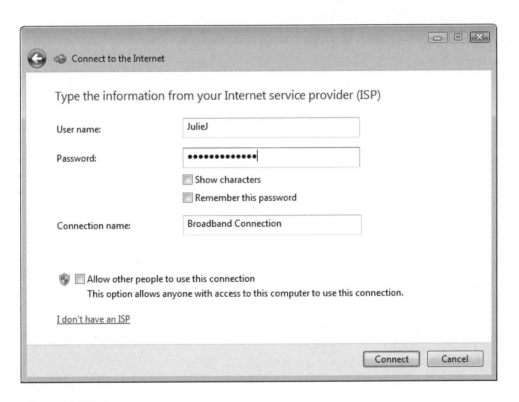

Figure 16-3

In many cases, if you have a disc from your ISP, you don't need to follow the preceding steps. Just pop that DVD into your DVD-ROM drive, and in no time, a window appears that gives you the steps to follow to get set up.

Navigate the Web

1. You need to learn how to get around the Web using a browser such as the popular Internet Explorer from Microsoft. Open IE by clicking the Internet Explorer icon in the Windows taskbar.

2. Enter a Web site address in the Address bar, as shown in **Figure 16-4** (www.ilookbothways.com is my company's Web site), and then press Enter.

Enter a Web address

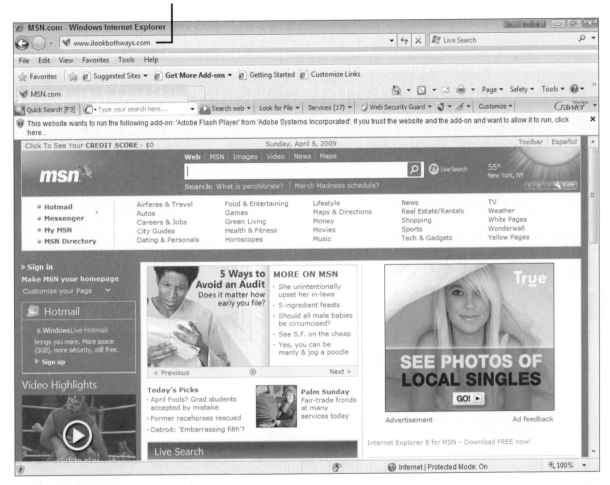

Figure 16-4

3. On the resulting Web site, click a link (short for *hyperlink;*
a *link* takes you to another online page or document),
display another page on the site using navigation tools on
the page such as the Education tab on the page in **Figure
16-4,** or enter another address in the Address bar to
proceed to another page.

 A link can be an icon or text. A text link is identifiable
by colored text, usually blue. After you click a link, it
usually changes to another color (such as purple) to

show that it's been followed.

4. Click the Back button to move back to the first page that you visited. Click the Forward button to go forward to the second page that you visited.

5. Click the down-pointing arrow at the far right of the Address bar to display a list of sites that you visited recently, as shown in **Figure 16-5.** Click a site in this list to go there.

Click the arrow

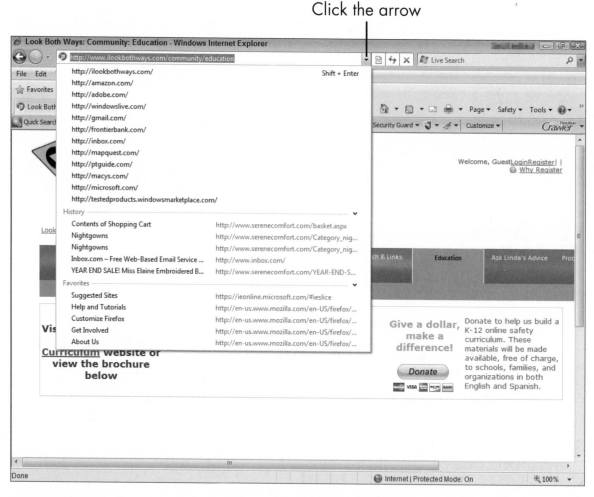

Figure 16-5

The Refresh and Stop buttons on the right end of the Address bar are useful for navigating sites. Clicking the Refresh button redisplays the current page. This is especially useful if a page updates information frequently, such as on a stock market site. You can also use the Refresh button if a page doesn't load correctly; it might load correctly when refreshed. Clicking the Stop button stops a page that's loading. So, if you made a mistake entering the address, or if the page is taking longer than you'd like to load, click the Stop button to halt the process.

 You can use the Pop-Up Blocker to stop annoying pop-up ads as you browse. Click the Tools menu button and choose Pop-up Blocker, Turn On Pop-up Blocker to activate this feature. You can also use the Pop-up Blocker Settings command on this same menu to specify sites you want to allow pop-ups to appear in.

Use Tabs in Browsers

1. Tabs allow you to have several Web pages open at once and easily switch among them. With Internet Explorer open, click New Tab (the smallest tab on the far right of the tabs).

2. In the new tab that appears, which displays some information about tabs (see **Figure 16-6**), enter a URL in the Address bar and press Enter. The URL opens in that tab. You can then click other tabs to switch among sites.

3. Click the Quick Tabs button (it consists of four little squares on the far left of the tabs) to display a thumbnail of all open tabs (see **Figure 16-7**), or click the Tab List

button (the arrow to the right of the Quick Tabs button) to display a text list of tabs.

The new tab

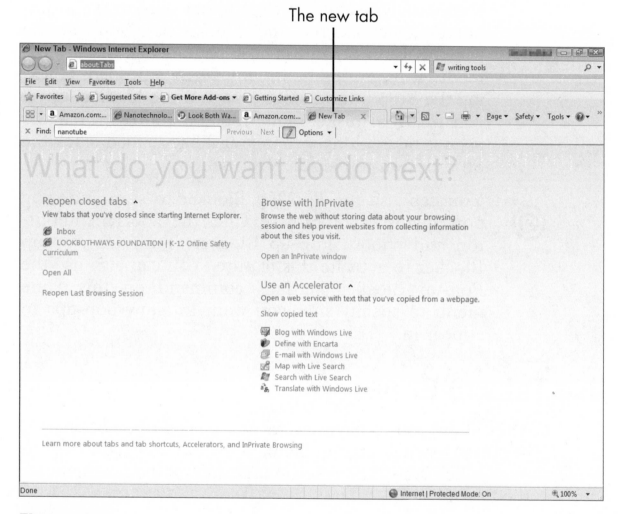

Figure 16-6

4. Close an active tab by clicking the Close button on the right side of the tab.

A *tab* is a sort of window you can use to view any number of sites. You don't have to create a new tab to go to another site. Having the ability to keep a few tabs open at a time means you can more quickly switch between two or more sites without navigating back and forth either with the Previous or Next buttons or by entering URLs. You can also create more than one Home Page tab that can appear every time you open IE. See the task "Set Up a Home Page" for more about this.

The Quick Tabs button

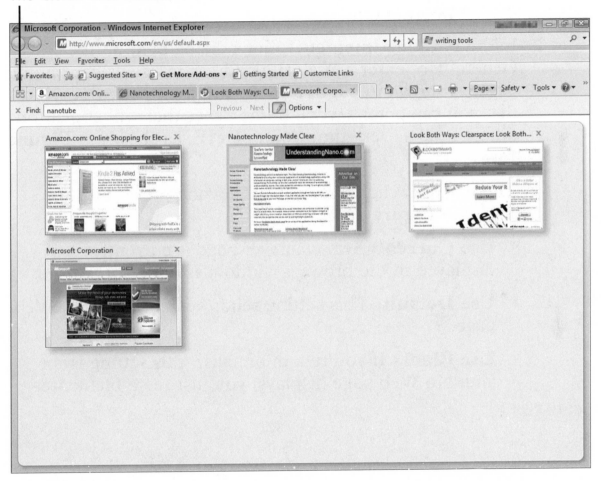

Figure 16-7

 You can also press Ctrl+T to open a new tab in Internet Explorer. Also, if you want to keep one tab open and close all others, right-click the tab you want to keep open and choose Close Other Tabs.

Set Up a Home Page

1. Your home page(s) appear automatically every time you log on to the Internet, so choose one or a few sites that you go to often for this setting. Open IE and choose Tools⇨Internet Options.

2. In the resulting Internet Options dialog box, on the General tab, enter a Web site address to use as your home page, as shown in **Figure 16-8,** and then click OK. Note that you can enter several home pages that will appear on different tabs every time you open IE, as shown in **Figure 16-8.**

Alternatively, click one of the following preset buttons shown in **Figure 16-8:**

- **Use Current:** Sets whatever page is currently displayed in the browser window as your home page.

- **Use Default:** This setting sends you to the MSN Web page.

- **Use Blank:** If you're a minimalist, this setting is for you. No Web page displays; you just see a blank area.

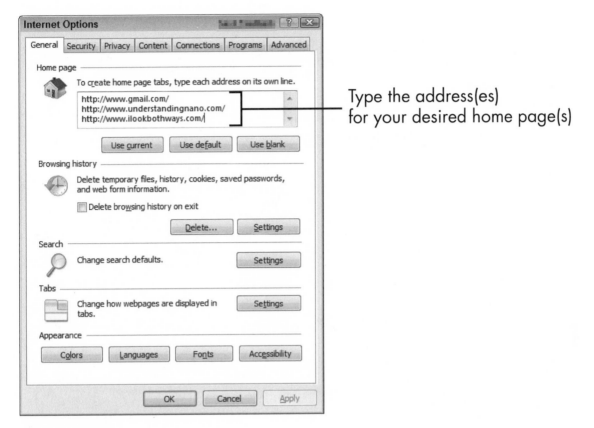

Type the address(es)
for your desired home page(s)

Figure 16-8

3. Click the Home Page icon (see **Figure 16-9**) on the IE toolbar (it looks like a little house) to go to your home page.

 If you want to have more than one home page, you can create multiple home page tabs that will display when you click the Home button. Click the arrow on the Home button and choose Add or Change Home Page. In the Add or Change Home Page dialog box that appears, click the Add This Webpage to Your Home Page Tabs radio button, and then click Yes. Display other sites and repeat this procedure for all the home page tabs you want.

The Home Page icon

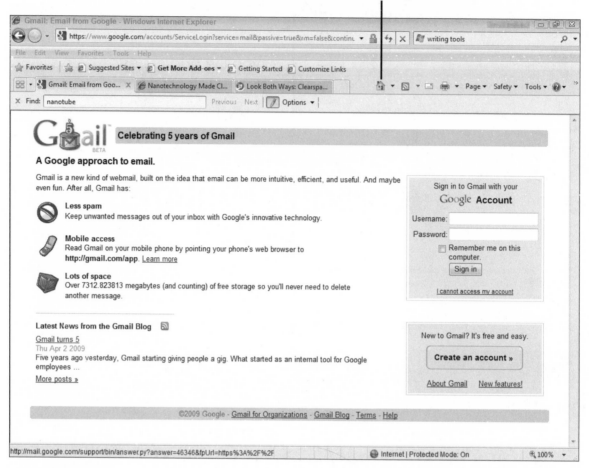

Figure 16-9

 To remove a home page you have set up, click the arrow on the Home Page button and choose Remove and then choose a particular home page, or choose Remove All from the submenu that appears.

Chapter 17

Browsing the Web with Internet Explorer

A *browser* is a program that you can use to move from one Web page to another, but you can also use it to perform searches for information and images. Most browsers, such as Internet Explorer (IE) and Mozilla Firefox

327

are available for free. Macintosh computers come with a browser called Safari built in.

Chapter 16 introduces browser basics, such as how to go directly to a site when you know the Web address, how to use the Back and Forward buttons to move among sites you've visited, and how to set up the home page that opens automatically when you launch your browser.

In this chapter you discover more ways of using Internet Explorer. By using IE you can

➨ **Navigate all around the Web.** Use the IE navigation features to go back to places you've been (via the Favorites and History features), and use Google to search for new places to visit.

➨ **Customize Internet Explorer.** You can modify what tools are available to you in Internet Explorer toolbars to make your work online easier.

➨ **Work with RSS Feeds**. On the Internet you can use RSS Feeds to get content from sites sent to you to keep you up to date on news or opinions from various sources.

➨ **Print content from Web pages.** When you find what you want online, such as a graphic image or article, just use the Print feature of IE to generate a hard copy.

➨ **Play Podcasts**. You can listen to podcasts, which are audio programs you find on many Web sites covering a variety of topics.

Search the Web

1. You can use words and phrases to search for information on the Web using a search engine. In this example, you'll use Google, a popular search engine. Enter `www.google.com` in your browser's Address bar.

2. Enter a search term in the text box and then click the Google Search button.

3. In the search results that appear (see **Figure 17-1**), you can click a link to go to that Web page. If you don't see the link that you need, click and drag the scrollbar to view more results.

 You can use the Internet Explorer search feature to perform searches (it's in the upper-right corner of IE, with a little magnifying glass button on the right edge). Change the search engine by clicking the arrow to the right of the Search field and choosing another provider listed there, or click the Find More Providers link to see a more comprehensive list.

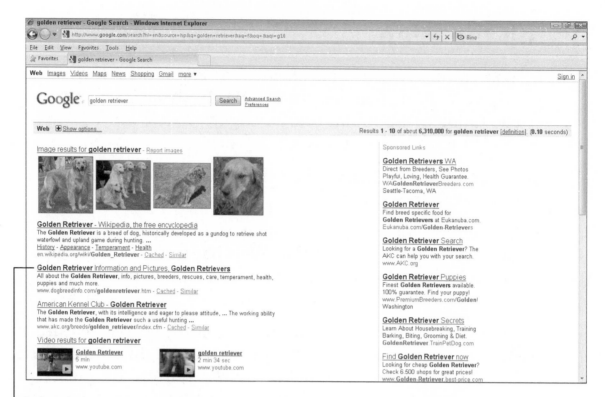

Click a link in the results list

Figure 17-1

4. Click the Advanced Search link on the Google home page to change Search parameters.

5. In the resulting Advanced Search page, shown in **Figure 17-2,** modify the following parameters:

- **Find Web Pages That Have:** These options let you narrow the way words or phrases are searched; for example, you can find matches for the exact wording you enter only.

- **But Don't Show Pages That Have:** Enter words that you want to exclude from your results. For example, you could search *flu* and specify you don't want results that involve swine flu.

330

- **Need More Tools:** Here you can control how many results are shown on a page, what language to search for, and which specific file types or domains to search.

- **Date, Usage Rights, Numeric Range, and More:** Click here for even more advanced search parameters.

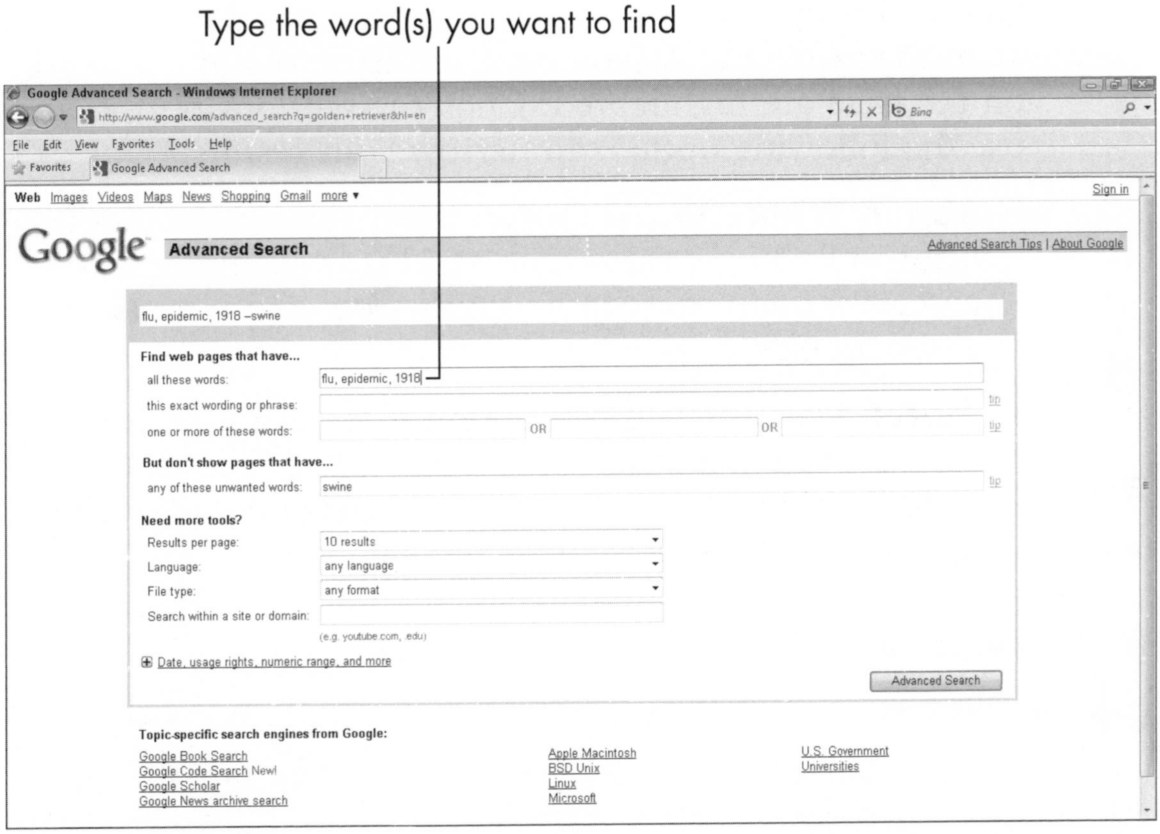

Type the word(s) you want to find

Figure 17-2

Knowing how search engines work can save you time. For example, if you search by entering *golden retriever,* you typically get sites that contain both words or either word. If you put a plus sign between these two keywords *(golden+retriever),* you get only sites that contain both words.

Find Content on a Web Page

1. With IE open and the Web page that you want to search displayed, click the arrow on the Search box, and choose Find on This Page.

2. In the resulting Find toolbar that appears on the active tab, as shown in **Figure 17-3,** enter the word that you want to search for. As you type, all instances of the word on the page are highlighted. Click the Options button and use the following options to narrow your results:

- **Match Whole Word Only:** Select this option if you want to find only the whole word (for example, if you enter *elect* and want to find only *elect* and not *electron* or *electronics*).

- **Match Case:** Select this option if you want to match the case (for example, if you enter *Catholic* and want to find only the always-capitalized religion and not the adjective *catholic*).

Enter the word to find

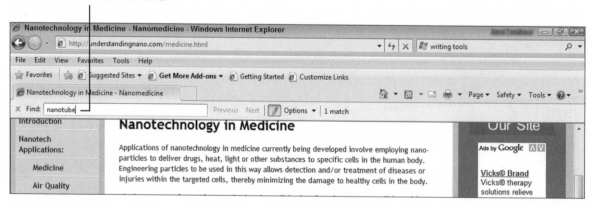

Figure 17-3

3. Click the Next button and you move from one highlighted instance of the word to the next (see **Figure 17-4**). If you want to move to a previous instance, click the Previous button.

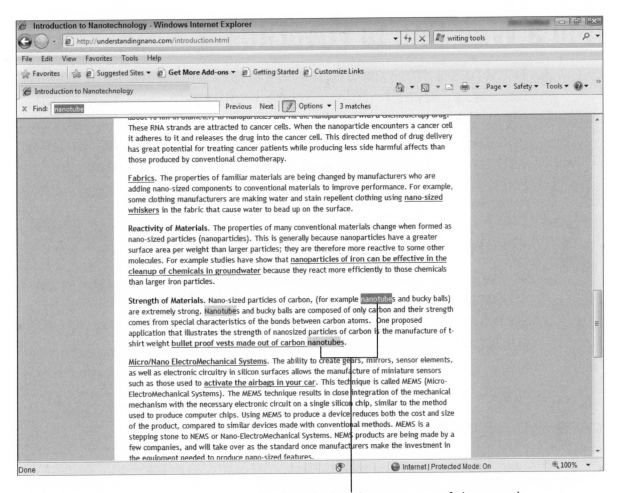

The highlighted instances of the word

Figure 17-4

4. When you're done searching, click the Close button on the left side of the Find toolbar.

 Many Web sites have a Search This Site feature that allows you to search not only the displayed Web page but all Web pages on a Web site, or to search by department or category of item in an online store. Look for a Search text box and make sure that it searches the site — and not the entire Internet.

Add a Web Site to Favorites

1. If there's a site you intend to revisit, you may want to save it to IE's Favorite folder so you can easily go there again. Open IE, enter the URL of a Web site that you want to add to your Favorites list, and then click Go (the button with two blue arrows on it to the right of the Address bar).

2. Click the Favorites button to display the Favorites pane, and then click the Add to Favorites button.

3. In the resulting Add a Favorite dialog box, shown in **Figure 17-5,** modify the name of the Favorite listing to something easily recognizable. If you wish, choose another folder or create a folder to store the Favorite in.

Change the favorite name here

Figure 17-5

4. Click Add to add the site.

5. Click the Favorites button and then click the name of the site from the list that's displayed (see **Figure 17-6**) to go to that site.

Click the Favorites button

Figure 17-6

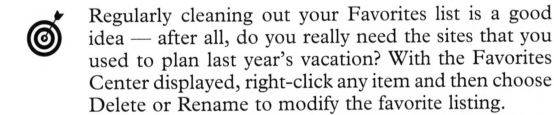

Regularly cleaning out your Favorites list is a good idea — after all, do you really need the sites that you used to plan last year's vacation? With the Favorites Center displayed, right-click any item and then choose Delete or Rename to modify the favorite listing.

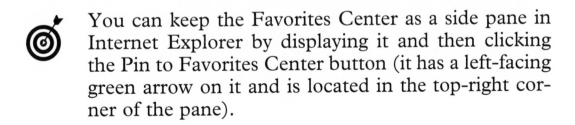

You can keep the Favorites Center as a side pane in Internet Explorer by displaying it and then clicking the Pin to Favorites Center button (it has a left-facing green arrow on it and is located in the top-right corner of the pane).

Organize Favorites

1. You can organize favorites into folders to make them easier to find. With Internet Explorer open, click the Favorites button to open the Favorites pane. Click the arrow on the right of the Add to Favorites button and then choose Organize Favorites.

2. In the resulting Organize Favorites dialog box (see **Figure** 17-7), click the New Folder, Move, Rename, or Delete button to organize your favorites.

Select a favorite...

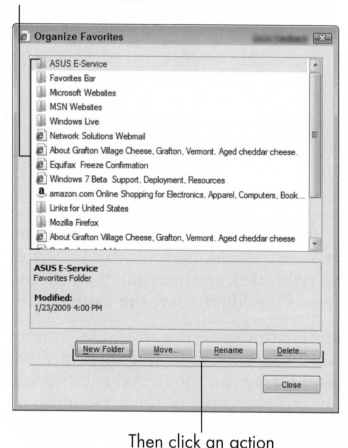

Then click an action

Figure 17-7

3. When you finish organizing your Favorites, click Close.

These steps provide a handy way to manage several sites or folders, but you can also organize favorite sites one by one by using the Favorites pane. (You display the Favorites pane by clicking the Favorites button.) Right-click any favorite site listed in the pane and choose a command: Create New Folder, Rename, or Delete, for example.

If you create new folders in the above steps, then you will have to manually transfer files into those folders. To do this just display the Favorites Center and click and drag files listed there on top of folders.

View Your Browsing History

1. If you went to a site recently and want to return there again but can't remember the name, you might check your browsing history to find it. Click the Favorites button and then click the History tab to display the History pane (see **Figure 17-8**).

The History tab

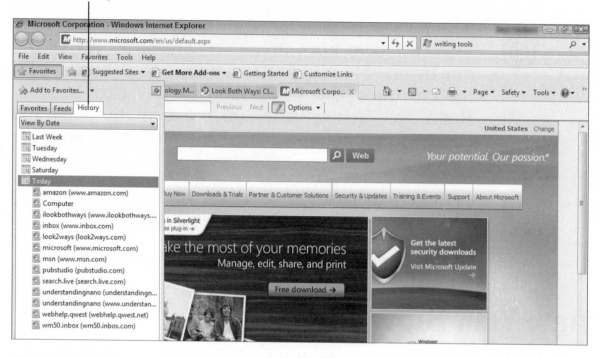

Figure 17-8

2. Click the down-arrow on the History button (see **Figure 17-9**) and select a sort method:

- **View By Date:** Sort favorites by date visited.

- **View By Site:** Sort alphabetically by site name.

- **View By Most Visited:** Sort with the sites visited most on top and those visited least at the bottom of the list.

- **View By Order Visited Today:** Sort by the order in which you visited sites today.

Click the arrow

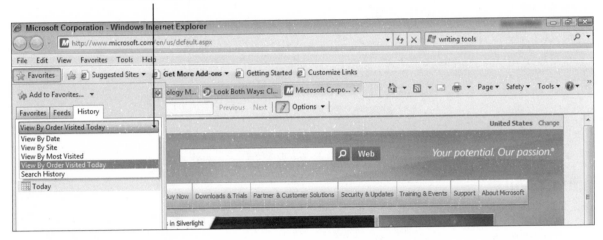

Figure 17-9

3. In the History pane, you can click a site to go to it. The History pane closes.

> You can also choose the arrow on the right of the Address bar to display sites you've visited.

> Choose Search History on the History menu to display a search box you can use to search for sites you've visited.

Customize the Internet Explorer Toolbar

1. You can customize the toolbars that offer common commands in IE so the commands you use most often are included. Open IE.

2. Click Tools⇨Toolbars⇨Customize. The Customize Toolbar dialog box (shown in **Figure 17-10**) appears.

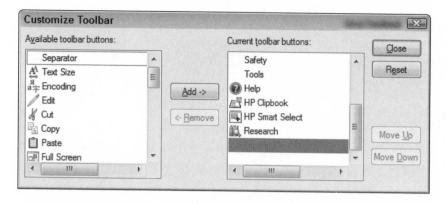

Figure 17-10

3. Click a tool on the left and then click the Add button to add it to the toolbar.

4. Click a tool on the right and then click the Remove button to remove it from the toolbar.

5. When you're finished, click Close to save your new toolbar settings. The new tools appear (see **Figure 17-11**); click the double-arrow button on the right of the toolbar to display any tools that IE can't fit on-screen.

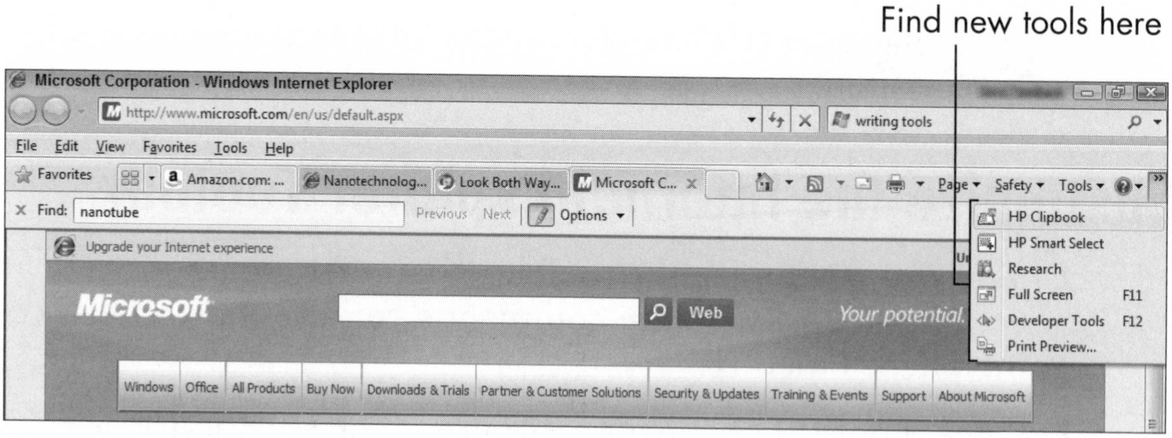

Find new tools here

Figure 17-11

You can use the Move Up and Move Down buttons in the Customize Toolbar dialog box to rearrange the order in which tools appear on the toolbar. To reset the toolbar to defaults, click the Reset button in that same dialog box.

If you want to add some space between tools on the toolbar so it's easier to see, click the Separator item in the Available Toolbar Buttons list and add it before or after a tool button.

View RSS Feeds

1. You can view information sent to you via RSS feeds using IE. Click the Favorites button; then click the Feeds tab to display a list of recently displayed RSS Feeds (see **Figure 17-12**).

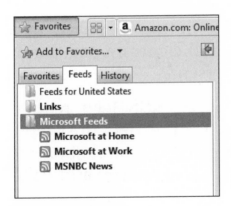

Figure 17-12

2. Double-click a folder to open it, and then click a feed to display it (see **Figure 17-13**).

Click a feed to view it

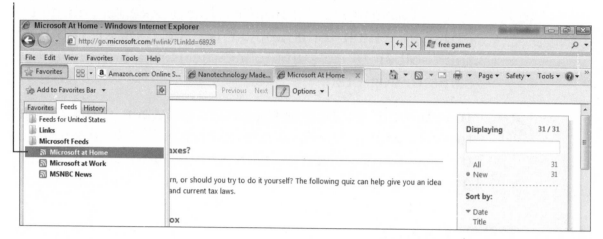

Figure 17-13

3. You can also click the View Feeds on This Page button on the toolbar to view any active feeds listed on the currently displayed page.

🎯 The View Feeds on This Page button is grayed out when there are no RSS feeds on the current page, and it turns Red when feeds are present.

🎯 Though Internet Explorer has an RSS feed reader built in, you can explore other feed readers. Just type **RSS feeds** into Internet Explorer's Search box to find more information and listings of readers and RSS feed sites.

Print a Web Page

1. If a Web page includes a link or button to print or display a print version of a page, click that and follow the instructions.

2. If the page doesn't include a link for printing, click the Print button on the IE toolbar.

3. In the resulting Print dialog box, decide how much of the document you want to print and then select one of the options in the Page Range area, as shown in **Figure 17-14.**

 Note that choosing Current Page or entering page numbers in the Pages text box of the Print dialog box doesn't mean much when printing a Web page — the whole document might print because Web pages aren't divided into pages as word-processing documents are.

4. Click the up-arrow in the Number of Copies text box to print multiple copies. If you want multiple copies collated, select the Collate check box.

Choose a page range option

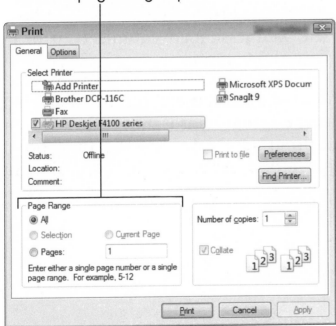

Figure 17-14

5. When you adjust all settings you need, click Print.

Play Podcasts

Many sites offer podcasts, which are audio recordings of interviews, opinions, or informative oral articles. To check this out, go to *The New York Times* site by entering this address in your browser's address bar: `www.nytimes.com/ref/multimedia/podcasts.html`.

Click on the little arrow on the right of any podcast, as shown in **Figure 17-15.** The podcast begins playing (in some cases podcasts open a new window with an animated display that plays during the podcast, though that doesn't happen at *The New York Times* site). Use the controls to do any of the following:

➼ Click the Stop button (it has two little vertical bars on it) to stop playback.

➼ Click and drag the wedge-shaped volume control to increase or decrease the volume.

➼ Click the diamond-shaped object on the bar that shows the podcast's progress to move forward or backward in the program. Note that the time point where you are in the podcast is displayed to the right of this bar.

Click the arrow to play the podcast

Figure 17-15

Chapter 18

Staying Safe While Online

Getting active online carries with it certain risks, like most things in life. But just as you know how to drive or walk around town safely when you know the rules of the road, you can stay relatively safe online.

In this chapter you discover some of the risks and safety nets that you can take advantage of to avoid risk, including:

➻ **Understand what risks exist.** Some risks are human in the form of online predators wanting to steal your money or abuse you emotionally; other risks come from technology such as computer viruses. For the former, you can use the common sense you use when interacting offline to stay much safer. For the latter, there are tools and browser settings to protect you.

➻ **Be aware of what information you share.** Abuses such as ID theft occur most often when you or somebody you know shares information about you that's nobody's business. Find out how to spot who is exposing information (including you) and what information to keep private and you'll become much safer online.

➻ **Avoid scams and undesirable content.** You can use the Content Advisor to limit the online locations that your computer can visit so you don't encounter sites you consider undesirable. You can also find out how to spot various e-mail scams and fraud so you don't become a victim.

➻ **Create safe passwords.** Passwords don't have to be hard to remember, just hard to guess. I provide some guidance in this chapter about creating passwords that are hard to crack.

Understand Technology Risks on the Internet

When you buy a car, it has certain safety features built in. After you drive it off the lot, you might find that the manufacturer slipped up and either recalls your car or requests that you go to the dealer's service department to have a faulty part replaced. In addition, you need to drive defensively to keep your car from being damaged in daily use.

Your computer is similar to your car in terms of the need for safety. It comes with an operating system (such as Microsoft Windows) built in, and that operating system has security features. Sometimes that operating system has flaws or new threats emerge after it's first released, and you need to get an update to keep it secure. And as you use your computer, you're exposing it to dangerous conditions and situations that you have to guard against.

Threats to your computer security can come from a file you copy from a disc you insert into your computer, but most of the time, the danger is from a program that you download from the Internet. These downloads can happen when you click a link, open an attachment in an e-mail, or download one piece of software without realizing that *malware* (malicious software) is attached to it.

You need to be aware of these three main types of dangerous programs:

➤ A *virus* is a little program that some nasty person thought up to spread around the Internet and infect computers. A virus can do a variety of things, but typically, it attacks your data by deleting files, scrambling data, or making changes to your system settings that cause your computer to grind to a halt.

→ *Spyware* consists of programs responsible for tracking what you do with your computer. Some spyware simply helps companies you do business with track your activities so that they can figure out how to sell you things; other spyware is used for more insidious purposes, such as stealing your passwords.

→ *Adware* is the computer equivalent of telemarketing phone calls at dinner time. After adware is downloaded onto your computer, you'll get annoying pop-up windows trying to sell you things all day long. Beyond the annoyance, adware can quickly clog up your computer. Its performance slows down, and it's hard to get anything done at all.

To protect your information and your computer from these various types of malware, you can do several things:

→ **You can buy and install an antivirus, anti-spyware, or anti-adware program.** It's critical that you install an antivirus program, such as those from McAfee, Symantec (see **Figure 18-1**), or Trend Micro, or the freely downloadable AVG Free. People are coming up with new viruses every day, so it's important that you use software that is up to date with the latest virus definitions and that protects your computer from them. Many antivirus programs are purchased by yearly subscription, which gives you access to updated virus definitions that the company constantly gathers throughout the year. Also, be sure to run a scan of your computer on a regular basis. For convenience, you can use settings in the software to set up automatic updates and scans. Consult your program's Help tool for instructions on how to use these features.

Figure 18-1

➤ **Install a program that combines tools for detecting adware and spyware.** Windows 7 has a built-in program, Windows Defender, which includes an anti-spyware feature. (I cover Windows Defender tools later in this chapter.) If you don't have Windows 7, you can purchase programs such as Spyware Doctor from PC Tools or download free tools such as SpyBot or Spyware Terminator.

➤ **Use Windows tools to keep Windows up to date with security features and fixes to security problems.** You can also turn on a *firewall,* which is a feature that stops other people or programs from accessing your computer without your permission. I cover Windows Defender and firewalls in Chapter 21.

350

>> **Use privacy and security features of your browser,** such as the Suggested Sites and InPrivate Browsing features new to IE 8.

Use Suggested Sites

1. To have Internet Explorer suggest sites you might like that are related to the currently displayed site, click the Tools button and choose Suggested Sites (a checkmark appears next to it as shown in **Figure 18-2**). When a prompt appears asking if you want to discover Web sites you might like based on sites you have visited, click Yes.

Choose Suggested Sites

Figure 18-2

2. Click the Suggested Sites button on the Favorites toolbar (if the toolbar isn't displayed, right-click the toolbar area and click on Favorites Bar). A list of suggested sites appears in a pop-up window (see **Figure 18-3**).

A list of suggested sites

Figure 18-3

3. Click on a site to display its URL.

 Suggested Sites uses your browsing history to come up with suggestions, so when you first activate it, it may take a little while before the feature comes up with useful suggestions.

Download Files Safely

1. Open a Web site that contains downloadable files such as www.adobe.com. Typically Web sites offer a Download button or link that initiates a file download.

2. Click the appropriate link to proceed. Windows might display a dialog box asking your permission to proceed with the download; click Yes.

Download dialog box, shown in
e either option:

wnload to a temporary folder.
nstallation program for software,
vever, beware: If you run a program
Internet, you could be introducing
s to your system. You might want
virus program to scan files before
n.

ve the file to your hard drive.
alog box, select the folder on your
ovable storage media (a USB Flash
e) where you want to save the file. If
you're downloading software, you need to locate the
downloaded file and click it to run the installation.

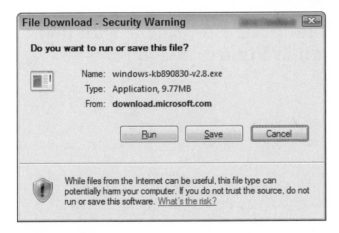

Figure 18-4

If you're worried that a particular file might be unsafe
to download (for example, if it's from an unknown
source and, being an executable file type, could contain a virus), click Cancel in the File Download dialog
box.

353

If a particular file will take a long time to download (some can take 20 minutes or more), you may have to babysit it. If your computer goes into standby mode, it could pause the download. If your computer automatically downloads Windows updates, it may cause your computer to restart automatically as well, cancelling or halting your download. Check in periodically to keep things moving along.

Turn on InPrivate Browsing and Filtering

1. InPrivate Browsing is a new feature that stops IE from saving information about your browsing session, such as cookies and your browsing history. InPrivate Filtering allows you to block or allow sites that are automatically collecting information about your browsing habits. To turn on InPrivate features, open IE.

2. Click Safety and choose InPrivate Browsing to turn that feature on. The tab shown in **Figure 18-5** appears.

The InPrivate tab

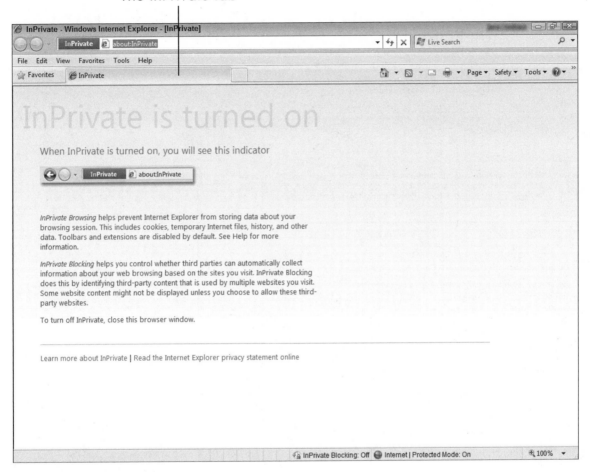

Figure 18-5

3. Click Safety and choose InPrivate Filtering Settings; if you haven't turned this feature on, a window appears asking you to turn it on; click the Block for Me link and again choose InPrivate Filtering Settings. The dialog box shown in **Figure 18-6** appears. Choose one of the following settings:

• **Automatically Block** blocks any site that uses content from other sites you've visited.

• **Choose Content to Block or Allow** allows you to

open the InPrivate Filtering Settings dialog box and use the Allow and Block buttons to select which sites to allow and which to block.

Choose a setting

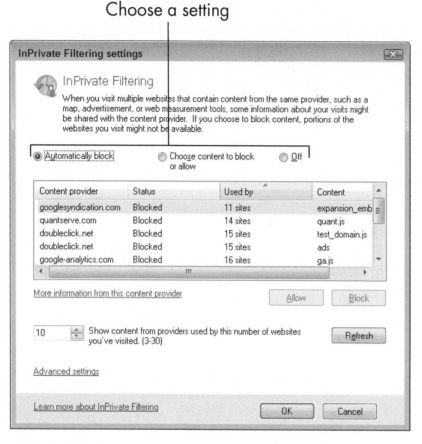

Figure 18-6

4. Click OK to save your settings. When you browse a bit and then reopen the InPrivate Filtering Settings dialog box (Safety⇨InPrivate Block), you see blocked and allowed sites listed.

If you don't want to use InPrivate Browsing but would like to periodically clear your browsing history manually, with IE open, you can press Ctrl+Shift+Delete to do so.

Use SmartScreen Filter

1. SmartScreen Filter lets you check Web sites that have been reported to Microsoft as generating phishing scams or downloading malware to your computer. To turn SmartScreen Filter on, click on the Safety button and then choose SmartScreen Filter⇨Turn On SmartScreen Filter. In the confirmation dialog box that appears, click OK.

2. To use SmartScreen Filter, go to a Web site you want to check. Click the Safety button and choose SmartScreen Filter⇨Check This Website.

3. The SmartScreen Filter window appears (see **Figure 18-7**), indicating whether it found any threats. Click the OK button to close the message.

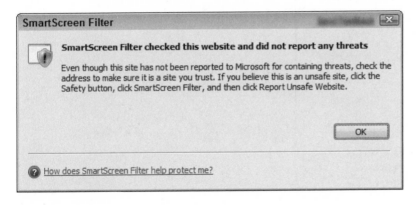

Figure 18-7

 Once turned on, SmartScreen Filter automatically checks Web sites and will generate a message if you visit one that has reported problems. However, that information only gets updated periodically, so if you have concerns about a particular site, use the procedure given here to check the latest information about the Web site.

Change Privacy Settings

1. You can modify how IE deals with privacy settings to keep information about your browsing habits or identity safer. With IE open, choose Tools⇨Internet Options and click the Privacy tab, as shown in **Figure 18-8.**

The Privacy tab

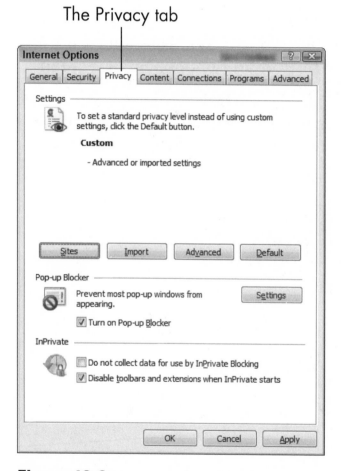

Figure 18-8

2. Click the slider and drag it up or down to make different levels of security settings.

3. Read the choices and select a setting that suits you.

4. Click the Sites button to specify sites to always or never allow the use of cookies. In the resulting Per Site Privacy Actions dialog box (shown in **Figure 18-9**), enter a site in the Address of Website box and click either Block or Allow.

Enter a Web site here

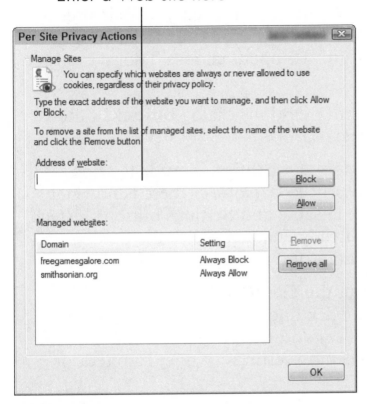

Figure 18-9

5. Click OK twice to save your new settings.

 The default setting, Medium, is probably a good bet for most people. To restore the default setting, click the Default button in the Internet Options dialog box's Privacy tab or use the slider to move back to Medium.

You can also use pop-up blocker settings on the Privacy tab to specify which pop-up windows to allow or block. Just click the Settings button, enter a Web site name, and then click Add to allow pop-ups.

Enable the Content Advisor

1. Use Content Advisor to alert you when you visit sites with certain types of content you or your family might find objectionable. With IE open, choose Tools⇨Internet Options.

2. In the resulting Internet Options dialog box, click the Content tab to display it.

3. Click the Enable button; if a confirmation dialog box appears, click Yes to proceed. (**Note:** If there is no Enable button, but there are Disable and Settings buttons instead, Content Advisor is already enabled. Click the Settings button to see the options and make changes if you wish.)

4. On the Ratings tab of the Content Advisor dialog box (see **Figure 18-10**), click one of the categories (such as Depiction of Drug Use) and then move the slider to use one of three site-screening settings: None, Limited, or Unrestricted.

5. Repeat Step 4 for each of the categories.

6. Click the Approved Sites tab (see **Figure 18-11**) and enter the name of a specific site that you want to control access to. Then click Always or Never.

   • **Always** allows users to view the site, even if it's included in the Content Advisor screening level you've set.

   • **Never** means that nobody can visit the site even if it's

360

acceptable to Content Advisor.

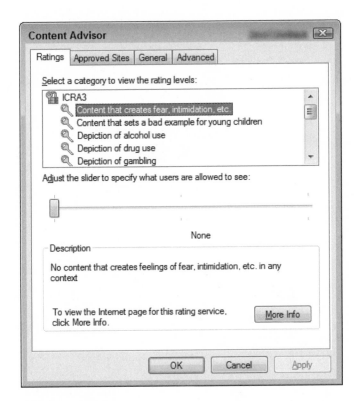

Figure 18-10

Enter a Web site here

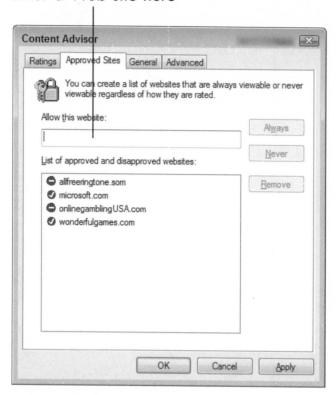

Figure 18-11

7. When you finish making your settings, click OK; if prompted to create a supervisor password, do so. Click OK again to save your settings.

   If you want to view sites that you don't want others to see, you can do that, too. On the General tab of the Content Advisor dialog box, make sure that the Supervisor Can Type a Password to Allow Viewers to View Restricted Content check box is selected, and then click Create Password. In the dialog box that appears, enter the password, confirm it, and then enter a hint and click OK. Now if you're logged on as the system administrator, you can get to any restricted site by using this password.

To find rating systems that various organizations have created and apply them to Internet Explorer, click the Rating Systems button on the General tab. Here you can choose a system already shown there. Or, click Add; then, in the resulting Open Ratings System File dialog box, choose another system to apply.

Understand Information Exposure

Many people think that if they aren't active online, their information isn't exposed. But you aren't the only one sharing your information:

➤ **Employers:** Many employers share information about employees. Consider carefully how much information you're comfortable with sharing through an employee bio posted on your company Web site. How much should be visible to other employees on your intranet? When you attend a conference, is the attendee list shown in online conference documents? And even if you're retired, there may still be information about you on your old employer's Web site. Review the site to determine if it reveals more than you'd like it to — and ask your employer to take down or alter the information if needed.

➤ **Government agencies:** Some agencies post personal information, such as documents concerning your home purchase and property tax (see **Figure 18-12**), on publicly available Web sites. Government agencies may also post birth, marriage, and death certificates, and these documents may contain your Social Security number, loan number, copies of your signature, and so on. You should check government records carefully to see if private information is posted and demand that it be removed.

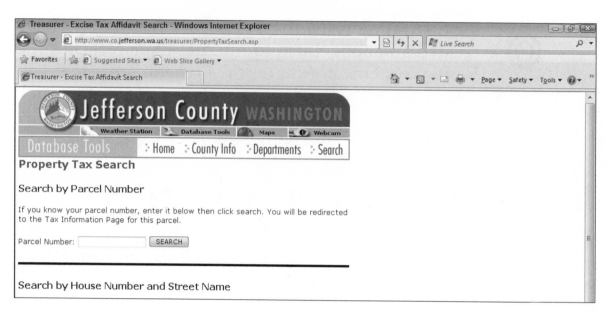

Figure 18-12

> ➤ **Family members and friends:** They may write about you in their blogs or mention you on special-interest sites such as those focused on genealogy.

> ➤ **Clubs and organizations:** Organizations with whom you volunteer, the church you attend, and professional associations may reveal facts such as your address, age, income bracket, and how money much you've donated.

> ➤ **Newspapers:** If you've been featured in a newspaper article, you may be surprised to find the story, along with a picture of you or information about your work, activities, or family, by doing a simple online search. If you're interviewed, ask for the chance to review the information that the newspaper will include, and be sure that you're comfortable with exposing that information.

➡ **Online directories:** Services such as `www.white pages.com`, shown in **Figure 18-13**, or `anywho. com` list your phone number and address, unless you specifically request that these be removed. You may be charged a small fee associated with removing your information — a so-called privacy tax — but you may find the cost worthwhile. Online directories often include the names of members of your family, your e-mail address, the value of your home, your neighbors' names and the values of their homes, an online mapping tool to provide a view of your home, driving directions to your home, and your age. The record may also include previous addresses, schools you've attended, and links for people to run background checks on you.

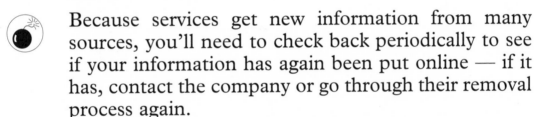 Because services get new information from many sources, you'll need to check back periodically to see if your information has again been put online — if it has, contact the company or go through their removal process again.

Try entering your home phone number in any browser's address line; chances are you'll get an online directory listing with your address and phone number (although this doesn't work for cell phone numbers).

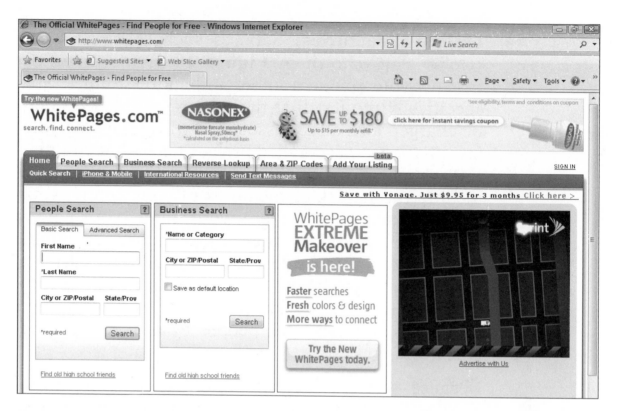

Figure 18-13

Keep Your Information Private

Sharing personal information with friends and family enriches your relationships and helps you build new ones. The key is to avoid sharing information with the wrong people and shady companies because, just as in the real world, exposing your personal information online is one of your biggest risks.

Criminals come in all flavors, but the more savvy ones collect information in a very systematic way. Each piece of information is like another drop of water that, over time, collects to form a very clear picture of your life. And after criminals collect and organize the information, they never throw it away because they may be able to use it many times over.

Fortunately, information exposure is a risk you have a great deal of control over. Before sharing information such as your date of birth, make sure that you're comfortable with how the recipient will use the information.

➤ **Address and phone number:** Abuse of this information results in you receiving increased telemarketing calls and junk mail. Although less common, this information may also increase a scammer's ability to steal your identity and make your home a more interesting target for break-ins.

➤ **Names of husband/wife, father, and mother (including mother's maiden name), siblings, children, and grandchildren:** This information is very interesting to criminals, who can use it to gain your confidence and then scam you, or use it to guess your passwords or secret question answers, which often include family members' names. This information may also expose additional family members to ID theft, fraud, and personal harm.

➤ **Information about your car:** Limit access to license plate numbers; VINs (vehicle identification numbers); registration information; make, model, and title number of car; your insurance carrier's name and coverage limits; loan information; and driver's license number. The key criminal abuse of this information includes car theft (or theft of parts of the car) and insurance fraud. The type of car you drive may also indicate your financial status, and that adds one more piece of information to the pool of data criminals collect about you.

➤ **Information about work history:** In the hands of criminals, your work history can be very useful for "authenticating" the fraudster and convincing people and organizations to provide them with more of your financial records or identity.

➤ **Information about your credit status:** This information can be abused in so many ways that any time you're asked to provide this online, your answer should be no. Don't fall for the temptation to check your credit scores for free through sites that aren't guaranteed reputable. Another frequent abuse of credit information is found in free mortgage calculators that ask you to put in all kinds of personal information in order for them to determine what credit you qualify for.

Many people leave messages on their e-mail letting people know when they'll be away from their offices. This is really helpful for colleagues, but exercise caution and limit who you provide the information to. Leaving a message that says, "Gone 11/2–11/12. I'm taking the family to Hawaii for ten days," may make you a prime target for burglary. And you'll probably never make the connection between the information you exposed and the offline crime.

You may need to show your work history, particularly on resumes you post on Internet job or business-networking sites. Be selective about where you post this information, create a separate e-mail account to list on the resume, and tell what kinds of work you've done rather than give specifics about which companies and what dates. Interested, legitimate employers can then contact you privately, and you won't have given away your life history to the world. After you've landed the job, **take down** your resume. Think of it as risk management — when you need a job, the risk of information exposure is less than the need to get the job.

Spot Phishing Scams and Other E-mail Fraud

As in the offline world, the Internet has a criminal element. These cybercriminals use Internet tools to commit the same crimes they've always committed, from robbing you to misusing your good name and financial information. Know how to spot the types of scams that occur online and you'll go a long way towards steering clear of Internet crime.

Before you click a link that comes in a forwarded e-mail message or forward a message to others, ask yourself:

➡ **Is the information legitimate?** Sites such as www. truthorfiction.com, www.snopes.com (see **Figure 18-14**), or http://urbanlegends.about. com can help you discover if an e-mail is a scam.

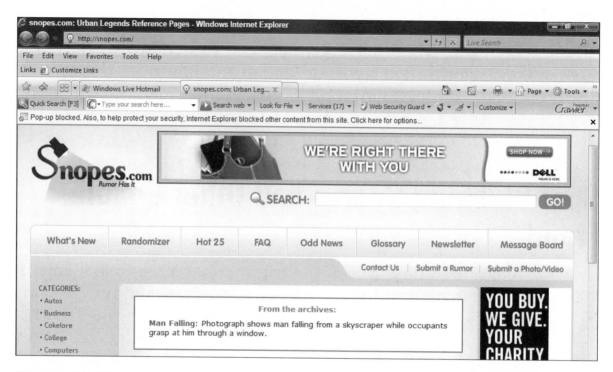

Figure 18-14

➤ **Does a message ask you to click links in e-mail or instant messages?** If you're unsure whether a message is genuinely from a company or bank that you use, call them, using the number from a past statement or the phone book. ***Remember:*** Don't call a phone number listed in the e-mail; it could be fake. To visit a company's or bank's Web site, type the address in yourself if you know it or use your own bookmark rather than clicking a link. If the Web site is new to you, search for the company using your browser and use that link to visit its site. Don't click the link in an e-mail, or you may land on a site that looks right — but is just a good fake.

➤ **Does the e-mail have a photo or video to download?** If so, exercise caution. If you know the person who sent the photo or video, it's probably fine to download, but if the photo or video has been forwarded several times and you don't know the person who sent it originally, be careful. It may deliver a virus or other type of malware to your computer.

In addition to these questions, also remember the following:

➤ **If you decide to forward (or send) e-mail to a group, always put their e-mail addresses on the Bcc: (or Blind Carbon Copy) line.** This keeps everyone's e-mail safe from fraud and scams.

➤ **Think *before* you click.** Doing so will save you and others from scams, fraud, hoaxes, and malware.

Create Strong Passwords

A strong password can be one of your best friends in protecting your information in online accounts and sites. Never give your password to others, and change passwords on particularly sensitive accounts, such as bank and investment accounts, regularly.

Table 18-1 outlines five principles for creating strong passwords.

Table 18-1	Principles for Strong Passwords
Principle	*How to Do It*
Length	Use at least ten characters.
Strength	Mix it up with upper- and lowercase letters, characters, and numbers.
Obscure	Use nothing that's associated with you, your family, your company, and so on.
Protect	Don't place paper reminders near your computer.
Change	The more sensitive the information, the more frequently you should change your password.

Look at **Table 18-2** for examples of password patterns that are safe but also easy to remember.

Table 18-2	Examples of Strong Passwords
Logic	*Password*
Use a familiar phrase typed with a variation of capitalization and numbers instead of words (text message shorthand).	`L8r_L8rNot2day` = Later, later, not today `2BorNot2B_ThatIsThe?=` To be or not to be, that is the question.
Incorporate shortcut codes or acronyms.	`CSThnknAU2day` = Can't Stop Thinking About You today `2Hot2Hndle` = Too hot to handle
Create a password from an easy to remember phrase that	`1mlook1ngatyahoo` = I'm looking at Yahoo (We

describes what you're doing, with key letters replaced by numbers or symbols.	replaced the ls with 1s.) `MyWork@HomeNeverEnds`
Spell a word backwards with at least one letter representing a character or number.	`$lidoffaD` = Daffodils (The $ replaces the s.) `y1frettuB` = Butterfly (The 1 replaces the l.) `QWERTY7654321` = This is the 6 letters from left to right in the top row of your keyboard, plus the numbers from right to left across the top going backwards.
Use patterns from your keyboard. (See **Figure 18-15.**) Make your keyboard a palette and make any shape you want.	`1QAZSDRFBHU8` is really just making a W on your keyboard. (Refer to **Figure 18-15.**)

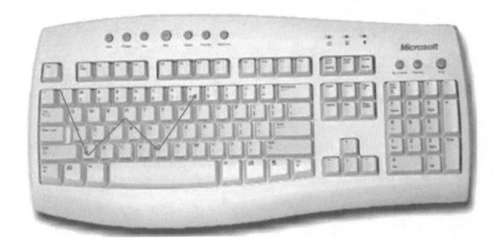

Figure 18-15

Chapter 19

Keeping In Touch with E-Mail

Get ready to . . .

An *e-mail program* is a tool you can use to send text messages to others. These messages are delivered to their e-mail *inbox*, usually within seconds. You can attach files to e-mail messages and even put graphic images within the message body. You can get an e-mail account through you Internet provider or through sites such as Yahoo! and Microsoft Live Hotmail. These accounts are typically free.

When you have an e-mail account, you can send and receive e-mail through the account provider's e-mail program online, or you can set up a program on your computer, such as Microsoft Outlook, which comes with Microsoft Office, or Windows Live Mail, which is built into Internet Explorer to access that account. These programs typically offer more robust e-mail and contact management features than the programs that providers such as Yahoo! offer.

To make your e-mailing life easy, this chapter takes a look at these tasks:

➼ **Choose an e-mail provider.** Find out how to locate e-mail providers and what types of features they offer.

➼ **Manage your e-mail account.** Make settings to send out messages with different e-mail addresses if you want to forward more than one e-mail account to Windows Live Mail so you can check all your messages in one place. This is useful if you use both work and home e-mail accounts, for example.

➼ **Receive, send, and forward messages.** Deal with the ins and outs of receiving and sending e-mail. Use the formatting tools that Windows Live Mail provides to make your messages more attractive and readable.

➡ **Add information into the Address Book.** You can quickly and easily manage your contacts as well as organize the messages you save in e-mail folders.

➡ **Set up the layout of all Windows Live features.** Use the Folder bar and Layout features to create the most efficient workspace.

Set Up an Internet-Based E-Mail Account

Your Internet service provider (ISP), whether that's your cable or phone company or a small local provider, probably offers you a free e-mail account along with your service. You can also get free accounts from many online sources, such as Yahoo!, AOL, Gmail, and Windows Live Mail.

Here are some tips for getting your own e-mail account:

➡ **Using e-mail accounts provided by an ISP:** Check with your ISP to see whether an e-mail account comes with your connection service. If it does, your ISP should provide instructions on how to choose an e-mail alias (that is the name on your account, such as `SusieXYZ@aol.com`) and password and sign in.

➡ **Searching for an e-mail provider:** If your ISP doesn't offer e-mail, or you prefer to use another service because of features it offers, use your browser's search engine to look for what's available. Don't use the search term *"free e-mail"* because results for any search with the word *free* included are much more likely to return sites that will download bad programs like viruses and spyware onto your computer. Alternatively, you can go directly to services such as Yahoo!, AOL, or Gmail by entering their addresses in your browser's address box (for example, www.gmail.com).

➥ **Finding out about features:** E-mail accounts come with certain features that you should be aware of. For example, they each provide a certain amount of storage for your saved messages. (Look for one that provides 4 gigabytes or more.) The account should also include an easy-to-use Address Book feature to save your contacts' information. Some services provide better formatting tools for text, calendar, and to-do list features. Whatever service you use, make sure it has good junk-mail features to protect you from unwanted e-mails. You should be able to control junk-mail filters to place messages from certain senders or with certain content in a junk-mail folder where you can review or delete them.

➥ **Signing up for an e-mail account:** When you find an e-mail account you want to use, sign up (usually there will be a Sign Up or Get An Account button or link to click) by providing your name and other contact information and selecting a username and password. The username is your e-mail address, in the form of UserName@service.com, where the service is, for example, Yahoo!, Windows Live Mail, or AOL. Some usernames might be taken, so have a few options in mind.

➥ **Make sure your username is a safe one:** Don't use your full name, your location, age, or other identifiers if possible. Such personal identifiers might help scam artists or predators to find out more about you than you want them to know.

Manage Accounts in Windows Live

1. In addition to providing your Windows Live e-mail address so others can send you mail directly, you can use settings in various e-mail programs to forward your mail to your Windows Live address so you can receive all your e-mail messages in one place. You can then make settings in Windows Live to use other e-mail addresses when responding to messages so your recipients assume the messages are coming from the originating account. Follow these steps to set up your accounts in Windows Live Mail. Open your browser and type `www.mail.live.com` in the address field and press Enter.

2. Windows opens your default browser and displays the Windows Live Mail sign-in window shown in **Figure 19-1**. If you need to start a new account at this point, click the Sign Up button and go through the sign-up procedure. If you already have an account, click the Sign In to Windows Live button and enter your password in the field that appears, and then click the Sign In button to sign in.

3. Click on the Mail link to go to the Mail portion of Windows Live.

4. Choose Options⇨More Options. In the resulting Options window, shown in **Figure 19-2**, click the Send and Receive Mail from Other E-Mail Accounts link.

5. In the resulting window (see **Figure 19-3**), click the Add Another Account to Send Mail From link.

6. In the following screen, enter an e-mail address and click the Send Verification E-mail button. An e-mail is sent to that account. Open the account and view the e-mail. Click the link in the e-mail to verify that it's okay for

Windows Live to send e-mail with that address on it.

7. Once verified, you are set up to send out messages with that account name. In a new e-mail form, simply click the arrow on the right of the From field and select the account you want the message to go from.

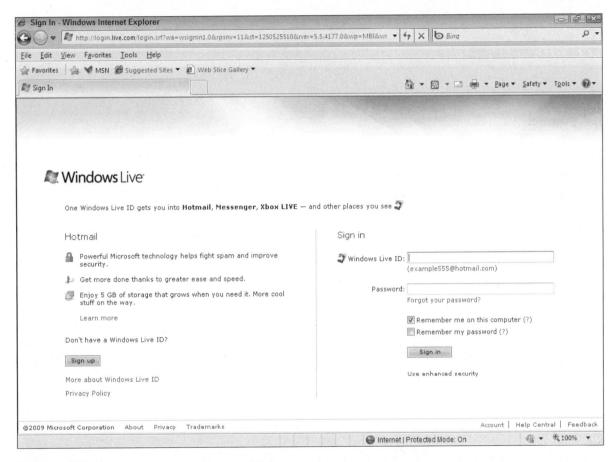

Figure 19-1

Click this link

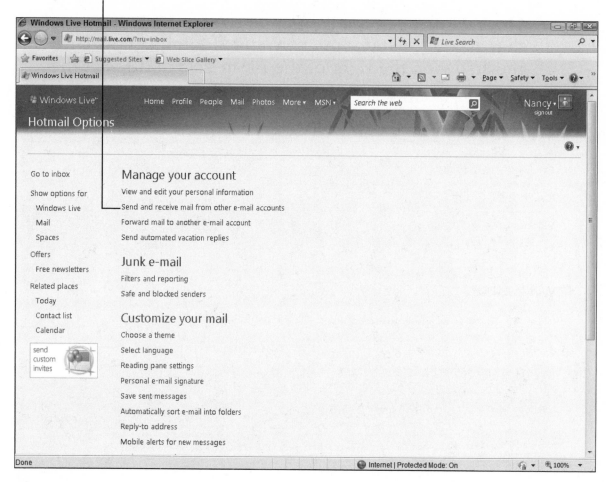

Figure 19-2

Get to Know Windows Live Mail

Windows Live (see **Figure 19-4**) is typical of many e-mail programs in that it includes both menus and tools to take actions such as deleting an e-mail, creating a new e-mail, and so on. There's also a list of folders on the left. Some typical folders are your Inbox, where most incoming mail appears; your Outbox or Drafts folder, where saved drafts of e-mails are saved ready to be sent; and your Sent folder, where copies of sent e-mails are stored.

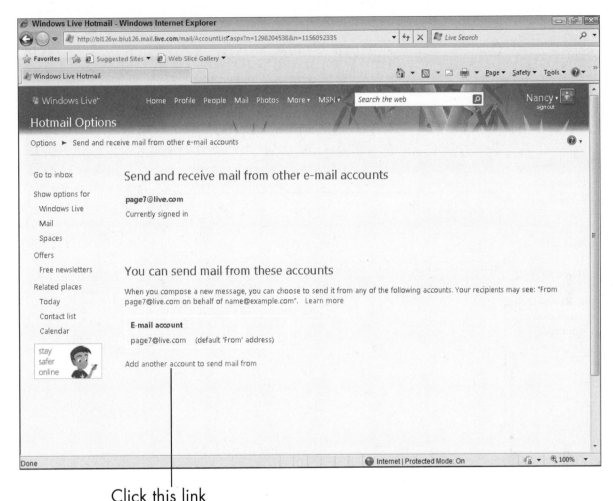

Click this link

Figure 19-3

Finally, the central area of the screen may display folder contents or, if you are creating or viewing a message, a preview pane that shows the contents of a selected message in the Inbox or other folder (in **Figure 19-4,** the contents of a message being composed are displayed).

 To organize messages in the Inbox, click the Sort By drop-down list and select an option, such as From (to sort the messages alphabetically by sender), Received (to sort by the date they were received), and so on.

Folders   Preview pane   Toolbar

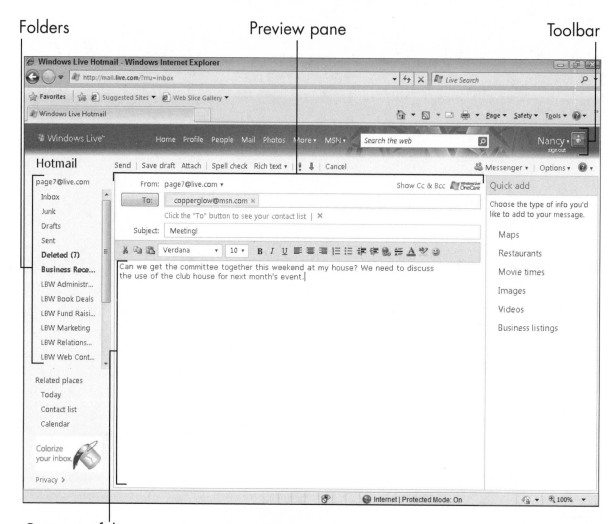

Contents of the message

Figure 19-4

When you access Windows Live Mail and many of the other online e-mail services, you are using a program that is hosted online, rather than software on your computer. That makes it easy to access your mail from any computer because your messages and

folders are kept online. If you use an e-mail program such as Outlook, the software and your messages are stored on your computer.

Open Windows Live Mail and Receive Messages

1. Use your browser to go to Windows Live (`www.mail.live.com`).

2. Windows opens your default browser and displays the Windows Live sign-in window shown in **Figure 19-5**.

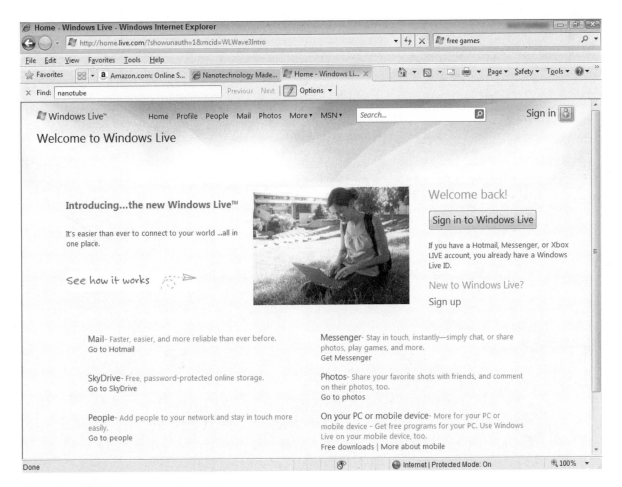

Figure 19-5

3. Click on the Sign In to Windows Live button and enter your password in the field that appears, and then click the Sign In button to sign in. Windows Live automatically sends and receives all messages.

4. Click the Mail link at the top of the page, if necessary, to view your Inbox, shown in **Figure 19-6**. New messages sport a small closed envelope icon; those with attachments have a paper clip icon as well.

Messages in the Inbox

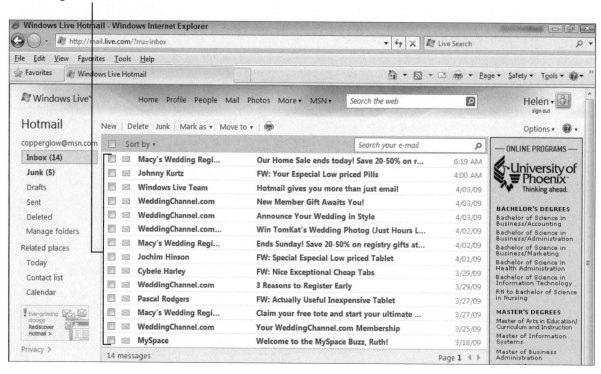

Figure 19-6

If your mail doesn't come through, it's probably because your e-mail provider's servers are experiencing technical problems. Just wait a little while. If you still can't get mail, make sure your connection to the Internet is active. Your browser may show you your Inbox, but if you've lost your connection, new messages can't be received.

 Note that if an e-mail has a little exclamation point next to it in your Inbox, somebody has flagged it as urgent. It's usually best to check out those e-mails first!

Create and Send E-Mail

1. Creating e-mail is as simple as filling out a few fields in a form. Open Windows Live Mail in your browser (`www.mail.live.com`).

2. Sign in, and then click the Mail button on the Windows Live Mail screen, if needed, to go to your Inbox.

3. Click the New button to create a new, blank e-mail form (see **Figure 19-7**).

A new, blank e-mail

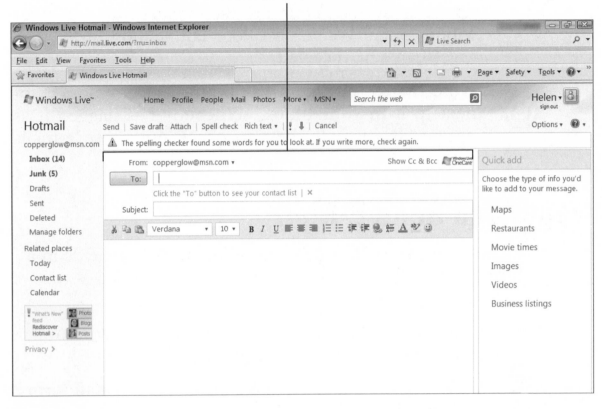

Figure 19-7

4. Type the e-mail address of the recipient(s) in the To field text box. If you want to send a copy of the message, click the Show Cc & Bcc link and enter an address(es) in the Cc or Bcc field text box.

5. Click in the Subject field text box and type a concise yet descriptive subject.

6. Click in the message window and type your message (see **Figure 19-8**).

Enter your message here

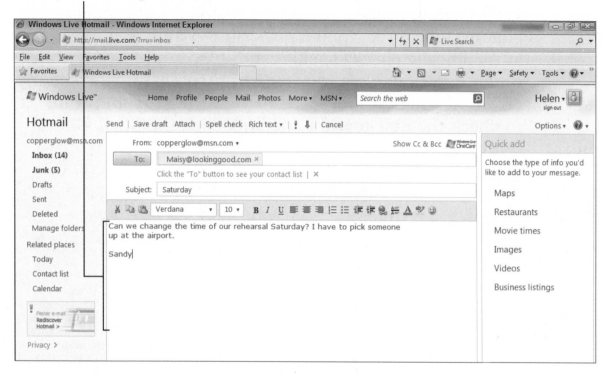

Figure 19-8

 Don't press Enter at the end of a line when typing a message. Windows Live has an automatic text wrap feature that does this for you. Do be concise. If you have lots to say, consider sending a letter by snail mail or overnight delivery. Most people tire of reading text on-screen after a short while.

 Keep e-mail etiquette in mind as you type. For example, don't type in ALL CAPITAL LETTERS. This is called *shouting,* which is considered rude. Do be polite even if you're really, really angry. Your message could be forwarded to just about anybody, just about anywhere, and you don't want to get a reputation as a hothead.

7. When you finish typing your message, you should check your spelling (unless you're the regional state spelling champ). Click the Spell Check button and Windows Live automatically checks spelling and places a red, wavy line under questionable words (see **Figure 19-9**). Correct any errors. If you add more text to your message and want to check the new text for spelling, click the Spell Check button again.

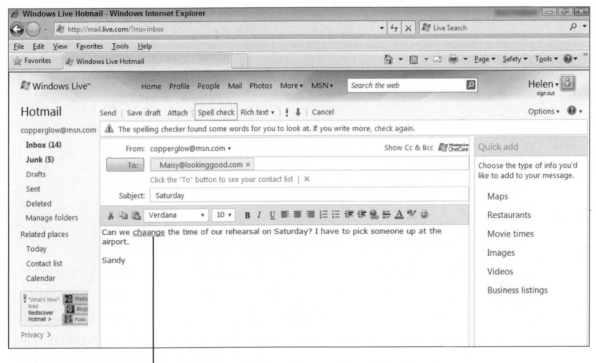

A questionable word

Figure 19-9

8. Click the Send button. A messages appears like the one in **Figure 19-10** telling you the message is on its way!

Confirmation of a sent message

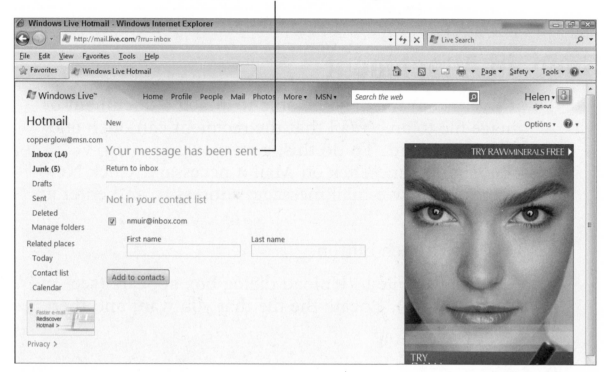

Figure 19-10

   If the message is really urgent, you might also click the High Importance button (it looks like a red exclamation point) to add a bright red exclamation mark to the message header to alert the recipient. Click the Low Importance button (it looks like a blue, downward-pointing arrow) to return the priority to Low.

   Remember that when creating an e-mail, you can address it to a stored address by using the Address Book feature. Click the To button, and your Address Book appears. You can then select a contact(s) from there. Windows Live Mail also allows you to just begin to type a stored contact in an address field (To or Cc), and it provides a list of likely options while you type.

Just click on the correct name when it appears in the list to enter it.

Send an Attachment

1. It's very convenient to be able to attach a document or image file to an e-mail that the recipient can open and view on his end. To do this, go to `www.mail.live.com`, sign in, and click on Mail if necessary. Click New to create a new e-mail message, address it, and enter a subject.

2. Click the Attach button.

3. The Choose File to Upload dialog box appears (see **Figure 19-11**). Locate the file that you want and then click Open.

Figure 19-11

4. The name of the attached file appears in the Attach field text box (see **Figure 19-12**) indicating that it's uploading. When the first attachment finishes uploading, you can click the Attach button again and repeat Step 3 as many times as you like to add additional attachments.

An attached file

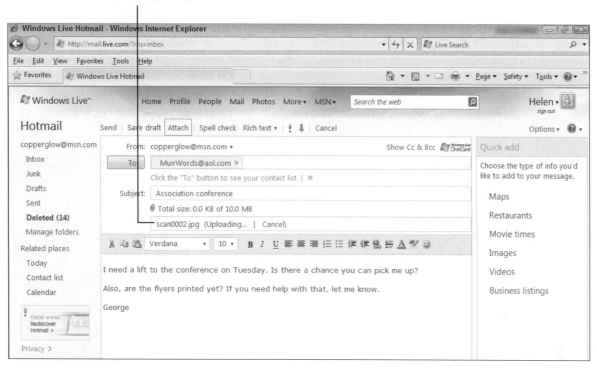

Figure 19-12

5. Click the Send button to send the message and attachment.

 You can attach as many files as you like to a single e-mail by repeating steps in this task. Your limitation is size. Various e-mail programs have different limitations on the size of attachments, and some prevent you from attaching certain types of files for security reasons. If you attach several documents and your e-

391

mail fails to get sent, just send a few e-mails and spread the attachments out among them.

Read a Message

1. When you receive an e-mail, your next step is to read it. Click an e-mail message in your Inbox or double-click it to open it in a larger window. Unread messages sport an icon of an unopened envelope to the left of the message subject.

2. Use the scrollbars in the message window to scroll down through the message and read it (see **Figure 19-13**).

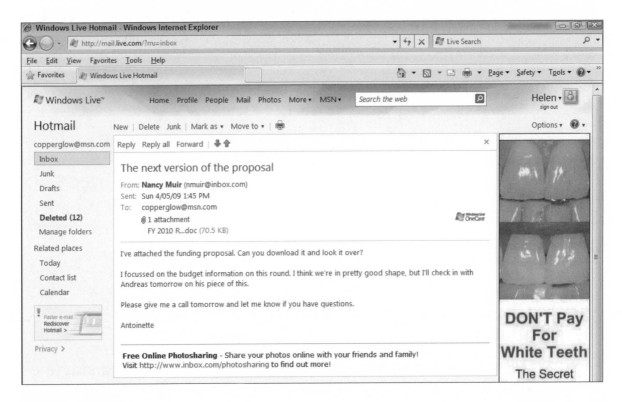

Figure 19-13

3. If the message has an attachment, it shows a paper

clip symbol when the message is closed in your Inbox; attachments are listed in the open message. To open an attachment, click it.

4. In the File Download dialog box (see **Figure 19-14**), click the Open button to open the file with the suggested program. The attachment opens in whatever program is associated with it (such as the Windows Fax and Picture Viewer for a graphics file) or the program it was created in (such as Microsoft Office Word).

 If you'd rather save an attachment to a storage disc or your hard drive, click the Save button in Step 4, choose the location to save the file to, and then click Save.

Click Open

Figure 19-14

Reply to a Message

1. If you receive an e-mail and want to send a message back, use the Reply feature. Open the message you want

393

to reply to, and then select one of the following reply options, as shown in **Figure 19-15:**

- **Reply:** Send the reply to only the author.

- **Reply All:** Send a reply to the author as well as to everyone who received the original message.

2. In the resulting e-mail form (see **Figure 19-16**), enter any additional recipient(s) in the To and/or Cc or Bcc text boxes and type your message in the message window area.

3. Click the Send button to send the reply.

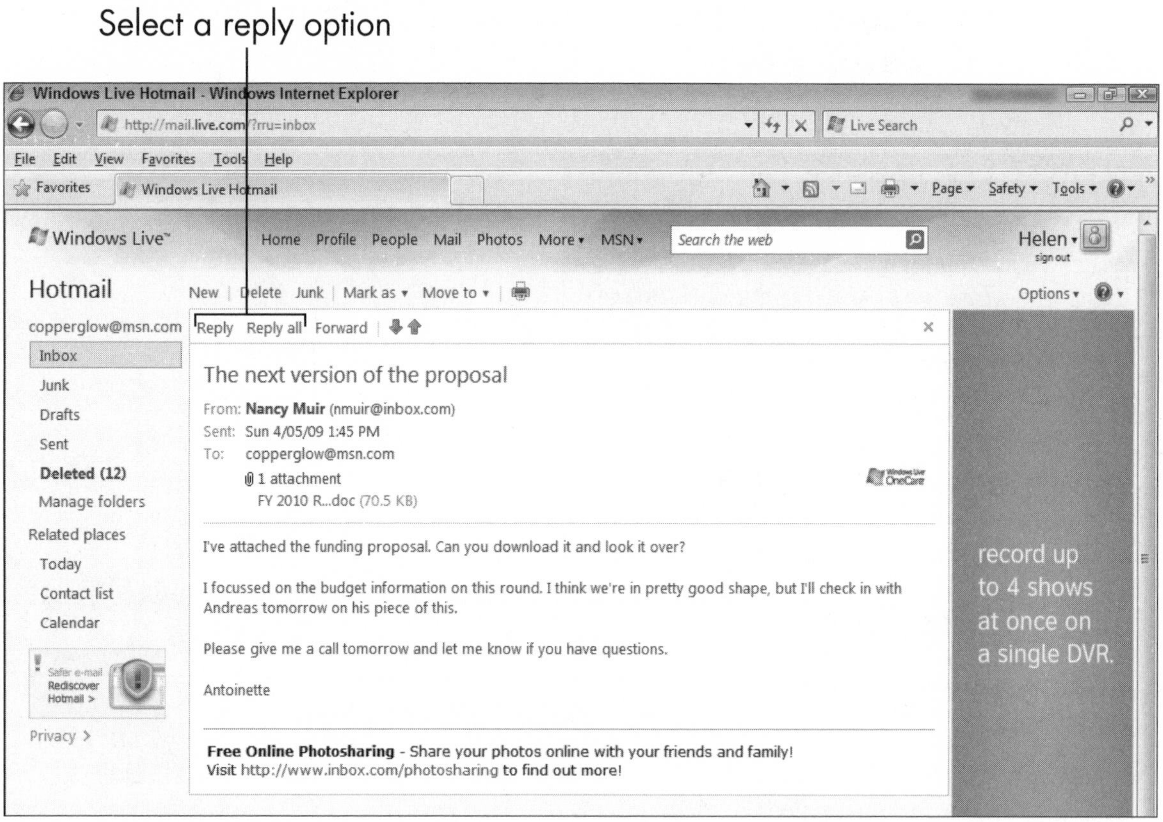

Select a reply option

Figure 19-15

Enter recipients here

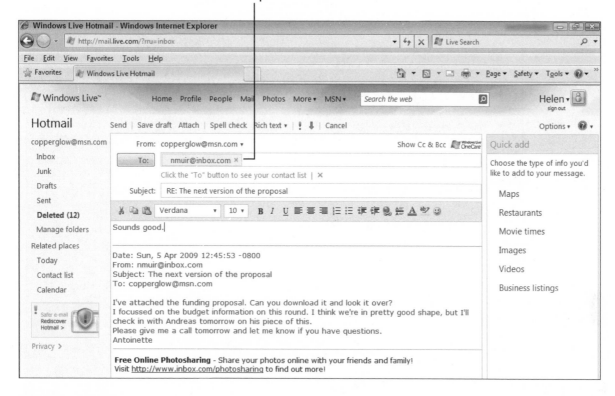

Figure 19-16

Forward E-Mail

1. To share an e-mail you receive with others, use the Forward feature. Open the e-mail message that you want to forward.

2. Click the Forward button on the toolbar.

3. In the message that appears with FW: added to the beginning of the subject line, enter a new recipient(s) in the To and/or Cc and Bcc fields, and then enter any message that you want to include in the message window area, as shown in the example in **Figure 19-17**.

Enter your message here

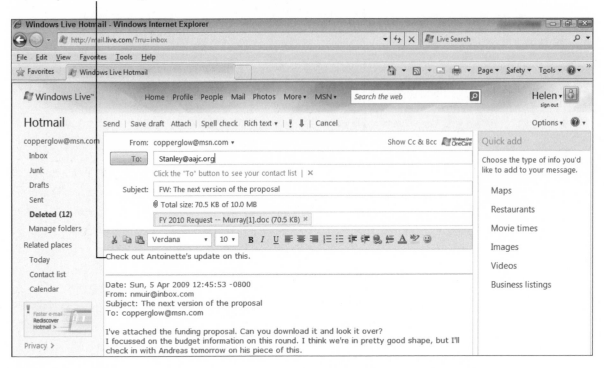

Figure 19-17

4. Click Send to forward the message.

Create and Add a Signature

1. A signature is a quick way to add some closing information such as your name and organization to the end of every message. Choose Options⇨More Options to open the Options page. Click the Personal E-mail Signature link (under Customize Your Mail) (see **Figure 19-18**).

2. In the Personal E-mail Signature form that opens (see **Figure 19-19**), type your signature. Use the tools on the toolbar to change the text formatting, such as changing the font or font size or applying effects such as bold or italic to it.

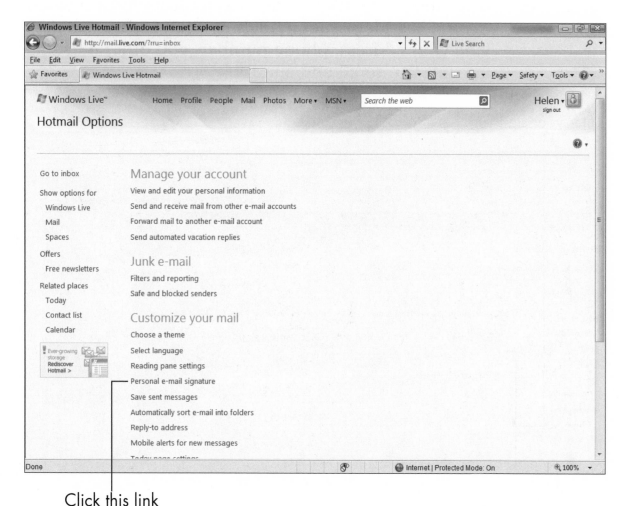

Click this link

Figure 19-18

3. Click Save to save the signature.

 If you have a Web site and want to include a link to it in your signature, click the Insert Hyperlink button in the toolbar shown in **Figure 19-19**. Enter the address in the text box that appears and then click OK.

Remember that if you attach your signature to every outgoing e-mail including e-mail replies, whoever you communicate with will get the information provided there. Consider issues of identity theft before you provide your address, phone number, and other personal information to all and sundry.

Enter your signature here

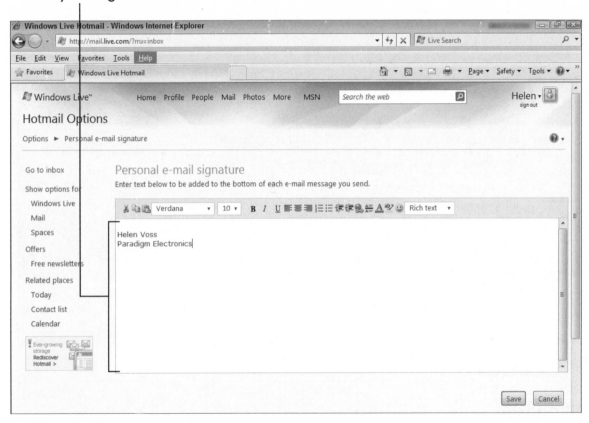

Figure 19-19

Format E-Mail Messages

1. Windows Live provides tools to format the text in your message to change fonts, add color, and more, just as you would in a word-processing document. Create a new e-mail message or open a message and click Reply or Forward.

2. Enter text, and then select the text that you want to format (see **Figure 19-20**).

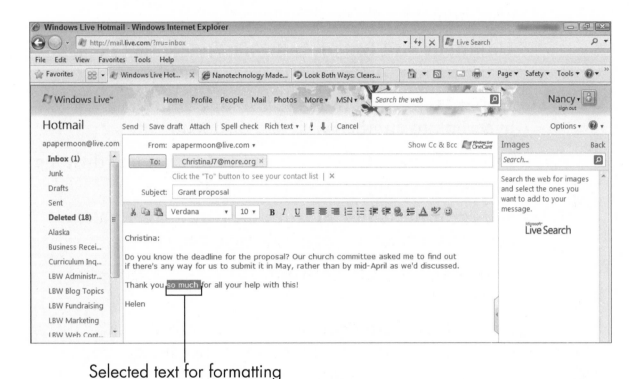

Selected text for formatting

Figure 19-20

3. Use any of the following options to make changes to the font. (See the toolbar containing these tools in **Figure 19-21.**)

- **Font Name drop-down list:** Choose an option from the drop-down list to apply it to the text.

- **Font Size drop-down list:** Change the font size here.

- **Bold, Italic, and Underline buttons:** Apply styles to

selected text.

- **Justify Left, Justify Center, and Justify Right buttons:** Adjust the alignment.

- **Insert Ordered List and Insert Unordered List buttons:** Apply numbering order to lists or precede each item with a round bullet.

- **Unindent and Indent buttons:** Indent that paragraph to the right or move (decrease) it to the left.

- **Insert Hyperlink button:** Use this to insert a hyperlink to another Web site or document.

- **Insert Horizontal Rule button:** Insert a line dividing the signature from the message body.

- **Foreground Color button:** Display a color palette and click a color to apply it to selected text.

- **Background Color button:** Add color to the background of the message.

- **Insert Emoticon button:** Click this to view a selection of graphical smiles and other images to include in your signature for a bit of fun.

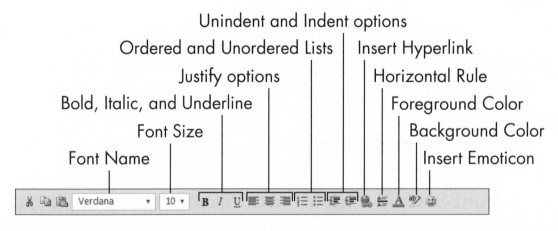

Figure 19-21

Apply a Theme

1. You can modify the appearance of Windows Live Mail by applying a theme which contains preset designs and colors to the window. Choose Options⇨More Themes.

2. In the Themes page that appears (see **Figure 19-22**), click on a theme from the list.

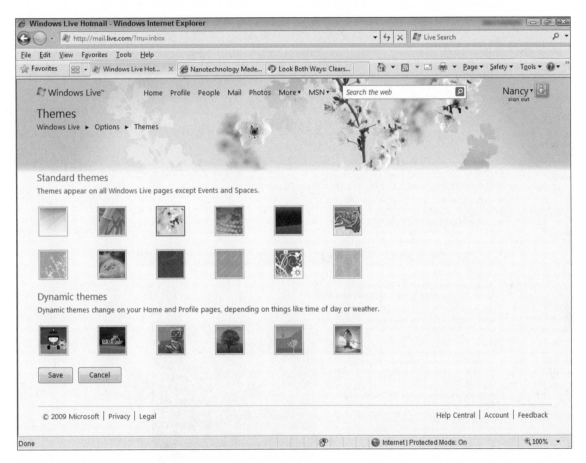

Figure 19-22

3. Click Save to apply the stationery to Windows Live Mail, and click the Mail link to return to your Inbox sporting the new look (see **Figure 19-23**).

If you are the visual type, you should know that you can also insert a picture in an e-mail message. With the e-mail form open, click the Images item in the Quick Add pane to the right. Enter a search term in the Search field text box to find an image online, and then click on any image result to insert it in your e-mail. You can also use Quick Add to add a map, movie time, video, business listing, or restaurant information.

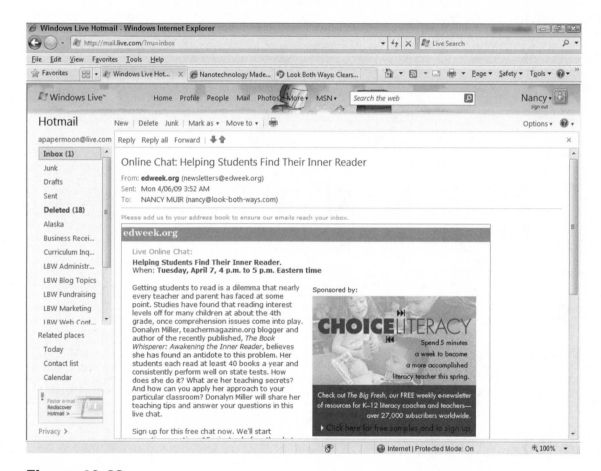

Figure 19-23

402

Add People to the Contact List

1. To make addressing e-mails faster, you can save people's e-mail addresses and more in a Contact List. In the Windows Live Mail main window, click the Contact List link in the left pane to open the People page, as shown in **Figure 19-24**.

2. To create a new contact, click the New button.

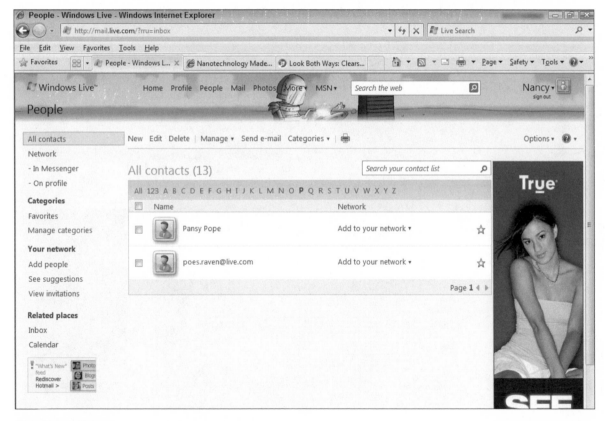

Figure 19-24

3. In the resulting Contact dialog box, as shown in **Figure 19-25**, enter contact information:

- **Name and E-mail:** Enter the person's first name and last name. (This is the only information you *must* enter

403

to create a contact.)

- **Personal Information:** Enter the person's e-mail address, home and mobile phone numbers, and home addresses.

- **Business Information:** Enter information about the company that the person works for as well as his work e-mail, phone, fax, and address.

- **Other Information:** Enter any other e-mail, phone, Web site, or birthday information for the person.

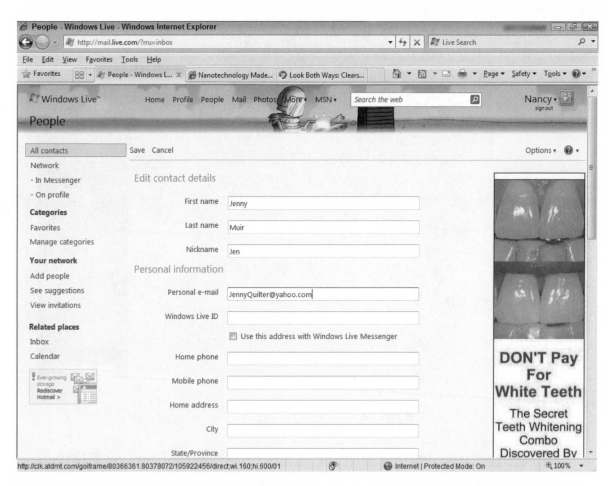

Figure 19-25

4. Click Save to save your new contact information, and then click Mail to return to your Inbox.

 You can search contacts by clicking on People in any Windows Live window and entering search text in the Search Your Contact List field. You can also click on the letters listed across the top of the Contacts window to look for people whose last names begin with that letter.

Customize the Reading Pane Layout

1. You can modify the layout of elements in the Windows Live main page to suit you. In the Mail portion of Windows Live, choose Options⇨More Options to open the Options window. Click on the Mail link in the left pane.

2. Click on Reading Pane Settings (under Customize Your Mail). Select various options in the Reading Pane Settings, as shown in **Figure 19-26**, to modify where the reading pane appears and when to show messages in the reading pane.

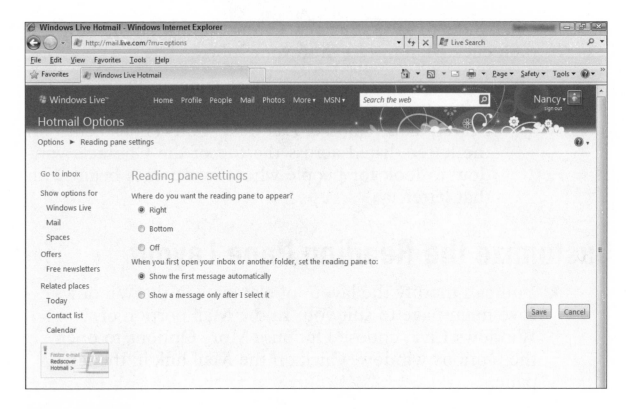

Figure 19-26

>   *3.* Click Save to save your reading pane settings.

Create Message Folders

>   *1.* Message folders are a way to organize your incoming
>   messages so you can find them easily. You can create
>   folders with a few simple steps. Choose the Manage
>   Folders link near the bottom of the list of folders within
>   the Inbox in the left pane to open the Manage Folders
>   window shown in **Figure 19-27**.

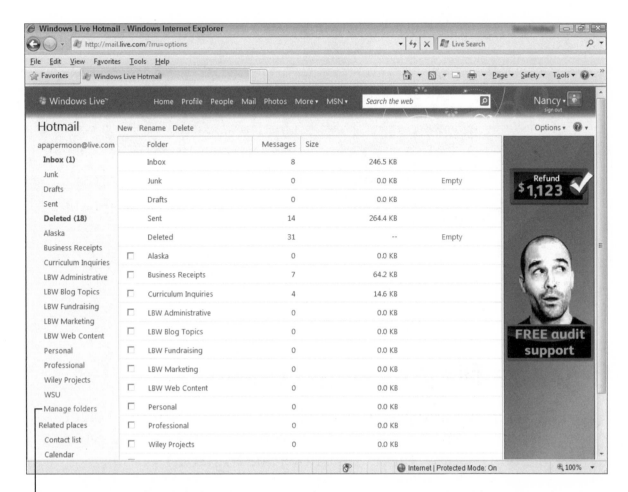

The Manage Folders link

Figure 19-27

2. Click New.

3. In the New Folder dialog box (see **Figure 19-28**), enter a folder name and click Save.

4. Click Mail to return to your Inbox.

 If you want to remove or rename a folder, you can use the tools in the Manage Folders window shown in **Figure 19-27** to do so.

Enter a name for the new folder

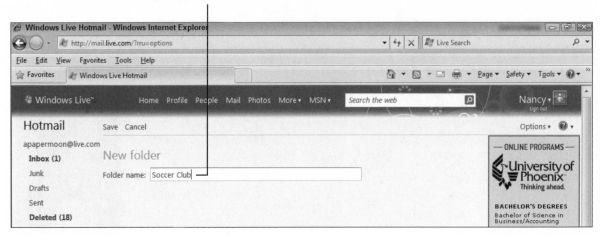

Figure 19-28

Organize Messages in Folders

1. To move a message in your Inbox into a folder, select
the checkbox in front of the message and choose Move
To⇨[Folder Name], as shown in **Figure 19-29**.

2. To move a message between folders, with a folder (such
as the Inbox) displayed, click a message and then drag it
into another folder in the Folders list.

3. To delete a message in a folder, click the folder name to
open it and click the checkbox in front of the message.
Click Delete.

 If you want to mark a message as junk mail so that
Windows Live Mail puts any message from that
sender in the Junk folder going forward, click the
checkbox in front of the message and then click
Junk.

The message being moved

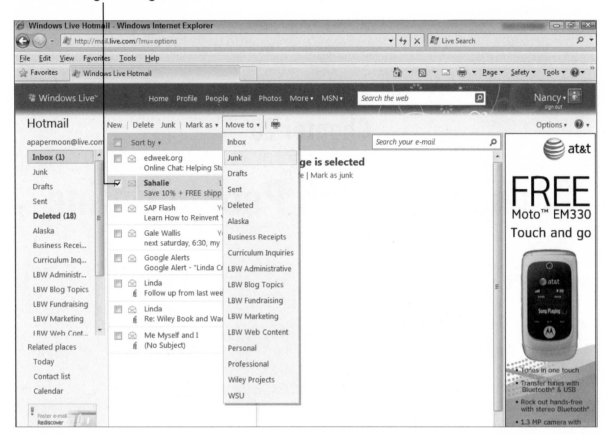

Figure 19-29

Chapter 20

Connecting with People Online

Get ready to . . .

The Internet offers many options for connecting with people and sharing information.

You'll find discussion boards and chat sites on a wide variety of sites, from news sites to recipe sites, sites focused around grief and health issues, and sites that host political-

or consumer-oriented discussions.

There are some great senior chat rooms for making friends, and many sites allow you to create new chat rooms on topics at any time.

Instant messaging (IM), on the other hand, isn't a Web site but a service. Using software such as Windows Live Messenger, IM allows you to chat in real time with your contacts. You can access instant messaging programs via your computer or your cell phone.

As with any site where users share information such as social networks and blogs, you can stay safer if you know how to sidestep some abuses, including data mining (gathering your personal information for commercial or criminal intent), social engineering ploys that try to gain your trust and access to your money, ID theft scams, and so forth. If you're careful to protect your privacy, you can enjoy socializing without worry.

In this chapter, I look at some ways of sharing information and tell you how to do so safely.

Use Discussion Boards

A *discussion board* is a place where you can post written messages, pictures, and videos on a topic. Others can reply to you, and you can reply to their postings.

Discussion boards are *asynchronous,* which means that you post a message (just as you might on a bulletin board at the grocery store) and wait for a response. Somebody might read it that hour — or ten days or several weeks after you make the posting. In other words, the response isn't instantaneous, and the message isn't usually directed to a specific individual.

You can find a discussion board about darn-near every topic under the sun, and these are tremendously helpful when you're looking for answers. They're also a great way to share your expertise — whether you chime in on how to remove an ink stain, provide history trivia about button styles on military uniforms, or announce the latest break-throughs in your given field. Postings are likely to stay up on the site for years for people to reference.

1. To try one, enter this URL in your browser's address field: `www.microsoft.com/communities/newsgroups/en-us/default.aspx`. (Note that some discussion boards require that you become a member with a user name and sign in before you can post, though this site doesn't.)

2. On the left side of the screen, click English (or another language of your choice) and then click a topic area, such as Home and Entertainment.

3. In the topic list that appears, click another topic, such as Games, to see more options. Continue to click until you get to a specific discussion board, such as the one shown in **Figure 20-1.**

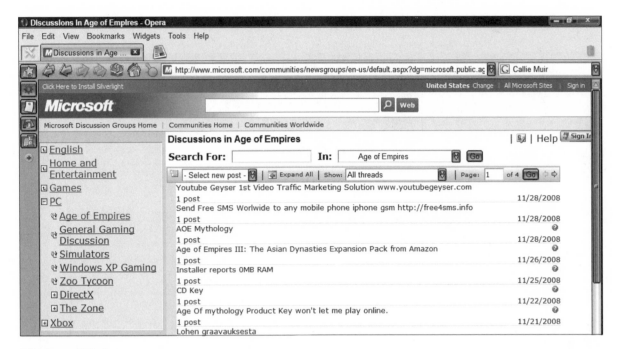

Figure 20-1

4. When you click a posting that has replies, you'll see that they are organized in the middle of the page in easy-to-follow *threads,* which arrange postings and replies in an outline-like structure. You can review the various participants' comments as they add their ideas to the entire conversation.

5. To reply to a posting yourself, first click the posting, and then click the Reply button, fill in your comments (see **Figure 20-2**), and click Post.

Enter your comments here

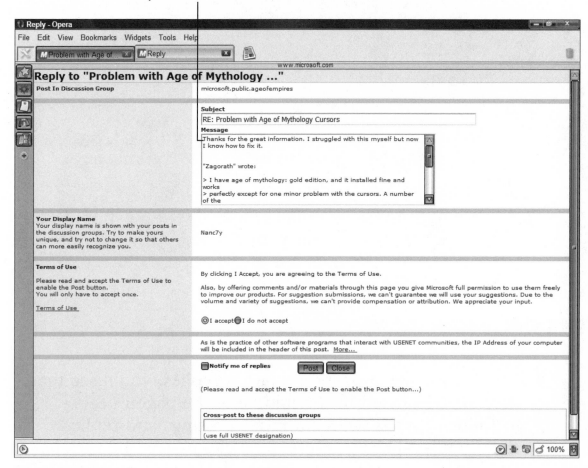

Figure 20-2

Participate in Chat

A *chat room* is an online space where groups of people can talk back and forth via text, audio, Web camera, or a combination of media. (See **Figure 20-3,** which shows a Web site that links to hundreds of chat rooms.) In chat, you're having a conversation with one or more people in real time, and your entire conversation appears in the chat window. Here are some characteristics of chat you should know:

➤ When the chat is over, unless you save a copy, the conversation is typically gone.

➤ Interactions are in *real time* (synchronous), which means you can interact with others in the moment.

➤ Several people can interact at once, although this can take getting used to as you try to follow what others are saying and jump in with your own messages.

➤ When you find a chat you want to participate in, sign up to get a screen name, and then you simply enter the chat room, enter your message, and submit it. It shows up in the stream of comments and others may — or may not — reply to it.

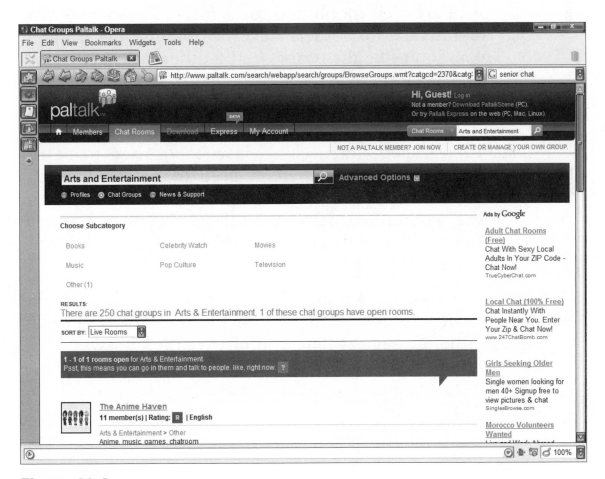

Figure 20-3

When you're talking to someone in a chat room with multiple people, you can, if you'd like, invite him to enter a *private chat room,* which keeps the rest of the folks who wandered into the chat room out of your conversation. Also, others can invite you into private chat rooms. Be careful who you interact with in this way, and be sure you understand the motivations for making your conversation private. This may be entirely reasonable, or it may be that you're dealing with someone with suspect motivations.

 Before you get started, check out the Web site's Terms of Use and privacy, monitoring, and abuse reporting procedures to understand the safety protections in place before joining a conversation. Some sites are well monitored for signs of abusive content or interactions; others have no monitoring at all. If you don't like the terms, find a different site.

Send and Receive Instant Messages (IMs)

Instant messaging (often called just *IMing)* used to be referred to as real-time e-mail. It used to be *synchronous,* meaning that two (or more) parties could communicate in real time, without any delay. It's still synchronous, but now you can also leave a message that the recipient can pick up later.

Instant messaging is a great way to stay in touch with the younger generations, who rarely use e-mail. IM is ideal for quick little messages where you just want an answer without forming a formal e-mail, as well as for touching base and saying hi. Text messaging on cell phones is largely the same phenomena: This isn't a tool you'd typically use for a long, meaningful conversation, but it's great for quick exchanges.

Depending on the IM service you use, you can do the following:

➤ Write notes to friends, grandchildren, or whoever, as long as they've installed the same IM service that you're using.

➤ Talk as if you were on the phone.

➤ Send photos, videos, and other files.

➤ Use little graphical images, called *emoticons* (such as smilies or winks) and *avatars,* to add fun to your IM messages.

➤ See participants via Web cameras.

➤ Get and send e-mail.

➤ Search the Web, find others using Global Positioning System (GPS) technology, listen to music, watch videos, play games, bid on auctions, find dates, and more.

➤ Track the history of conversations and even save transcripts of them to review later.

Instant messaging programs vary somewhat, and you have several to choose from, including Windows Live Messenger (available at `http://download.live.com/?sku=messenger`), Yahoo! Messenger (available at `http://messenger.yahoo.com`), and AOL Instant Messenger, also know as AIM (available at `www.aim.com`). Google mail (gmail) has a built-in IM feature.

To get started with a new messaging program, you need to follow the general steps in the upcoming list. But as with any software, if you aren't sure how to use its features, consult its Help documentation for specific instructions.

1. Download and install the messaging program according to the instructions on the provider's Web site.

2. Set up an account and sign in; this may simply involve entering your e-mail address and password.

You can send IMs from a computer to a mobile phone (and vice versa) and from one mobile phone to another. If you include your mobile phone number as part of your IM profile, anyone who can see your profile can view it. This is useful information for friends *and criminals,* so it's important to consider whether you want your number exposed — especially if you have many people on your contact list who you don't personally know.

3. Double-click a contact to initiate chat. (You can import contacts from your e-mail contacts when you sign up, or you can add them yourself.)

4. Click the phone button or icon to initiate a phone call.

IM programs let your contacts see when you're online, unless you change your settings to hide this information — something that's good to know when you're busy and don't have time to chat. You can choose availability settings such as Online, Busy, Be Right Back, Out to Lunch, or even display your status as Offline, even when you aren't. In the Windows Live Messenger IM program shown in **Figure 20-4,** click the arrow next to your name to access such a list.

IM is one place where people use shortcut text. Some of this will be familiar to you, such as FYI (for your information) and ASAP (as soon as possible). Other short text may be less familiar, such as LOL (laughing out loud). Visit `www.swalk.com` for a table of common shortcut text terms. Knowing these will make communicating with younger folks more fun.

Click this arrow

Figure 20-4

Consider what you're saying and sharing in IM and how you'd feel if the information was made public.

419

IM allows you to store your conversation history, which is super useful if you need to go back and check something that was said. But it has its downside. Anything you include in IM can be forwarded to others. If you're at work, keep in mind that many employers monitor IM (and e-mail) conversations.

 If you run across illegal content — such as child pornography — downloading or continuing to view this for any reason is illegal. Report the incident to law enforcement immediately.

Use Web Cams

Web cams are relatively inexpensive, and many laptops now come with Web cams embedded in their lids. (See **Figure 20-5.**) A Web cam can be a great way to communicate with friends and family, but it can quickly become risky when you use it for conversations with strangers.

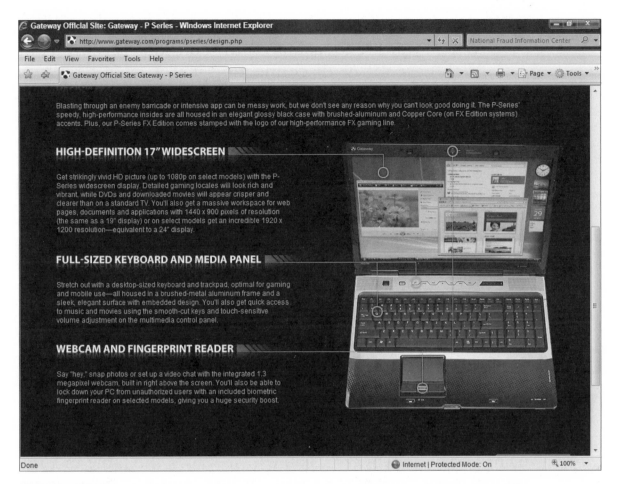

Figure 20-5

➡ Giving your image away, especially one that may show your emotional reactions to a stranger's statements in real time, simply reveals too much information that can put you at risk.

➡ If you use a Web cam to meet with someone you don't know online, they may expose you to behavior you'd rather not see.

➡ Note that Web cams can also be high-jacked and turned on remotely. This allows predators to view

421

and listen to individuals without their knowledge. When you aren't using them, consider turning your Web cam off or disconnecting it if it isn't a built-in model.

 Teens in particular struggle to use good judgment when using Web cams. If you have grandchildren or other children in your care, realize that normal inhibitions seem to fall away when they aren't physically present with the person they're speaking to — and many expose themselves, figuratively and literally. In addition to having a conversation about appropriate Web cam use with children and teens, it may be wise to limit access to Web cams.

Overview of Collaborative and Social Networking Sites

Although you may think kids are the only active group using social networking, you can see from the table in **Figure 20-6** that it isn't the case. In fact, persons 35–54 years old make up a large segment of social networkers.

US Internet Users Who Visit Social Networks, by Gender and Age, Q2 2008 & Q2 2009 (% of respondents in each group)	Q2 2008	Q2 2009
Gender		
Male	21.3%	37.6%
Female	31.1%	48.0%
Age		
<35	52.4%	71.5%
35-54	21.3%	43.1%
55+	6.4%	18.9%
Source: TNS and The Conference Board, "Consumer Internet Barometer: Second Quarter 2009," June 16, 2009		
105201		www.eMarketer.com

Figure 20-6

There are several types of sites where people collaborate or communicate socially. The following definitions may be useful:

➤ **Wiki:** A Web site that allows anyone visiting to contribute (add, edit, or remove) content. Wikipedia, for example, is a virtual encyclopedia built by users providing information in their areas of expertise. Because of the ease of collaboration, wikis are often used when developing group projects or sharing information collaboratively.

➤ **Blog:** An online journal (*blog* is short for *web log*) that may be entirely private, open to select friends or family, or available to the general public. You can usually adjust your blog settings to restrict visitors from commenting on your blog entries, if you'd like.

➤ **Social networking site:** This type of Web site (see **Figure 20-7**) allows people to build and maintain an online Web page and create networks of people that they're somehow connected to — their friends, work associates, and/or other members with similar interests. Most social networking sites also host blogs and have social networking functions that allow people to view information about others and contact each other.

➤ **Social journaling sites:** Sites such as Twitter allow people to go online with short notes which are typically about what they're doing at the moment. Many companies and celebrities are now tweeting, as posting comments on Twitter is referred to. You can "follow" individuals on Twitter so you're always informed if somebody you are a fan of makes a post.

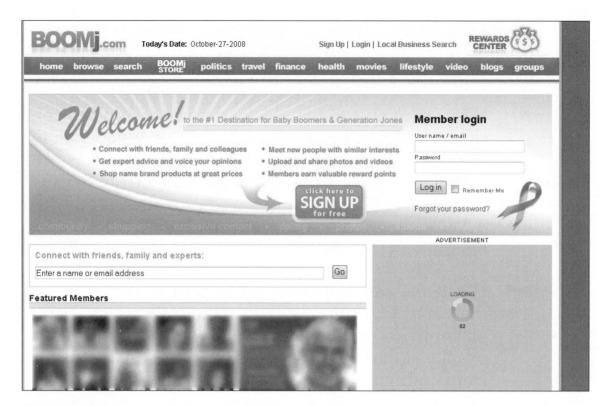

Figure 20-7

Sign Up for a Social Networking Service

Many social networking sites, such as Facebook or My-Space, are general in nature and attract a wide variety of users. Facebook, which was begun by some students at Harvard, has become today's most popular general site, and many seniors use its features to blog, exchange virtual "gifts," and post photos. Other social networking sites revolve around particular interests or age groups.

When signing up for a service, understand what is *required* information and what is optional. You should clearly understand why a Web service needs any of your personally identifiable information and how they may use that information — before providing it. Consider carefully the ques-

424

tions that sites ask users to complete in creating a profile.

 Accepting a social networking service's default settings may expose more information than you intend.

Walk through the signup process for Eons, a senior social networking site, to see the kinds of information they ask for. Follow these instructions to do so:

1. Type this URL into your browser's address line: `www.eons.com`.

2. Click the Sign Up button.

3. In the signup form that appears (see **Figure 20-8**), enter your name, e-mail address, a password, your birthdate, gender, and zip code.

   Note that the site requires your birthdate to verify that you are a senior, but you can choose to hide this information from others later if you don't want it displayed. (We recommend hiding your birthdate.)

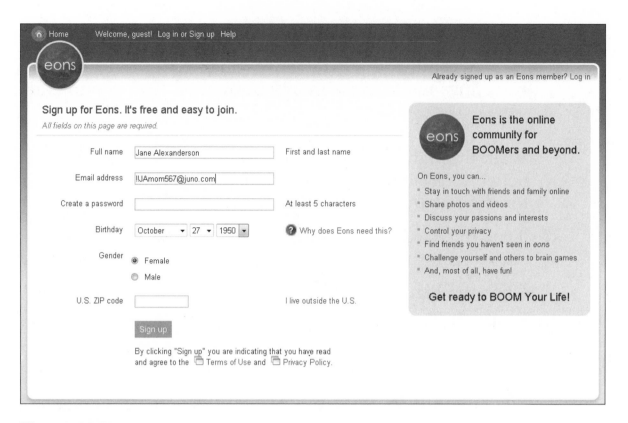

Figure 20-8

4. Click the Sign Up button. On the screen that appears (see **Figure 20-9**), note that your actual name is the screen name that members will see. We recommend you change this by highlighting the text and typing your alias over it.

Consider nicknames and the messages they send. Names like `lookin' forlove` or `lonelyinHouston` may send a message that you're lonely and emotionally vulnerable.

426

Change your screen name

See if your new screen name is available

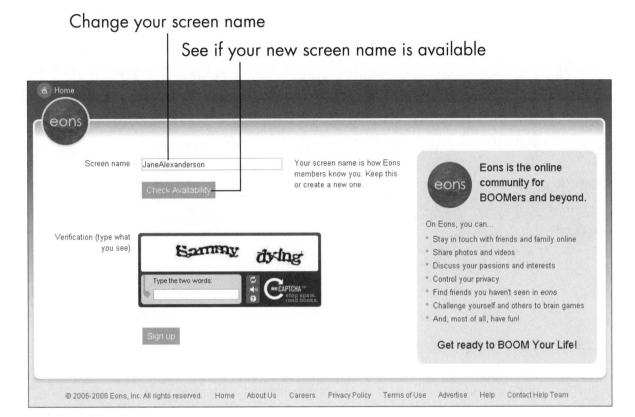

Figure 20-9

5. Click Check Availability to see if the alias you entered is not already in use as a screen name. If the screen name you request is already taken, choose another screen name and try again.

6. Type the word or phrase shown in the Verification field and click Sign Up.

7. At this point, you're instructed to check your e-mail account for a message. When you receive the message, click the link in it to confirm your e-mail address.

8. Note that after you confirm your e-mail address, a confirmation appears, offering a link to enhance your profile. Click that link.

9. Scroll to the bottom of the page. In the last paragraph on the page, click the Privacy Settings link.

10. On the Privacy Settings page (see **Figure 20-10**), note which settings default to Everyone, allowing anyone on the site to view your information, see your recent activity, comment on your blog, contact you, and so on.

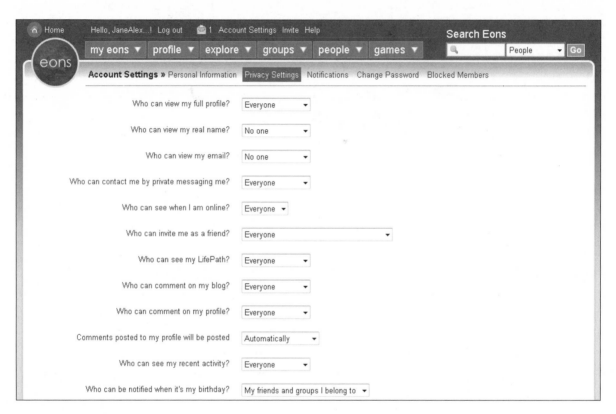

Figure 20-10

11. Change any privacy settings you wish and click Save.

Remember that social networking sites sometimes ask for information during signup that they use to provide you with a customized experience that suits your needs. But sometimes the information isn't needed for the service they're providing you at all — they sim-

428

ply want it for marketing purposes, to show to other members, or to sell.

 It's often very difficult to remove information from sites if you later regret the amount of information you've shared. It's best to be conservative in the information you share during the signup process; you can always add more later.

How Online Dating Works

Many seniors are making connections with others via online dating services, and if you've been wondering if this route could be for you, here's how you can jump into the world of online dating:

➥ Choose a reputable dating site. (See the section, "Select a Dating Service," later in this chapter.)

➥ Sign up and provide information about your likes, dislikes, preferences, and so on. This often takes the form of a self-guided interview process.

➥ Create and modify your profile to both avoid exposing too much personal information and ensure that you're sending the right message about yourself to prospective dates.

➥ Use search features on the site (see **Figure 20-11**) to find people who interest you and send them messages or invitations to view your profile.

➥ You'll get messages from other members of the site, to which you can respond (or not). Use the site's chat and e-mail features to interact with potential dates. You may also be able to read comments about the person from others who've dated him or her, if the site has that feature.

➥ When you're comfortable with the person and feel there might be a spark, decide if you want to meet the person offline.

Identify the type of people you'd like to meet

Figure 20-11

 Formal dating sites aren't the only places that people meet online, but they typically have the best safeguards in place. If you want to interact with people you meet on other sites, you should provide your own safeguards. Create a separate e-mail account (so you can remain anonymous and abandon the e-mail address if needed). Many dating sites screen participants and provide strong reporting measures that are missing on other types of sites, so be particularly careful. Take your time getting to know someone first before connecting.

Select a Dating Service

Select your online dating service carefully.

➤ Look for an established, popular site with plenty of members and a philosophy that matches your own.

➤ Review the site's policy regarding your privacy and its procedures for screening members. Make sure you're comfortable with them.

➤ Use a service that provides an e-mail system that you use for contacting other members only (sometimes called *private messaging*). By using the site's e-mail rather than your own e-mail address, you can maintain your privacy.

➤ Some sites, such as `http://saferdates.com`, shown in **Figure 20-12,** offer stronger levels of authenticating members. Safer Dates, for example, uses fingerprint identification and screening to make you more confident that you know who you're interacting with.

➤ Visit a site such as `www.consumerrankings.com/Dating.com` for comparisons of sites. Whether you choose a senior-specific dating site such as Dating-ForSeniors.com or a general population site such as

PerfectMatch.com, reading reviews about them ahead of time will help you make the best choice.

Figure 20-12

 If you try a site and experience an unpleasant incident involving another member, report it and make sure the service follows through to enforce its policies. If it doesn't, find another service.

Part IV

Taking Care of Your Computer

The 5th Wave   By Rich Tennant

"A centralized security management system sounds fine, but then what would we do with all the dogs?"

Chapter 21

Protecting Windows

Your computer contains software and files that can be damaged in several different ways. One major source of damage is from malicious attacks that are delivered via the Internet. Some people create damaging programs called *viruses* specifically designed to get into your computer's hard drive and destroy or scramble data. Companies might download adware on your computer, which causes pop-up

435

ads to appear, slowing down your computer's performance. Spyware is another form of malicious software that you might download by clicking a link or opening a file attachment; spyware sits on your computer and tracks your activities, whether for use by a legitimate company in selling you products or by a criminal element to steal your identity.

Microsoft provides security features within Windows 7 that help to keep your computer and information safe, whether you're at home or travelling with a laptop computer.

In this chapter, I introduce you to the major concepts of computer security and cover Windows 7 security features that allow you to do the following:

➡ Understand computer security and why you need it.

➡ Run periodic updates to Windows, which installs security solutions and patches (essentially, patches fix problems) to the software.

➡ Enable a *firewall,* which is a security feature that keeps your computer safe from outsiders and helps you to avoid several kinds of attacks on your data.

➡ Set up a password to protect your computer from others.

➡ Protect yourself against spyware.

Understand Computer Security

When you buy a car, it has certain safety features built in. After you drive it off the lot, you might find that the manufacturer slipped up and either recalls your car or requests that you go to the dealer's service department to get a faulty part replaced. In addition, you need to drive defensively to keep your car from being damaged in daily use.

Your computer is similar to your car in terms of the need for safety. It comes with an operating system (such as Microsoft Windows) built in, and that operating system has security features. Sometimes that operating system has flaws, and you need to get an update to keep it secure. And as you use your computer, you're exposing it to dangerous conditions and situations that you have to guard against.

Threats to your computer security can come from a file you copy from a disc you insert into your computer, but most of the time the danger is from a program that you downloaded from the Internet. These downloads can happen when you click a link, open an attachment in an e-mail, or download a piece of software without realizing that the malware is attached to it.

There are three main types of dangerous programs (called *malware*) to be aware of:

➤ A **virus** is a little program that some nasty person thought up to spread around the Internet and infect computers. A virus can do a variety of things, but typically it attacks your data, deleting files, scrambling data, or making changes to your system settings that cause your computer to grind to a halt.

➤ **Spyware** consists of programs whose main purpose in life is to track what you do with your computer. Some spyware simply helps companies you do business with track your activities so they can figure out how to sell you things; other spyware is used for more insidious purposes, such as stealing your passwords.

➤ *Adware* is the computer equivalent of telemarketing phone calls at dinner time. Once adware gets downloaded onto your computer, you'll get annoying pop-up windows trying to sell you things all day long. Beyond the annoyance, adware can quickly clog up your computer, so its performance slows down, and it's hard to get anything done at all.

To protect your information and your computer from these various types of malware, you can do several things:

➤ **You can buy and install an antivirus, antispyware, or antiadware program.** Programs such as McAfee Antivirus, Norton Antivirus from Symantec (see **Figure 21-1**), or the freely downloadable AVG Free from Grisoft can help stop the downloading of malicious files, and they can detect files that have somehow gotten through and delete them for you. Remember that after you install such a program, you have to get regular updates to it to handle new threats, and you need to run scans on your system to catch items that might have snuck through. Many antivirus programs are purchased by yearly subscription, which gives you access to updated virus definitions that the company constantly gathers throughout the year.

➤ **Some other programs such as Spyware Doctor from PC Tools combine tools for detecting adware and spyware.** Windows 7 has a built-in program, Windows Defender, that includes an antispyware feature. Windows Defender tools are covered later in this chapter.

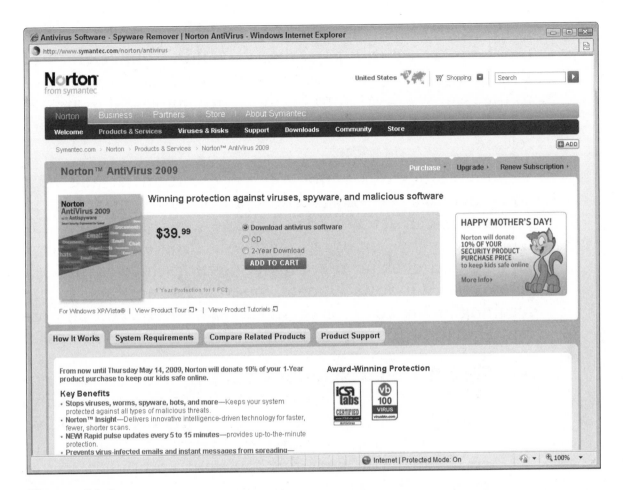

Figure 21-1

> **You can use Windows tools to keep Windows up to date with security features and fixes to security problems.** You can also turn on a firewall, which is a feature that stops other people or programs from accessing your computer without your permission. These two features are covered in this chapter.

Understand Windows Update Options

When a new operating system like Windows 7 is released, it has been thoroughly tested; however, when the product is in general use, the manufacturer begins to find a few problems or security gaps that it couldn't anticipate. For that reason, companies such as Microsoft release updates to their software, both to fix those problems and deal with new threats to computers that appeared after the software release.

Windows Update is a tool you can use to make sure your computer has the most up-to-date security measures in place. You can set Windows Update to work in a few different ways by choosing Start➪All Programs➪Windows Update and clicking the Change Settings link on the left side of the Windows Update window that appears. In the resulting dialog box (see **Figure 21-2**), click on the Important Updates drop-down list and you find these settings:

➤ **Install Updates Automatically:** With this setting, Windows Update starts at a time of day you specify, but your computer must be on for it to work. If you've turned off your computer, the automatic update will start when you next turn on your computer, and it might shut down your computer in the middle of your work to complete the installation.

➤ **Download Updates But Let Me Choose Whether to Install Them:** You can set up Windows Update to download updates and have Windows notify you (through a little pop-up message on your taskbar) when they're available, but you get to decide when the updates are installed and when your computer reboots (turns off and then on) to complete the installation. This is my preferred setting because I have control and won't be caught unawares by a computer reboot.

Click this arrow for drop-down list

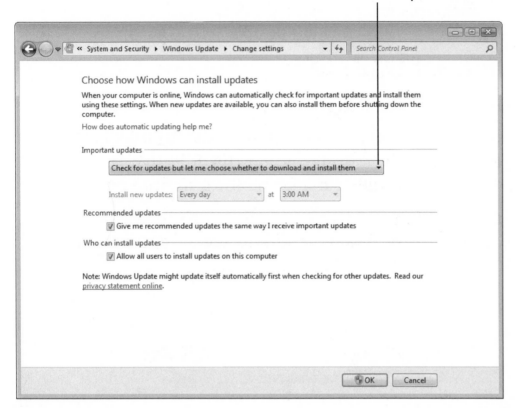

Figure 21-2

➡ **Check for Updates But Let Me Choose Whether to Download and Install Them:** With this setting, you neither download nor install updates until you say so, but Windows notifies you that new updates are available.

➡ **Never Check for Updates:** You can stop Windows from checking for updates and check for them yourself, manually (see the following task). This puts your computer at a bit more risk, but it's useful for you to know how to perform a manual update if you discover a new update is available that you need to proceed with a task (such as getting updated drivers or a language pack).

Run Windows Update

1. Choose Start➪All Programs➪Windows Update.

2. In the Windows Update window, click Check for Updates. Windows thinks about this for a while, so feel free to page through a magazine for a minute or two.

3. In the resulting window, as shown in **Figure 21-3,** click the Updates Are Available link to see all optional or important updates link.

Click this link

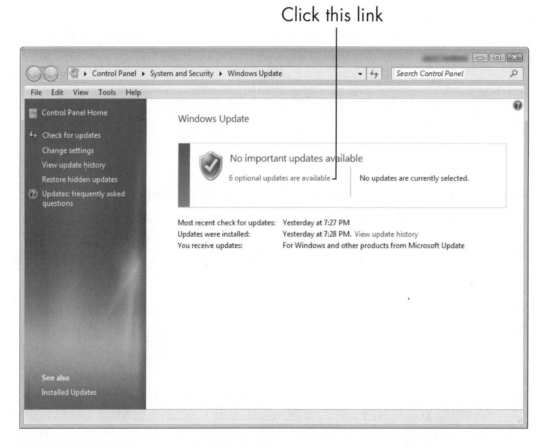

Figure 21-3

4. In the following window, which shows the available updates (see **Figure 21-4**), click to select available critical or optional updates that you want to install. Then click the OK button.

Select update to install

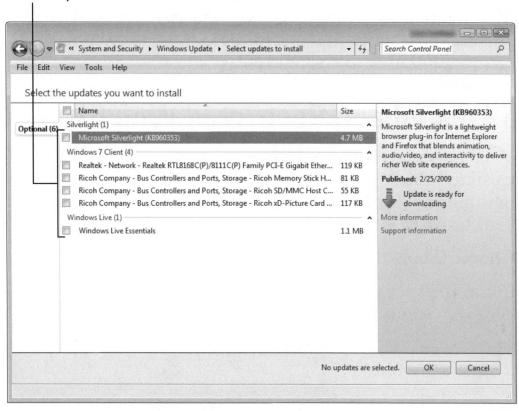

Figure 21-4

5. In the Windows Update window that appears, click the Install Updates button. A window appears showing the progress of your installation. When the installation is complete, you might get a message telling you that it's a good idea to restart your computer to complete the installation. Click Restart Now.

You can set up Windows Update to run at the same time every day. Click the Change Settings link in the Windows Update window and choose the frequency (such as every day) and time of day to check for and install updates.

Running Windows Update either automatically or manually on a regular basis ensures that you get the latest security updates to the operating system, so it's a good idea to stay current.

Set Up Trusted and Restricted Web Sites

1. You can set up Internet Explorer to recognize sites you trust and those you don't want IE to take you to. Click the Internet Explorer icon in the Windows taskbar to start your browser.

2. Choose Tools⇨Internet Options.

3. In the Internet Options dialog box (see **Figure 21-5**), click the Security tab.

Security tab

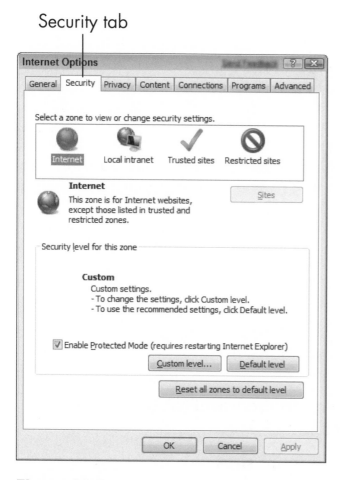

Figure 21-5

4. Click the Trusted Sites icon and then click the Sites button.

5. In the resulting Trusted Sites dialog box, enter a URL in the Add This Web Site to the Zone text box for a Web site you want to allow your computer to access. If you want any locations for a particular company, such as Microsoft, to be allowed, you can use a wildcard in the form of an asterisk, as shown in **Figure 21-6.**

An asterisk serves as a wildcard

Figure 21-6

6. Click Add to add the site to the list of Web sites, as shown in **Figure 21-6.**

7. Repeat Steps 3–6 to add more sites.

8. When you're done, click Close and then click OK to close the dialog boxes.

9. Repeat Steps 1–8, clicking the Restricted Sites icon rather than Trusted Sites in Step 4 to designate sites that you don't want your computer to access.

 If the Require Server Verification (https:) for All Sites In This Zone checkbox is selected in the Trusted Sites dialog box, any trusted site you add must use the `https` prefix, which indicates that the site has a secure connection.

 You can establish a Privacy setting on the Privacy tab of the Internet Options dialog box to control which

446

sites are allowed to download *cookies* to your computer. *Cookies* are tiny files that a site uses to track your online activity and recognize you when you return to the source site. *Trusted sites* are ones that you allow to download cookies to your computer even though the privacy setting you have made might not allow many other sites to do so. *Restricted sites* can never download cookies to your computer, no matter what your privacy setting is.

Enable the Windows Firewall

1. A firewall keeps outsiders from accessing your computer. Choose Start⇨Control Panel⇨System and Security⇨Windows Firewall.

2. In the Windows Firewall window that appears (see **Figure 21-7**), check that the Windows Firewall is marked as On. If it isn't, click the Turn Windows Firewall On or Off link in the left pane of the window.

3. In the resulting Customize Settings window (see **Figure 21-8**), select the Turn on Windows Firewall radio button for Home or Work (Private) Network Location Settings and/or Public Network Location Settings and then click OK.

4. Click the Close button to close Windows Security Center and the Control Panel.

Verify the firewall is on

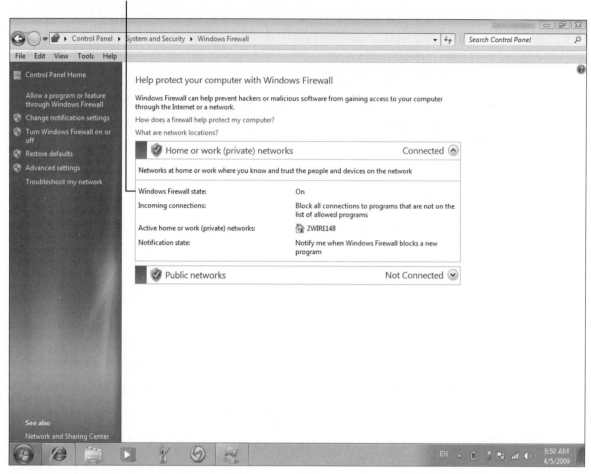

Figure 21-7

 A *firewall* is a program that protects your computer from the outside world. This is generally a good thing, unless you use a Virtual Private Network (VPN). Using a firewall with a VPN results in you being unable to share files and use some other VPN features.

 Antivirus and security software programs may offer their own firewall protection and may display a message asking if you want to switch. Check their features against Windows and then decide, but usually most firewall features are comparable. The important thing is to have one activated.

Select this option

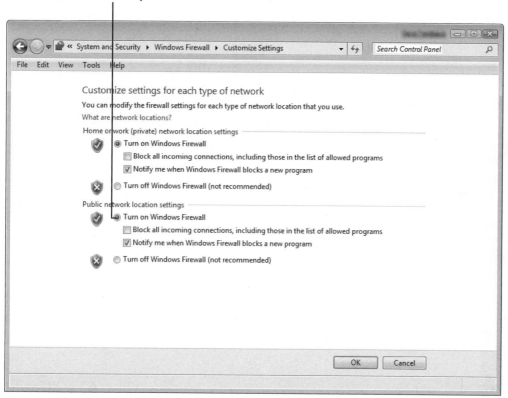

Figure 21-8

Set Up a Password for Your Computer

1. To set up a password so others can't get at your computer and files without entering that password, choose Start⇨Control Panel, and then click User Accounts and Family Safety.

2. In the resulting window, shown in **Figure 21-9,** click the Change Your Windows Password link. Then, if you have more than one user account, click an account to add

the password to. Click the Create a Password for Your Account link.

3. In the Create a Password for Your Account screen, shown in **Figure 21-10,** enter a password, confirm it, and add a password hint.

Click this link

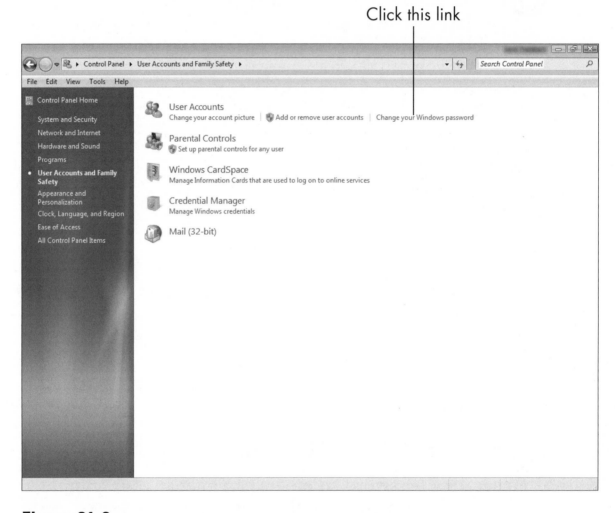

Figure 21-9

4. Click the Create Password button.

5. You return to the Make Changes to Your User Account

window. If you wish to remove your password at some point, you can click the Remove Your Password link here.

6. Click the Close button to close the User Accounts window.

 If you forget your password, Windows shows the hint you entered to help you remember it, but remember that anybody who uses your computer can see the hint when it's displayed. So, if lots of people know that you drive a Ford and your hint is "My car model," your password protection is about as effective as a thin raincoat in a hurricane.

Enter and confirm the new password

Figure 21-10

 After you create a password, you can go to the User Accounts window and change it at any time by clicking Change Your Password. You can also change the name on your user account by typing Change Your Account Name.

Check Your Computer's Security Status

1. Choose Start➪Control Panel➪System and Security.

2. In the resulting System and Security window (see **Figure 21-11**), click the Review Your Computer's Status and Resolve Issues link.

Click this link

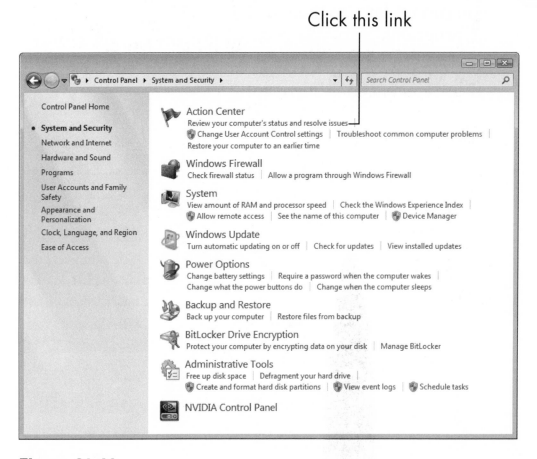

Figure 21-11

3. In the Action Center window that appears (see **Figure 21-12**), check to see if the Security item states whether Windows found any antivirus software on your computer.

4. If Windows did not find such software, click the Find a

Program Online button and review the recommended security software partners that Microsoft recommends. If you want to purchase one of these solutions, click the logo of the company you want to buy from and you are taken to their site where you can buy and download the software.

 It's very important that you do have antivirus and anti-spyware software installed on your computer, and that you run updates to them on a regular basis. These types of programs help you avoid downloading malware to your computer that could cause advertising pop-ups, slow your computer's performance, damage computer files, or even track your keystrokes as you type to steal your identity and more. If you don't want to pay for such a program, consider a free solution such as Spy-ware Terminator (www.spywareterminator.com).

Find out if you have antivirus software

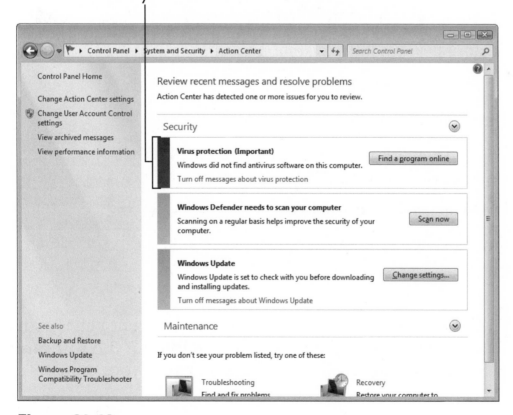

Figure 21-12

Chapter 22

Maintaining Windows

All the wonderful hardware that you've spent your hard-earned money on doesn't mean a thing if the software driving it goes flooey. If any programs cause your system to *crash* (meaning it freezes up and you have to take drastic measures to revive it), you can try a variety of tasks to fix it. You can also keep your system in good shape to help you avoid those crashes. In this chapter, you find out how to take good care of your programs and operating system in these ways:

➤ When a program crashes, you can simply shut that program down by using the Windows Task Manager. This utility keeps track of all the programs and processes that are running on your computer.

➤ If you've got problems and Windows isn't responding, sometimes it helps to restart in Safe Mode, which requires only basic files and drivers. Restarting in Safe Mode often allows you to troubleshoot what's going on, and you can restart Windows in its regular mode after the problem is solved.

➤ Use the System Restore feature to first create a *system restore point* (a point in time when your settings and programs all seem to be humming along just fine), and then restore Windows to that point when trouble hits.

➤ You can clean up your system to delete unused files, free up disk space, and schedule maintenance tasks.

➤ If you need a little help, you might run a troubleshooting program to help you figure out a problem you're experiencing with a program.

Shut Down a Nonresponsive Application

1. If your computer freezes and won't let you proceed with what you were doing, press Ctrl+Alt+Del.

2. In the Windows screen that appears, click Start Task Manager.

3. In the resulting Windows Task Manager dialog box (see **Figure 22-1**), click the Applications tab and select the application that you were in when your system stopped responding.

4. Click the End Task button.

5. In the resulting dialog box, the Windows Task Manager tells you that the application isn't responding and asks whether you want to shut it down now. Click Yes.

 If pressing Ctrl+Alt+Del doesn't bring up the Task Manager, you're in bigger trouble than you thought. You might need to press and hold your computer's power button to shut down. Note that some applications use an AutoSave feature that keeps an interim version of the document that you were working in — you might be able to save some of your work by opening that last-saved version. Other programs don't have such a safety net, and you simply lose whatever changes you made to your document since the last time you saved it. The moral? Save, and save often.

 You may see a dialog box appear when an application shuts down that asks if you want to report the problem to Microsoft. If you say yes, information is sent to Microsoft to help them provide advice or fix the problem down the road.

The Applications tab

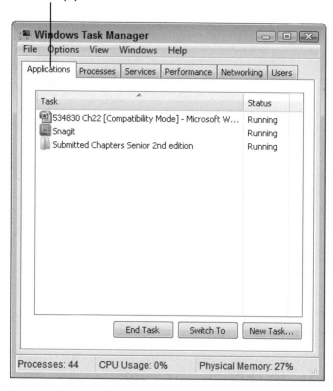

Figure 22-1

Start Windows in Safe Mode

1. To start Windows in a mode that loads only the most vital files, allowing you to get started and fix problems (for example, by performing a system restore to a time before the problems), remove any CDs or DVDs from your computer.

2. Choose Start, click the arrow on the right of the Shut Down button, and then choose Restart to reboot your system (see **Figure 22-2**).

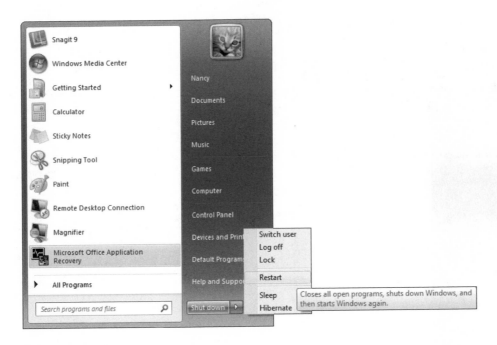

Figure 22-2

3. When the computer starts to reboot (the screen goes black), begin pressing F8.

4. If you have more than one operating system, you might see the Windows Boot Manager menu. Use the up- and down-arrow keys to select the Windows 7 operating system. Or, type the number of that choice, press Enter, and then continue to press F8.

5. In the resulting Advanced Boot Options window (a plain-vanilla, text-based screen), press the up- or down-arrow key to select the Safe Mode option from the list and then press Enter.

6. Log in to your computer with administrator privileges; a Safe Mode screen appears (see **Figure 22-3**). Use the tools in the Control Panel and the Help and Support system to figure out your problem, make changes, and

then restart. When you restart again (repeat Step 2), let your computer start in the standard Windows 7 mode.

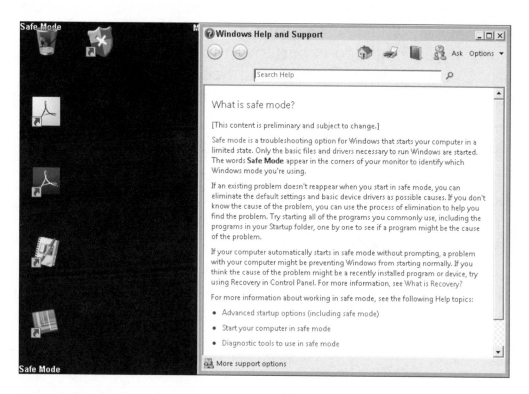

Figure 22-3

 When you reboot and press F8 as in Step 2, you're in the old text-based world that users of the DOS operating system will remember. It's scary out there! Your mouse doesn't work a lick, and no fun sounds or cool graphics exist to sooth you. In fact, DOS is the reason the whole *For Dummies* series started because *everybody* felt like a dummy using it, me included. Just use your arrow keys to get around and press Enter to make selections. You're back in Windowsland soon. . . .

Create a System Restore Point

1. You can back up your system files, which creates a restore point you can later use to return your computer to earlier settings if you begin to experience problems. Choose Start⇨Control Panel⇨System and Security and in the resulting System and Security dialog box, click the System link.

2. In the System dialog box, click the System Protection link in the left panel. In the System Properties dialog box that appears (see **Figure 22-4**), click the Create button.

Click this button

Figure 22-4

3. In the Create a Restore Point dialog box that appears, enter a name to identify the restore point, such as the current date or the name of a program you are about to install, and click Create.

4. Windows displays a progress window. When the restore point is created, the message shown in **Figure 22-5** appears. Click Close to close the message box, click Close to close the System Protection dialog box, and Close again to close the Control Panel.

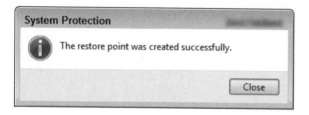

Figure 22-5

 Every once in a while, when you install some software and make some new settings in Windows, and when things seem to be running just fine, create a system restore point. It's good computer practice, just like backing up your files, only you're backing up your settings. Once a month or once every couple of months works for most people, but if you frequently make changes, create a system restore point more often.

 A more drastic option to System Restore is to run the system recovery disc that probably came with your computer or that you created using discs you provided. However, system recovery essentially puts your computer right back to the configuration it had when it was carried out of the factory. That means you lose any software you've installed and documents you've created since you began to use it. A good argument

461

for creating system restore points on a regular basis, don't you think?

Restore the Windows System

1. Choose Start⇨Control Panel⇨Back Up Your Computer (under System and Security).

2. In the Back Up and Restore window, click the Recover System Settings On Your Computer link. In the Recovery window, shown in **Figure 22-6**, click the Open System Restore button.

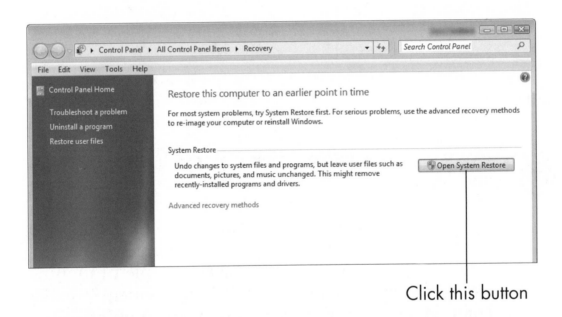

Click this button

Figure 22-6

3. The System Restore feature shows a progress dialog box as it starts. In the resulting System Restore window, click Next.

4. In the System Restore dialog box that appears, click the system restore point to which you want to restore the

462

computer and click the Next button.

5. A dialog box confirms that you want to run System Restore and informs you that your computer will need to restart to complete the process. Close any open files or programs, and then click Finish to proceed.

6. The system goes through a shutdown and restart sequence, and then displays a dialog box that informs you that the System Restore has occurred.

7. Click OK to close it.

 System Restore doesn't get rid of files that you've saved, so you don't lose your Ph.D. dissertation. System Restore simply reverts to Windows settings as of the restore point. This can help if you or some piece of installed software made a setting that is causing some conflict in your system that makes your computer sluggish or prone to crashes. If you're concerned about what changes will happen, click the Scan for Affected Programs button shown in the window displayed in **Figure 22-7**.

 System Restore doesn't always solve the problem. Your very best bet is to be sure you create a set of backup discs for your computer when you buy it. If you didn't do that, and you can't get things running right again, contact your computer manufacturer. They may be able to send you a set of recovery discs, though they may charge a small fee. These discs restore your computer to its state when it left the factory, and in this case you lose applications you installed and documents you created, but you get your computer running again.

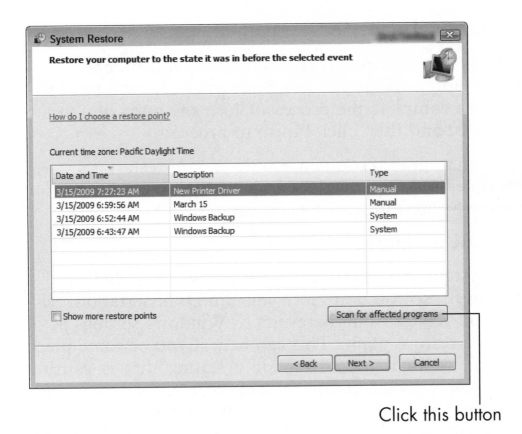

Click this button

Figure 22-7

Defragment a Hard Drive

1. To clean up files on your hard drive, choose
   Start⇨Control Panel⇨System and Security and then click
   Defragment Your Hard Drive in the Administrative Tools
   window.

2. In the resulting Disk Defragmenter window (see **Figure
   22-8**), to the left of the Defragment Disk button is the
   Analyze Disk button. Use this to check whether your disk
   requires defragmenting. When the analysis is complete,
   click the Defragment Disk button. A notation appears
   (see **Figure 22-9**) showing the progress of defragmenting

464

your drive.

3. When the defragmenting process is complete, the Disk Defragmenter window shows that your drive no longer requires defragmenting. Click Close to close the window and then close the Control Panel.

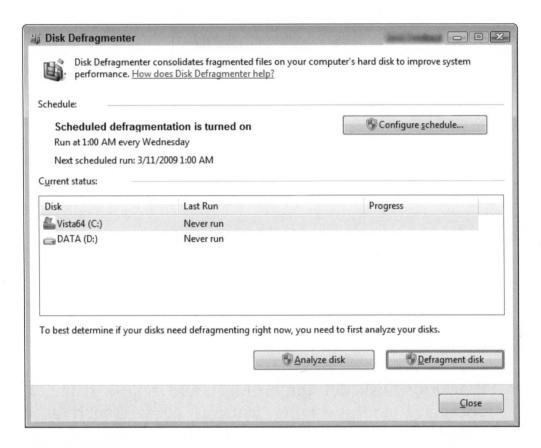

Figure 22-8

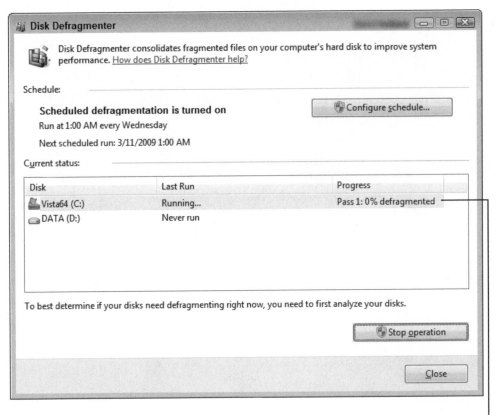

Progress is indicated here

Figure 22-9

 Warning: Disk defragmenting could take a while. If you have energy-saving features active (such as a screen saver), they could cause the defragmenter to stop and start all over again. Try running your defrag overnight while you're happily dreaming of much more interesting things. You can also set up the procedure to run automatically at a preset period of time, such as once every two weeks by using the Configure Schedule button in the Disk Defragmenter window.

Free Disk Space

1. To run a process that cleans unused files and fragments of data off of your hard drive to free up space, choose Start⇨Control Panel⇨System and Security and then click Free Up Disk Space in the Administrative Tools.

2. In the Disk Cleanup dialog box that appears, choose the drive you want to clean up from the drop-down list and click OK. Disk Cleanup calculates how much space you will be able to free up (see **Figure 22-10**).

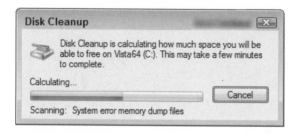

Figure 22-10

3. The resulting dialog box, shown in **Figure 22-11,** tells you that Disk Cleanup calculated how much space can be cleared on your hard drive and displays the suggested files to delete in a list (those to be deleted have a check mark). If you want to select additional files in the list to delete, click to place a check mark next to them.

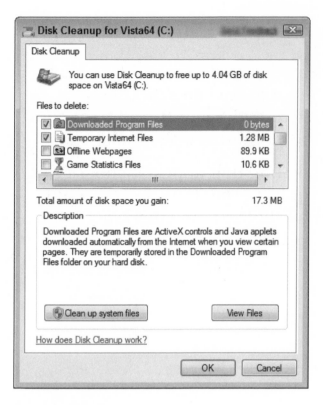

Figure 22-11

4. After you select all the files to delete, click OK. The selected files are deleted. Click the Close button to close the Control Panel.

 Click the View Files button in the Disk Cleanup dialog box to see more details about the files that Windows proposes to delete, including the size of the files and when they were created or last accessed.

 If you can't free up enough disk space for your needs, you might consider replacing your hard drive with one that has more capacity.

Delete Temporary Internet Files by Using Internet Explorer

1. When you roam the Internet, various files may be downloaded to your computer to temporarily allow you to access sites or services. To clear these away, first open Internet Explorer.

2. Choose Tools⇨Internet Options.

3. On the General tab of the resulting Internet Options dialog box (see **Figure 22-12**), click the Delete button in the Browsing History section.

4. In the resulting Delete Browsing History dialog box, shown in **Figure 22-13**, click the Temporary Internet Files checkbox to select it if it's not already selected and click Delete.

5. A confirmation message asks whether you want to delete the files. Click Yes. Click Close and then click OK to close the open dialog boxes.

Click this button

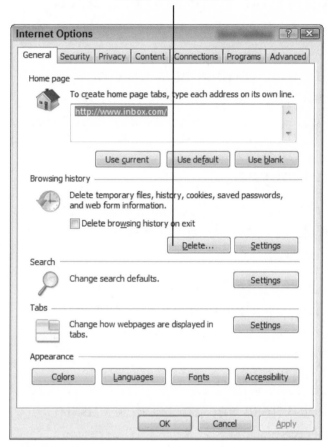

Figure 22-12

 Temporary Internet files can be deleted when you run Disk Cleanup (see that task earlier in this chapter), but the process that I describe here allows you to delete them without having to make choices about deleting other files on your system.

 Windows 7 offers a feature for rating and improving your computer's performance. From the Control Panel, click System and Security, and then click the Check the Windows Experience Index Base Score link. In the resulting dialog box, click the Rate This

470

Computer button to get a rating of your processor speed, memory operations, and more.

Verify this option is selected

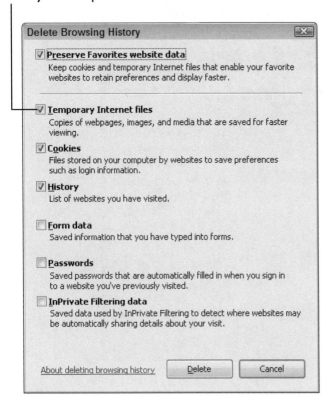

Delete Browsing History

☑ **Preserve Favorites website data**
Keep cookies and temporary Internet files that enable your favorite websites to retain preferences and display faster.

☑ **Temporary Internet files**
Copies of webpages, images, and media that are saved for faster viewing.

☑ **Cookies**
Files stored on your computer by websites to save preferences such as login information.

☑ **History**
List of websites you have visited.

☐ **Form data**
Saved information that you have typed into forms.

☐ **Passwords**
Saved passwords that are automatically filled in when you sign in to a website you've previously visited.

☐ **InPrivate Filtering data**
Saved data used by InPrivate Filtering to detect where websites may be automatically sharing details about your visit.

About deleting browsing history   Delete   Cancel

Figure 22-13

Schedule Maintenance Tasks

1. Choose Start⇨Control Panel⇨System and Security and then click Schedule Tasks in the Administrative Tools window.

2. In the resulting Task Scheduler dialog box, shown in **Figure 22-14**, choose Action⇨Create Task.

3. In the resulting Create Task dialog box (see **Figure 22-**

15), enter a task name and description. Choose when to run the task (either only when you are logged on, or whether you're logged on or not).

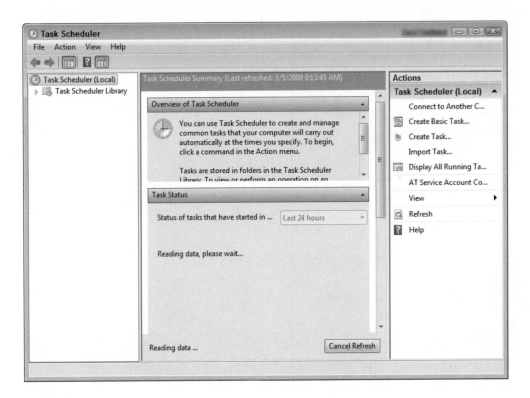

Figure 22-14

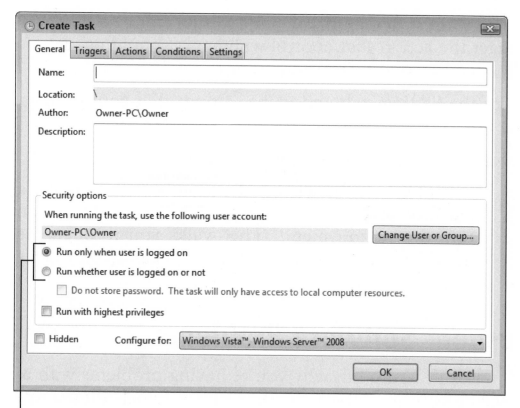

Choose when to run the task

Figure 22-15

4. Click the Triggers tab and then click New. In the New Trigger dialog box, choose a criteria in the Begin the Task drop-down list and use the settings to specify how often to perform the task as well as when and at what time of day to begin. Click OK.

5. Click the Actions tab and then click New. In the New Action dialog box, choose the action that will occur from the Action drop-down list. These include starting a program, sending an e-mail, or displaying a message. Depending on what you choose here, different action dialog boxes appear. For example, if you want to send an e-mail, you get an e-mail form to fill in. Click OK.

473

6. If you want to set conditions in addition to those that trigger the action that control whether it should occur, click the Conditions tab and enter them.

7. Click the Settings tab and make settings that control how the task runs.

8. After you complete all settings, click OK to save the task.

 If you like a more wizard-like interface for building a new task, you can choose the Create Basic Task item from the Action menu. This walks you through the most basic and minimal settings you can make to create a new task.

Troubleshoot Software Problems

1. If you can't figure out why you're having problems with a piece of software, choose Start⇨Control Panel⇨Find and Fix Problems (under System and Security).

2. In the resulting Troubleshooting window (see **Figure 22-16**), click Programs.

Click this link

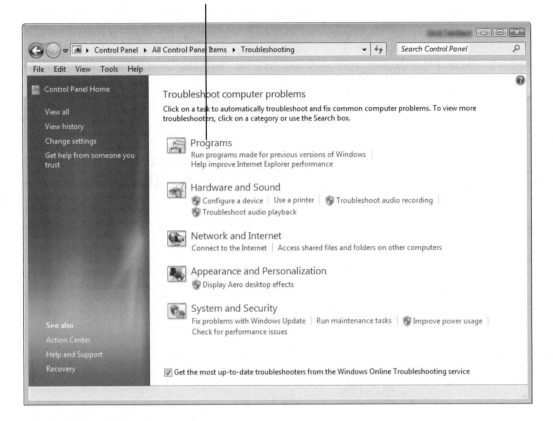

Figure 22-16

3. In the resulting Troubleshooting Problems–Programs window, choose what you want to troubleshoot:

- **Network** allows you to troubleshoot a connection to the Internet.

- **Web Browser** helps you figure out problems you may be having with the Internet Explorer browser.

- **Program Compatibility** is a good choice if you have an older program that doesn't seem to be functioning well with this version of Windows. Program compatibility is a common cause of problems running software.

475

- **Printing** allows you to find out why you're having difficulty with your printer, including checking for the correct printer driver software.

- **Media Player** troubleshooting can be used to pinpoint problems with general settings, media files, or playing DVDs.

4. Follow the sequence of instructions for the item you selected to let Windows help you resolve your problem (see **Figure 22-17**).

 In some cases you'll be asked for administrator permission for the troubleshooter to perform an action, so it's a good idea to run the troubleshooting wizard through an administrator level account. See Chapter 2 for more about user accounts and administrators.

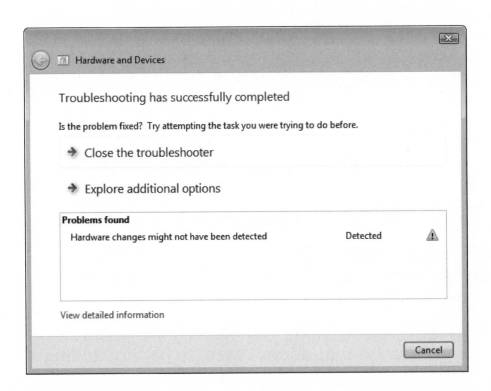

Figure 22-17

476

Index

Internet connection
browsers, 311. *See also* Internet Explorer
browsing. *See* Internet Explorer; searching the Web
browsing history
   deleting, 469–71
   viewing, 337–39
burning CDs or DVDS
   backing up files, 192–94
   music, 278–80
   photos, 265–68
   recovery disks, 42–43
buying a computer
   customized computers, 45–47
   DVD or CD drive choices, 42
   guidelines, 38–40
   hard drive choices, 43–44
   Internet connection concerns, 44–45
   monitor choices, 40–41
   price ranges, 38–40
   processor choices, 43–44
   RAM choices, 43–44
   reasons for, 28–31, 38–39
   return policies, 39
   shipping costs, 39
   types of computers, 34–36
   Windows 7 versions, 37

C

cable Internet connection, 44, 45, 314. *See also* Internet
    connection
calculations (spreadsheet), 239–41
Calendar gadget, 202–3
CDs. *See* DVDs and CDs
central processing unit (CPU), 32, 36, 43, 208–9
challenges, physical. *See* assistive options

syncing music devices, 280–81

The employees of Thorndike Press hope you have enjoyed this Large Print book. All our Thorndike, Wheeler, and Kennebec Large Print titles are designed for easy reading, and all our books are made to last. Other Thorndike Press Large Print books are available at your library, through selected bookstores, or directly from us.

For information about titles, please call:

(800) 223-1244

or visit our Web site at:

http://gale.cengage.com/thorndike

To share your comments, please write:

Publisher
Thorndike Press
295 Kennedy Memorial Drive
Waterville, ME 04901